REACHING BEYOND THE WAVES

A Teacher's Sixth Graders' Inspirational Search
for the WW II Survivors of a Downed B-17
and the Men Who Rescued Them

Suzanne Kelly

Suzanne Zobrist Kelly

HELLGATE PRESS   HELLGATE PRESS   ASHLAND, OREGON

Reaching Beyond the Waves

Published by Hellgate Press

(An imprint of L&R Publishing, LLC)

Hellgate Press
PO Box 3531
Ashland, OR 97520
email: info@hellgatepress.com

Editor: Harley B. Patrick
Cover Design: L. Redding
Cover photo credits: All photos Bob Kelly except: B-17 drawing, Chad Watson; Western Union telegram, Jim Reynolds; Men and rafts, National Archives

Library of Congress Cataloging-in-Publication Data

Printed and bound in the United States of America
First edition 10 9 8 7 6 5 4 3 2 1

SPECIAL APPRECIATION

To my husband Bob and son Ryan who lived these adventures with me, providing the love and support I always needed,

To the sixth graders who were always my best teachers,

To the men who allowed us to hear echoes of history and touched our hearts,

To my parents, Edith and Herman Zobrist; my neighbors, Ruth and Randy Matson; my educational colleagues, Ruth Walker and Lee Himan; and my sixth grade teacher, Hazel Jacobson, who helped students learn,

To the many librarians, historians, and strangers who found ways to answer students' questions,

To all who met the curiosity of pre-adolescents and embraced their search,

Thank you for reaching out and teaching us that when people go beyond a fleeting wave and connect with people, it is quite an experience to take those life's unsuspected journeys together.

SPECIAL ACKNOWLEDGMENT

To John Forssman who used his golden gift of teaching.

To Scott Erickson, and Dan and Donna Ryherd, who shared their interest in Tuvalu.

To Lynn Matson, who encouraged and listened to Update.

SPECIAL HOPE

To Charlie and Quinn, may your awesome adventures with books lead to continued learning, amazing research, and abounding joy.

CONTENTS

PREFACE

IN OCTOBER 1942, CAPTAIN (CAPT.) WILLIAM T. CHERRY, JR., member of the United States Army Air Corps and with the Air Transport Command, was forced to ditch a B-17 plane into the Pacific Ocean, because of faulty navigational equipment. On board were Eddie Rickenbacker, a civilian on a special mission for the War Department, and his military aide, Colonel (Col.) Hans Adamson. Eight crew members and passengers survived the emergency landing. All but one person survived for three weeks on rafts. The co-pilot, James Whittaker, wrote about his experience in a 1943 book, *We Thought We Heard the Angels Sing.*

When I was in sixth grade, my teacher, Hazel Jacobson, read the book to me, and I subsequently read it to all my sixth graders when I became a teacher. Forty-two years after the men's ordeal in the rafts, my students wanted to know what had happened to the men. Their curiosity started research that ultimately led to a reunion of the survivors and some of their rescuers. At Meeker Elementary in Ames, Iowa, this reuniting of the men was referred to as the Rescue Reunion, and the students became known as the Sixth Grade Super Sleuths.

In the decade that followed, more sixth graders continued the search to locate other men involved in the separate rescues of the three rafts. Before the technology of the Internet and Google searches, students wrote hundreds of letters to locate men from this World War II event. They found the raft builders, medical corpsmen, New Zealand coastwatchers, Navy scouting squadrons and construction battalions. They located the men who had been on the motor patrol torpedo boats, flew search planes from coded bases in the Pacific, and U.S. Marines who were on a remote coral island. They found Toma, a young native islander, who had rescued some of the men in his outrigger canoe.

The sixth graders and I started our research with information from Whittaker's book, old copies of *LIFE* magazine, and declassified documents from the military and the National Archives. We continued to develop extensive research with assistance from public librarians, newspaper reporters, military organizations, and even the State Department. Due to national publicity of our Rescue Reunion, people who had been involved in this incident then began to contact us. Each clue they provided was used to find more people and information.

What started as a sixth grade class research project to find eight men led to thirty years of contact with survivors, rescuers, and others involved in this historic event. Through correspondence and personal visits, the men told us their stories. Sometimes they asked our help to locate former military buddies or find members of a group for an upcoming reunion. We developed friendships with them and their families.

As our research skills grew, so did our admiration for the courage and sacrifice of these veterans. *Reaching Beyond the Waves* is a chronicle of the sixth graders' search for those men of World War II and the personal stories that connected us all.

Chapter One

———

CHOSEN PATHWAY

IFE'S JOURNEY IS A COMBINATION OF chosen pathways and unsuspected side trips. During World War II, a routine military flight became an unforeseen three-week ordeal of survival. This incident happened a year before I was born but impacted my life for over fifty years.

In October 1942, Captain William T. Cherry, Jr. was forced to ditch a B-17 plane into the Pacific Ocean. On board was Eddie Rickenbacker, a civilian on a special mission for the War Department. Eight crew members and passengers survived the emergency landing. All but one person survived three weeks on rafts, before each raft had a separate rescue. The plane's crew was unknown to the public, but Rickenbacker was famous around the world as the American Ace from the previous world war.

The co-pilot, James Whittaker, kept a diary of his experience and wrote *We Thought We Heard the Angels Sing*. In the mid-1950s I sat in the front row of a sixth grade classroom and listened spellbound as my teacher, Hazel Jacobson, read Whittaker's book to our class.

The book was rather an unassuming one, but the story was riveting. I marveled at the men's courage as they faced being lost because of faulty navigational equipment and then running out of fuel. I held my breath as Mrs. Jacobson read how pilot Captain Cherry ditched the plane into the Pacific with expertise that kept the four-motored land plane resting on the waves long enough for the crew to launch three small life rafts. I had tears when my teacher read about Alex dying and being buried at sea. It was hard to imagine the lack of water and food (only four scrawny oranges), the equatorial heat, threats of sharks, and towering waves.

There were many reasons why the book interested me. Growing up on a farm in Dallas County in the middle of Iowa, I was far removed from the salty Pacific Ocean. Other than frequent squabbles with my older brother Dale, usually over who could reach the mailbox first at the end of the driveway, my childhood was rather peaceful. This event from the war seemed distant and almost unreal.

I was also fascinated with flying. I often rambled around the farm, sometimes climbing to a high branch of the maple tree or on top of a small, pitched-roof hog house, and listened to planes fly over the farm to the rural airport about three miles away. I thought pilots were dashing heroes. I wondered what had happened to Captain Cherry after he was rescued.

Mostly, I was intrigued with the details of the story. Written during the war, many facts were obscured. Where were the men headed on their mission? Island X. I scanned maps in the encyclopedia and looked for clues in the public library in the small town of Adel, Iowa. But Island X, of course, was a coded location.

Although I was a shy child, who found it difficult to interact with others in a public setting, I liked people. As a youngster, I alternated between wanting to become a teacher or an even better Nancy Drew, the fictional detective character I loved to read about in the Carolyn Keene books. That sixth grade year, I was particularly intrigued with the old Lindeman Place, which was located a half-mile north of our farm. One autumn night, three friends and I, armed with notepads and flashlights, pushed open the sagging front door of the abandoned farmhouse. Entry was unsafe, but we dutifully recorded each observed detail. The memory of that adventure has remained with me. In the fall of 1955, however, I had no idea that investigative work and public communication would be integral parts of my future.

But the most auspicious thing about sixth grade was my teacher. Since I adored Mrs. Jacobson and she read that book to us, I then planned to read it to my future students. After graduating from Iowa State University, I accepted a sixth grade teaching assignment. My parents presented me with a gift—a used book, now out-of print, and the same book Mrs. Jacobson had read to me. I had no perception how much that book would connect future pathways in my life.

This is the story of how my sixth graders researched history and how I guided their steps. Before the days of school computers, the Internet, Google, or smart phones, finding answers to questions meant reading an encyclopedia. This is an account of the World War II event, how it captured my curiosity, motivated my students, and ultimately connected my sixth graders with people around the world.

As a teacher, I soon discovered that sixth graders in my class always had particular parts of the book they found fascinating, such as how the men rationed the segments of oranges, withstood the equatorial heat, and prayed nightly to the "Old Master" for food, water, and rescue. Students listened intently to the description of the men's painful saltwater ulcers, agonizing thirst, and their cramped endurance in the small life rafts. They thrilled at the invention of Captain Cherry's undershirt sail attached to an oar propped against the side of the raft. They almost always touched their own noses at the account of Bill Cherry's encounter with a ten-foot shark that broke *his* nose.

Sometimes students begged for more reading time, almost unable to withstand the suspense if I stopped in the middle of a particular spot, such as where the men were discussing using parts of their own flesh as a solution for needed bait to catch fish. An ear lobe? A piece of a little finger? But before the men reached a decision, there came what Whittaker called "a startling interruption."

Predicted protests always came rapidly. "Mrs. Kelly, you can't stop reading!" But I always did. Somehow, it was time to go to another class, or noon recess, or....Soon I could not resist, and I would continue reading. Students listened pensively to the author's forthright description of possibly carving bits of themselves for bait; so desperate were they for food.

Then when I read on about a sea swallow landing on Rickenbacker's head, students' reactions ranged from cheers to quiet clutching of their hands with reverent relief the men had found food. When I read about the men eating the sea swallow, or later, miniscule bites of shark or other fish, students usually sat quietly. Some years I had to add, "Do you understand that they had to eat it raw?" Then the light dawned and responses ranged from reflexive clutching of their abdomen to calm acceptance of survival necessities.

But most of the men's ordeal dealt with thirst. Once during a rainsquall the men were able to catch a little water and store it in their inflatable life preservers, called Mae Wests—so named after the popular buxom actress of the 1940s. I had learned to grab a drink at the hall water fountain before I read those passages to my class. It was all I could do to keep my mouth from being so dry the words could not form. How could the men have survived that long without a cold glass of water?

In World War II, when the men were reported missing, searched for, and given up for lost, major media covered the events. I had read newspaper clippings and even seen an old movie about the ordeal. Eddie Rickenbacker had been famous before he was lost, but became even more so, when the men were found. He and his military aide, Colonel Hans Adamson, another passenger on the B-17, had also written books about their survival. However, it was the copy of James Whittaker's, *We Thought We Heard the Angels Sing*, that became a fixture in my classroom. To my sixth graders it was a capitalized wonder known appropriately as "The Book."

After almost three weeks on the rafts, the men spotted United States Navy Kingfisher planes flying dawn and dusk patrols. The planes, however, did not see the rafts. So near death, the men's agony of hearing the planes drone on was almost unbearable. Finally, after twenty days of drifting together, the rafts separated. Cherry believed that if they spread over a larger distance, they had a better chance of being seen. Therefore, each raft had a separate rescue. Students wondered how each one occurred. Although Whittaker detailed his own rescue, not as many facts were provided about the others. Students always had questions.

I did not know when I first started reading The Book to sixth graders that it would be forty years after the war before some of those questions would be answered—and that they would be answered by my sixth graders with their infinite curiosities that could reach beyond the waves.

Suzanne Kelly's 1984-85 Language Arts Class, Room 14, Meeker Elementary. *Top Row*: Mr. Himan (Principal), Niki Nilsen, Jennifer Jones, Chad Watson, Cathy Watson, Derrick Boden, Lisa Moore, and Mrs. Kelly. *Middle Row*: Nicki Moreland, Michele Mitchell, Brad Arnold, Travis Senne, Erik Smedal, and David Jurgens. *Front Row*: Amy Larson, Ben Jackson, David Abelson, Amy Murphy, Christy Scott, Amy LeMay, and Doug Haynes. (*Photo Bob Kelly*)

Chapter Two

THE COURSE IS CHARTED

T HE SCHOOL YEAR STARTED MUCH LIKE OTHER YEARS. I now was in my nineteenth year of elementary teaching. I already knew this year's class had energy to burn, and although I appreciated their enthusiasm, I had not yet channeled it. When my husband Bob asked how my class was the first week, I had replied, "They're great, but their constant chatter is a challenge."

Although the students were always different, there was a certain rhythm to the beginning of a new school year. I had read The Book to the sixth graders, and they were as enthused as usual. However, this year when I finished reading, one boy asked, "Mrs. Kelly, what happened to the men?" I gave my standard answer that Rickenbacker was no longer living, but I did not know about the others. Travis Senne was insistent. "But I want to know. What happened to the men?" It was a thought-provoking question, but one to which I had no answer.

Sixth graders are a rare breed—individualistic yet social, predictable but full of surprises. Independently feisty, they crave a group to survive. Sarcastically mouthy, they melt your heart with a word or phrase. As one mother once told me, "You have to love them a lot, but don't have to like them at all." Myself? Licensed to teach from pre-school through secondary, I ended up caught in the middle, exactly where I belonged. I adored sixth graders.

Too old to be little kids and too young to be big kids, sixth graders are perpetually active. Their growing spurts are huge, and muscles beg to be used. Jumping up to touch the hallway doorframes was as much a rite of passage for pre-adolescence as discovering their first acne. "Bet you can't do that, Mrs. Kelly," was always accompanied with a smirky grin. The students used me, at five foot three, as a measure of how much they had grown. I always loved how smirky grins could become even smirkier.

Always wanting change and variety, sixth graders fluctuate from "This is boring!" to "How cool!" Individually, they can be naively innocent and yet concerned about the complexities of life. They can be punching a sibling while worrying about world peace.

Meeting the needs of all students at all times can be a daunting task, and an almost impossible goal, even for a dedicated teacher. But between the unique moments of daily routines and reaching lofty dreams are a few hours in a day to make a difference—a difference that can only occur if a motivation to learn is part of the student's burning desire to "find out."

We had been in school less than four weeks when I noticed my neck was swollen on one side. In the three days since I made a doctor's appointment, the swelling had become noticeably larger. The doctor was forthright. He thought the tumor was benign, but it needed to be removed as soon as possible. Surgery was scheduled within the week.

A week! That was not much time. There were things I wanted to say and do with my husband Bob and our six-year-old son Ryan. Personal preparations had to be made, even facing the positive odds that confronted me.

The next day I talked to the class. Not wanting to be too dramatic about my health concern, and yet needing to prepare my students, I said, "I hope the doctor is correct and I'll be fine. If I get to return to class soon, let's think of a way to celebrate."

Guessing they would choose a pizza party, I was surprised when they were adamant. "*Mrs. Kelly, we want to find the men.*" Usually eleven and twelve-year-olds are interested in books about friends, football, or science fiction—not historical biographies. To them, history was past and had very little connection to the present. At this point I was unaware it was the beginning of one of my professional unexpected side trips.

Two weeks later, I faced my sixth graders the first day back from surgery on October 15, 1984. Weak, but grateful for my health, I remember the day clearly. I had just finished a lesson and had given an assignment. Still not having the strength to stand for long periods, I slipped into my desk chair and looked around the room.

Quietly, Travis approached my desk. "You said when you got well we could find the men." (I actually had said *if* I got well and came back to school, but Travis had heard *when*.)

But I had been waiting for his question. "We'll talk about it later."

Sixth graders do not like the word *later* connected to something they want to do. They are *now* people. Later only slows them down. Sixth graders do not like to be slowed down—not when they are running in the halls, and certainly not when they have an idea of something they want to do.

Eight men had been thrust on three small life rafts. Among them were names—Cherry, Reynolds, Bartek, Whittaker, DeAngelis, Kaczmarczyk, Adamson—and one famous person, Eddie Rickenbacker. What *had* happened to the men?

The time was now. I could feel an excitement I had never felt before. That may seem strange. I do not believe it was a premonition or a vision of some kind; it was just a feeling, but deeper yet, a knowing that I did not understand. And so, I faced the class.

I explained that I had former students who also had wanted to find out what happened to the men, but they never followed through with clues. But now I was a more experienced teacher. I was more familiar with references and researching skills. I could help students organize and structure their learning around this project. The school district's required learning objectives could be met in a variety of ways. To the class I said, "I have specific lessons that I must prepare for you to learn. The way you learn these lessons can be changed. But this is not a game. In fact, if you research this Word War II incident right, you will work harder than any sixth graders I have ever had. The choice will be yours. However, don't make the decision lightly thinking it's a way of getting out of work."

I looked around the room. A few sheepish grins were covered amidst the direct glances of expectation. Most faces held the combination of innocence and total guilt that I so loved about this aged child.

Captain William T. Cherry, Jr. was the B-17 pilot from Texas.

Lieutenant James C. Whittaker, the co-pilot, was author of the book, *We Thought We Heard the Angels Sing*.

Sergeant James W. Reynolds was the radio operator from California.

All photos pages 10-11 courtesy Auburn University Libraries Special Collections and Archives.

Lieutenant John J. DeAngelis was the navigator.

Private John F. Bartek was the engineer from New Jersey.

Sergeant Alex Kaczmarczyk, recently released from the hospital and flying to rejoin his group, was assigned as an engineer for the flight.

"Okay," I acknowledged. "How do you want to begin?"

"You tell us," replied one student.

"That's not the way this is going to work. You will be the detectives. You must plan and work together to find clues and follow up on them. You will read information and summarize it, pulling facts that need to be documented and connected with other facts. You will write letters asking questions. Then you will write more letters thanking people for the answers they gave that led to more questions. Eventually, your clues will form a pattern, and you will be hot on the trail of the case you wanted to handle. But whether you will solve it or not, I do not know. No detective ever does. If you did, it wouldn't be a mystery."

I paused and looked at each student. Every upturned face met mine. No one slouched in a chair. I could read their eyes. Children hear with their ears, but they really listen with their eyes. These students understood. I continued, "I will teach you research skills. You will also teach each other and me. Together we can share strategies to find the men. But it will probably take the entire school year. It will be difficult to find the answers we want. After all, the B-17 incident happened forty-two years ago."

That fall of 1984, teaching was different than it is now. Before the "No Child Left Behind" legislation, teachers still prepared lessons, tried to meet the needs of individual students, and assessed student achievement of a prescribed curriculum. However, traditional classrooms also contained numerous workbooks and practice sheets for students to work individually at their desks. I taught in a semi-departmentalized situation, exchanging classes with two other teachers. Known as the science teacher, I taught three science classes each day, along with my homeroom language arts. These students went to other teachers for their social studies and math. We would only be able to do this research during our language arts time together.

By the end of the year, students would have covered all required skills, but in different ways. I would adapt the school district's language arts curriculum to fit this specific research project. The reading, writing, and research skills would be learned not only by individual lessons but also by team sharing and real-world application. I started with a few fundamental guidelines.

(1) I would teach them how to problem solve. I already advocated "hands on" science learning with investigative labs. But I had never specifically incorporated problem solving into a language arts curriculum. I would guide their research, but the students would be involved in selecting and following the pathways we would attempt. Teachers help students learn to be better thinkers, but this investigative research would involve more skills than I had ever emphasized with sixth graders. Research also meant use of reference materials. We were limited to shaggy red dictionaries, outdated encyclopedias, one old world atlas, wall-hanging maps of the United States and Europe, and a rusty metal globe that sixth graders loved to spin but hated to use.

(2) All research would be shared with the class. There would be no competition between students, only energy to achieve our common goals. We would have class meetings to brainstorm ideas and time to share progress reports. We would break the over-all task of finding the men into smaller chunks, so individual students could participate in different ways. Students would need more self-discipline to stay on task in a classroom where many different lessons were being learned at the same time.

(3) We would follow all clues at once. We would not wait for answers before asking further questions. If we had multiple ways to find answers, we would explore more than one path simultaneously.

(4) We would make copies of all correspondence to have a paper trail of documentation. Notes would be kept on sources, a journal would be recorded of all activities, and information would be filed in a central location. Students would have access to what other students had discovered. We

would learn research skills by doing research, and we would tell a story with that research.

(5) I personally would absorb extra costs for the project. Schools have budgets, but they do not have money. I would provide envelopes and postage stamps for correspondence, three-ring binders and dividers for the information, and page protectors for documents. For the moment, we would not use telephone calls for various reasons. First, other than the office phones and a phone for teachers in the hallway, no telephones were available for students. Second, long distance calls were expensive. Third, with phone calls there were no paper trails. Any verbal conversation would have to be recorded as notes.

After these guidelines were explained, we started our research with a large class meeting to organize a plan of action. Students brainstormed ideas.

"I think we need to form groups. There were eight men, but Mrs. Kelly says that Eddie Rickenbacker isn't living. So let's form seven groups."

"No. We need six groups. Remember Alex died at sea and wasn't rescued."

"I have another idea," came a quieter voice from the midst of the hubbub. *"We can't forget about Alex. It wasn't his fault he died."*

A louder voice chimed in, *"Yeah. Remember the Alamo. Remember Alex."*

"We're not talking about the Alamo. We're talking about people."
"Same thing."
"Is not."
"Is so."
"Mrs. Kelly, what should we do?"

I was tired. Would my full strength and energy level ever return? Surely, using a textbook and assigning pages of written work was easier than this. I looked at the expectant faces in front of me. Some day they would be employees applying teamwork for a business or spouses learning the give and take of marriage. Right now, however, they were sixth graders. They needed time and opportunity to learn communication skills, as well as traditional reading and writing skills. So I began, "What do you want to know?"

Travis was emphatic. "I want to know what happened to the men!"

"Yeah," came support from across the aisle. "We want to know if they have any kids."

Someone giggled. "First, we want to know if they got married!"

A classmate added, "Some of them were engaged. I forgot who. But some weren't."

Another student piped up, "I wanna know what they did. I mean, were they real people?"

"Of course they were real people."

"You know what I mean. In The Book it talked about John Bartek, the engineer, wanting to be a minister. Was he—like a real minister?"

Finally, the students reached a conclusion. There were eight men on the rafts. Each man was important, living or not. All the students in the class would be divided into seven groups, each group to research one of the men who was rescued. In addition, all groups would work to find information on Alex, who died at sea.

The Book was our best resource. As the author, James Whittaker had written an account of the event from his point of view. For him, the rescue of the men had strengthened his belief that God had intervened to save them. This was a perfect example to help students understand an author's purpose, which was one of our reading skills. We discussed the difference between facts and opinions, another reading skill. This was done in context of The Book. When I first read *We Thought We Heard the Angels Sing*, I omitted some of the passages Whittaker had quoted from John Bartek's little New Testament. I told students they were welcome to read those parts on their own. I never wanted anyone to be uncomfortable with what I was teaching, and therefore, made a distinction between the actual event that had occurred with Whittaker and his interpretation of how it had changed his life. But the students were interested in their pursuit of the men.

Besides Eddie Rickenbacker, Col. Hans Adamson was also a passenger on the plane. He was a military aide for Rickenbacker while on this mission for the War Department. Alex Kaczmarczyk, a sergeant who had been hospitalized, was returning to his assignment in the Pacific. He was designated as an engineer for the flight, because he had more experience than Bartek. The rest of the crew consisted of pilot Bill Cherry and co-pilot James Whittaker, along with James Reynolds, the radio operator; Johnny J. DeAngelis, the navigator; and John Bartek, the flight engineer.

Thus, the seven groups of students began their research with any clues they had. For example, Whittaker wrote that the pilot Bill Cherry had lived in the Dallas-Fort Worth area before the war. Obviously, this was a starting point. My task was to help students take that clue, problem solve, and use it to gain more information.

"If you know a city where somebody lives, how do you find their address?" I asked.

"But we don't know if Captain Cherry lives in Dallas or Fort Worth. Maybe he's not even living," responded one sixth grader.

"That's right," I agreed. "But we have to start with the clue we have. Let us assume that Captain Cherry is living, that he returned from the war, and that his home now is still in Texas. How can we find him?"

"Ask somebody," a student suggested.

"Whom should we ask?" I prodded.

I could see the looks on their faces. To them, if you have a question, you ask it. If you have a question, someone else answers it. But there were no easy answers. Even the questions were difficult.

I backed up, trying to channel their thinking. "If I knew you lived in Ames, Iowa, how could I find where you live?" I asked, realizing the closer the big picture came to their level, the easier for them to relate.

One student's eyes lit up. "I'd call you up on the phone."

A student turned to look at the speaker while he pondered the idea. "But what if you didn't know my phone number?"

The room was silent, but it was filled with energy. You could see on the faces how ideas were shaping. Phone book! Look up Captain Cherry's address in the telephone book! Christy Scott's group was ecstatic. They had a plan. Christy was to go to the Ames Public Library and find a Dallas-Fort Worth telephone book and copy the address for Captain Cherry. Students could hardly wait until tomorrow.

The next morning Christy appeared in the classroom doorway. "Mrs. Kelly, I don't know, but I may have found something." Quickly we organized a class meeting, so we all could hear her report.

"Last night I went to the public library and looked in the phone book. I copied the addresses for fifty-three names of Cherry, but there wasn't one that was a Bill Cherry."

Students expressed their disappointment in many ways—forlorn looks, sighs, and shakes of their heads. But Christy continued, "I still had some time before my dad picked me up, so I turned to the section in the phone book for the suburbs."

"What's a suburb?" one student wondered.

Another answered, "You know, like a smaller city connected to a bigger city, like West Des Moines is connected to Des Moines."

Students were learning, sharing, and teaching each other. Christy began again. "I found a suburb called Grapevine that is between Ft. Worth and Dallas. In that phone directory I found a listing for 'Cherry, Wm T III.'"

I explained what "the third" was and students raced to The Book. We had been calling the pilot "Captain Cherry" for so long, we did not know if the author had indicated anything else. We looked, and there it was. The pilot of the plane was William T. Cherry, Jr. Surely that meant that William T. Cherry, III was Captain Cherry's son.

The group helped Christy compose a letter. We had taken our first clue and followed it. Later that afternoon, while the students were at recess, I took the letter dated November 15, 1984, to the school's office. I paid for a stamp and deposited our first letter in the mail for postal pick-up at the end of the day. I remember clearly that a warm wave of anticipation swept over me. The principal, Lee Himan, came out of his office.

I am very hopeful that you might be Captain William Cherry, or his son or maybe even grandson of the veteran. I am hoping for very promising results, and am eager to receive any information or leads in our difficult search.
I will be awaiting your reply!
Cordially yours,
Christy Scott
Room # 14

Christy Scott and her group composed a letter for the pilot, William T. Cherry, Jr. Later, Capt. Cherry related how much he loved Christy's beautiful handwriting.

"What's up, Mrs. Kelly?" he asked.

"I'm not sure, " I said, "but I'll let you know." Our investigation had begun. I hoped our story had started to be written. But after thirty years of wondering, I felt that something was going to happen.

Chapter Three

THE JOURNEY BEGINS

ATE SUNDAY AFTERNOON ON DECEMBER 2, 1984, our home phone rang. When I answered, a rich Texas accent said, "Mrs. Kelly, you don't know me. My name is Bill Cherry."

Although I had hoped the students' research might locate the men and had felt the letter they sent held promise, I still was not prepared to hear the voice on the phone. As I related afterwards, however, I am certain I behaved in a mature, professional manner...I screamed! I remember being afraid we would lose connection. Turning aside, I directed our son, Ryan, who had been making chains to hang for Christmas decorations, to find me something so I could write notes. Usually very good at following directions, this time he asked, "Pen or pencil?" followed by, "Scratch paper or colored paper?" I really did not care. This was Captain Cherry, a man I had thought about for almost thirty years!

"Where were you?" I asked.

"Texas, visiting my son. I live in California now."

"Not where you lived," I clarified, "where were you when you were lost?"

In my flustered state, I actually asked a question that would take a great deal of research to be answered. He did not know where he was when he was lost, but he knew where he should have been.

We knew their flight destination had been "Island X" about 1,700 miles southwest of Hawaii. This had been established after the men were rescued in November 1942, still during the war. One of the leading questions my students had was, "Where was Island X?"

Captain Cherry knew. It was Canton Island in the Phoenix Island group. They were scheduled to refuel there and then take Eddie Rickenbacker to his ordered destination, Port Moresby, New Guinea. But, because the navigational equipment was faulty, they were off course, passing probably either northwest or southeast of Canton.

My next thought was, how could Captain Cherry talk with our class? My husband Bob, also an educator, suggested a telephone conference call. Early Monday morning I went to my principal, Lee Himan. "Lee, do you remember when you asked me what was up? Well, I have some news." Excited about our research, he immediately helped organize our call to Captain Cherry. We arranged for the students to fill the staff lounge and workroom, where there were facilities for a phone hook-up and plenty of space for the sixth graders.

The students sat in eager anticipation as Captain Cherry answered his phone at our pre-arranged time. (A speakerphone, which is common now, was very uncommon then.) As his wonderful Texas twang filled the room, with his rapid-fire delivery of details, I sat in awe that this event was happening. It was an example of what education should look like— curiosity, communication, and the search for knowledge. I was very glad I was a teacher and that these were my students.

The most valuable information we received from Captain Cherry was the name of the island group where they were rescued—the Ellice Islands. Our main references, The Book and World War II newspaper accounts, had been printed soon after the men had been found and did not reveal the actual names of the islands. Now we could use our old globe and atlas to find the islands. In addition, Captain Cherry helped clarify that two of the Ellice Islands, Funafuti and Nukufetau, were the ones involved in the rescue of the men. Funafuti was the main island and had a U.S. military base. Nukufetau was a neighboring island where Whittaker and the others in one raft had rowed ashore.

Besides the group that found Captain Cherry, other student groups had been equally busy. The sixth graders researching John Bartek started with information from The Book that said the crew engineer was from New Jersey. Whittaker had described young Bartek as being "red-haired and freckled." That was not much of a clue. However, two years earlier, I had contacted the *Air Force Times*, an Army Times Publishing Company. During the war, the B-17 crew was part of the Army Air Corps Transport Command (before the days of the United States Air Force). The associate editor agreed to place my request in the locator service part of their publication. Joyce Horne from Lompoc, California, answered my notice. She wrote that she had attended school with John Bartek's brother, George. They had lived in Freehold, New Jersey. I had never done anything with this information. Now students confirmed from an old newspaper clipping that this had been Bartek's hometown during the war.

This group of students now had a state and a city. All they needed was an address. Our local public library did not have a telephone book from Freehold, but it did have addresses for public libraries in the United States. Sixth grader, Paul Kubichek, wrote to the Freehold Public Library and explained our research project. The director responded with John Bartek's address in Mercerville, New Jersey. However, by this time Paul had moved away, so classmate Erik Smedal sent a letter to John Bartek on November 28. John responded to the class saying, "You did a good job of finding me. I can say much better than they did in 1942 when we were lost in the Pacific Ocean."

Finding John Bartek produced an address for John J. DeAngelis, the crew's navigator. Although we located him in Pennsylvania, for personal reasons he chose not to correspond with the class. The students, particularly those in his research group, were very disappointed. "But we didn't learn anything," they complained. I remember telling them a story I once heard about Thomas Edison. Each time Edison invented a new material for a filament in the electric light bulb, he gained information. Even if the material did not work, he had learned something, so that specific experiment was not a failure. I reminded the students they *had* located another member of the crew. We needed to respect his wishes not to participate more in our project.

Students knew the radio operator on the B-17 was Staff Sergeant (Staff Sgt.) James Reynolds from Oakland, California. The group researching him wrote to the Oakland Public Library. A library assistant, Elizabeth Watts, searched through old city directories and found two listings in a current Oakland phone book—one a James R. and the other a James W. She contacted James W. Reynolds, now in Alameda, California, and found he was the person we were trying to reach. She relayed back to us that he would like the students to write him. Sixth grader Cathy Watson did so immediately. I had no idea that later, and for many years to come, I would refer to this detail of finding Jim Reynolds when I would call him on the phone and ask, "Is this James W.?"

Students were responding to my suggestion that they send out several leads at once. This strategy accomplished several purposes. First, it provided jobs for each member of a group, so all students were learning writing skills. Also, it involved numerous resources and references for students to use as they learned researching skills. In addition, this process softened the disappointments when a clue ran into a dead end. Hope was kept alive that another clue would solve the mystery. While one clue was being researched, students already were working on another possibility. I had also observed that the perpetual hope and optimism sixth graders display, kept them motivated. Students were enthused when they received any response.

"We got a letter back! You open it."

"It says they don't know anything, but they wish us luck in our endeavors."

"What are endeavors?"

"Our project."

"Oh, okay. Mark this address off the list. How many more do we have to hear from?"

"Um. Let's see. I think...four."

"It's my turn to file the research."

"I know that. But ask Mrs. Kelly first to make copies for our folders."

"Right."
"What should we do next?"

During this time, I realized a shift was occurring in our research. The students were not only interested in finding the men; they were becoming more intrigued about the event. As some students focused on particular survivors, others looked at maps and analyzed details about the war.

Of the five rescued crewmembers, we had located four. How strange that the one we knew the most about from his writing, we had not yet found. Although we knew James Whittaker had been from California, we had not been able to find him or any members of his family.

The rafts had stayed together for three weeks, strung out on the Pacific tied together with rope, before they separated and had different rescues. Whittaker had written in detail about his own rescue in the raft with Johnny DeAngelis and Jim Reynolds. They had eventually spotted palm trees. Whittaker had rowed over seven hours to reach land. According to him, they beached on November 11, 1942, on a small coral island, which we now knew was Nukufetau.

The men slept for a while and drank rainwater that had collected in pockets, or mounds, of coral. They ate coconuts from the ground that DeAngelis collected and small rodent-like rats that Whittaker killed with his sheath knife. That night it rained, and they turned the raft over them for shelter as they slept.

The next day they again saw planes, flying in formation, which they assumed were looking for submarines. They went looking for water, but high waves had polluted the pockets with salt water. The next plane they saw was much closer, so they went out in the raft, hoping to be seen. Travelling along side the island, they saw a deserted thatched hut and went ashore. Here they found more fresh water (with wigglers) in the base of palm trees. Again, they spotted a plane, but it did not see them. Needing rest, they fell asleep around noon. Whittaker shook DeAngelis when he saw boats coming toward them. The boats were outrigger canoes.

Unknown to Whittaker, Bill Cherry's raft had already been found. Those patrol planes were not looking for submarines, but other rafts. Earlier, one of the Navy scouting planes had dropped a note to a military post, manned by a "friendly power" that maintained a radio station on the island. They had requested help from the natives to look for the other rafts, which explained why the islanders were out in the heat of mid-day.

By early afternoon, some islanders had spotted Whittaker, DeAngelis, and Reynolds. One native, Toma, and his companions then placed DeAngelis and Reynolds on mats stretched across the supports between the outrigger float and the main part of one canoe. Rowing Whittaker in the raft, they left the open sea and entered a lagoon, taking the men to a village where women made them chicken soup. Soon two officers from that nearby garrison came, gave them fruit juices, and radioed the United States military.

Later, a Kingfisher plane arrived with a Navy physician, Lieutenant (Lt.) Hall, who began injections of glucose to save Jim Reynolds's life. The pilot, Lt. (jg.) Fred E. Woodward, then had told what he knew of the other rafts' rescues. Lieutenant Woodward's radioman, Lester Boutte, had spotted Bill Cherry's tiny raft, which led to their rescue.

We also knew from The Book that Lt. Bill Eadie had picked up Rickenbacker, Adamson, and Bartek from the third raft. Lieutenant Eadie set his Kingfisher seaplane down at dusk near the raft. He had strapped Colonel Adamson into the rear cockpit and lashed Rickenbacker and Bartek to the plane's wings. Now, too heavy to fly, they taxied until they met a motor torpedo boat, where Rickenbacker and Bartek were transferred. Colonel Adamson, too ill to be moved, stayed in the plane, which taxied the rest of the way to Island X-2, which we later found out was Funafuti. Only by talking with Bill Cherry did we learn that the distance between these two islands was over sixty miles.

After the initial success of finding some of the crew, the students wanted to know more about each rescue. Sometimes they wrote to Cherry, Bartek, and Reynolds for details. We soon discovered, however, that although each of these men had been involved in each of the raft rescues, they really did not know many details. They had been too busy staying alive.

Students' curiosity about the individual raft rescues led to searches, not only for the survivors, but also for the rescuers. Students wanted to find the men mentioned in The Book and newspaper articles. Specifically, they began searching for a radioman, Boutte; two Kingfisher pilots, Woodward and Eadie; a physician, Hall; and a native islander, Toma.

In January, Travis Senne wrote to the United States Army Military History Institute at Carlisle Barracks, Pennsylvania. John J. Slonaker, Chief of the Historical Reference Branch, wrote back that he did not have any addresses for the men we were seeking, but he did cite Whittaker's book telling about Rickenbacker and Bartek being transferred to a motor torpedo (PT) boat. He provided us with an address for an organization dedicated to recording the history of PT boats. He also furnished a list of references that contained information about the rescue. Students now made plans to go to the local public library. Mr. Slonaker's letter ended with, "You and your class are cordially invited to visit the Military History Institute, which is open Monday through Friday..." The sixth graders immediately pounced on this opportunity for a field trip. As they waited expectantly for confirmation, I remember contemplating how much endurance it would take for a bus trip with sixth graders from Iowa to Pennsylvania and back. I quickly shook my head *no*. "Party pooper!" one of them mumbled with a grin.

By now the students were feeding their own curiosity and quite capable of asking their own questions.

"How far were the men from Canton Island where they were supposed to land?"

"Where were all these islands? How far apart were they?"

"If the raft landed on an island, why did they paddle to another island for soup?"

"What's an outrigger canoe?"

"Who was the friendly power that had a radio station there?"

"Who's Lieutenant Hall?"

"How had they picked up Captain Cherry if a plane spotted him?"

"What happened to Radioman Boutte? And how do you pronounce his name?"

"If John Bartek was lashed to the wing of a plane, was it the left one or the right one?"

I must admit that when the student added this last question to the list, I lifted my eyebrows in a familiar "you-have-to-be-kidding" gesture. To the sixth grader's credit, he defended his question. "Mrs. Kelly, you said to write down any question we wanted answered, and that's definitely a question I want answered!"

But to the sixth graders, the most burning question of all was, "What happened to Toma?" They sent dozens of letters to locate him. Sixth grader Derrick Boden's letter to the Managing Editor of the *Army Historian*, U.S. Army Center of Military History in Washington, D.C. summarized our goal. "If you have any information on the rescuers or Toma who was nineteen at the time, please send it to us."

Since Toma actually lived on one of the Ellice Islands, he was enshrouded in an aura of mystery that the students wanted to solve. We all wondered if Toma had survived the war and if he had ever left his island home. The sixth graders considered him a hero. He had saved three men who were fast becoming special people to us.

The first letter-writing experiences were new and held a purpose. Now students still had a purpose for writing, but they were also frustrated with lack of details, long waits for letters to be answered, and the repetition of applying writing skills. Some students had become bored with the task of writing letters *error-free, in ink.*

One sixth grader, in particular, was having a difficult afternoon. After several tries, he was discouraged, but determined, to finish the letter during language arts class. He sighed when it was time for recess, and he still had not finished his letter to the Naval Historical Center, requesting information on Lester Boutte. I encouraged him by saying, "Go out to recess, David. You'll feel refreshed and can write your letter tomorrow." I will always be grateful to his parents, because the next day he arrived with a new writing utensil—an erasable ink pen—and a new attitude.

By February, David Abelson received a letter back from Dean C. Allard, Head of the Operational Archives Branch of the Naval Historical Center. Not only had he sent biographical data on Captain Lester H.

Boutte (pronounced "boo-TAY"), but he had also sent a "Report of the Rescue of Captain Rickenbacker and His Party on 11-12 November 1942." David enthusiastically wrote a thank-you letter. Part of it read, "I was thrilled by all the information on the rescue mission…[It] also gave the first name of the doctor on the island, Doctor William J. Hall."

The document that had been sent to the class was stamped *Secret and Confidential*. There were two lines through the word *Confidential* and another stamp had been added that said *Declassified*. I clarified to the class that during the war, military documents recorded facts about events. However, the documents were confidential, so information would not be given to the enemy. This report, written by G. F. Good, Jr., was a record by the commanding officer about the rescue of Eddie Rickenbacker and the others. Since the war ended it was okay for people to see the report. We now could have a copy to use for clues in our research.

The bell rang for recess and chatter erupted full force as the sixth graders headed to hall lockers for winter coats and boots. While I supervised the hallway activity, I overheard two students talking. "Just think," one of them said, "at first it was a secret, and then because of us—*because of us*—it's declassified!" I did not intend to dampen their enthusiasm.

David Abelson's perseverance had really paid off. Much information was packed into the document's four pages. According to the report, on 11 November 1942, at 1545 five Navy OS2U-3 (Kingfisher) planes had taken off from Funafuti, in the Ellice Islands, Central Pacific, to fly their normal evening plane patrol. At 1635 one of the plane's radiomen, Aviation Radioman Second Class L. H. Boutte, spotted an "irregular object" in the water. The pilot of the Kingfisher, Lt. (jg.) Frederick E. Woodward, flew lower and observed a small yellow life raft containing one man. Then he returned to Funafuti, made a message drop to report the discovery, and returned to the raft. The message was taken to the Force Commander, who instructed the PT tender, U.S.S. *Hilo*, to dispatch a PT boat to the area. PT Boat #21, commanded by Lt. A. F. Cluster, USN, located the raft by observing Lt. Woodward circling over it. We learned that Captain Cherry, in what we called Raft #1, was the first to be spotted. He was rescued at latitude 8° 22' 20" south and longitude 178° 39' 10" east.

The sixth graders soon renamed the United States Marine Corps document of the men's rescue that was written by Gen. George F. Good, Jr. as the "Rescue Report." It contained invaluable information for our research, but without extensive military knowledge, almost each fact also held a question for us.

One of the first questions involved time. Students researched how military time uses 00 to 23 to express hours, and, therefore, a.m. and p.m. are unnecessary. Students reasoned how 1635 military time meant Captain Cherry was seen at 4:35 p.m. in regular time.

But what really confused the students was how some dates did not match. Ben Jackson and Doug Haynes were two sixth graders quite interested in maps and had been making several of them to document our research. Only by plotting the latitude/longitude coordinates did we realize that this incident occurred across the International Date Line. The date for the rescuers was on one side, and the date for the survivors was on the other. I tried to explain about time zones, but I really preferred one student's explanation. "Cool!" he summarized. "The men were actually rescued before they were found!"

When Captain Cherry identified himself as the pilot of the B-17 that was carrying Eddie Rickenbacker, the search began for the other two rafts at dawn the following day. According to the Rescue Report, the Commanding Officer of the U.S.S. *Hilo* requested permission to accompany the search and was directed to maintain contact among the four motor torpedo boats and the five Kingfisher patrol planes.

The aviation unit ground crew worked all night to put all five planes in the air that morning at 0640. The search area was divided into section A, B, and C designated areas. Three of the five Kingfisher planes returned to Funafuti at 1005, were serviced, and took off again at 1100. Pilot Bill Eadie made a message drop on Nukufetau, requesting a lookout for possible survivors. Two other patrol planes were passing through Section A, when they sighted a raft with Rickenbacker, Adamson, and Bartek. Then one pilot remained in the air over the raft, while another pilot

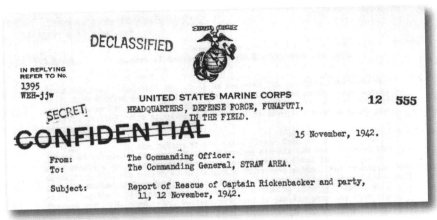

DECLASSIFIED

IN REPLYING
REFER TO No.
1395
WEH-jjw

SECRET

UNITED STATES MARINE CORPS
HEADQUARTERS, DEFENSE FORCE, FUNAFUTI,
IN THE FIELD.

12   555

~~CONFIDENTIAL~~

15 November, 1942.

From: The Commanding Officer.
To: The Commanding General, STRAW AREA.

Subject: Report of Rescue of Captain Rickenbacker and party,
             11, 12 November, 1942.

The header from General George F. Good, Jr.'s 1942 report of the men's rescue, which was called the "Rescue Report" by the sixth graders. It was sent to the students by Dean C. Allard at the Naval Historical Research Center in Washington, D.C.

returned to the base at Funafuti for fuel and to report the siting. Now, after ten hours of searching, pilots continued to switch places, leaving to refuel and, still not breaking radio silence, standing guard over the vulnerable raft below. By 1740 the Force Commander decided to break radio silence and send the U.S.S. *Hilo* and PT boats to the raft at latitude 8° 10' 30" south and longitude 178° 38' east. This raft had now been found, but the men were not yet rescued.

At 1830 the base received a message from a coastwatcher radio on Nukufetau that a raft and three survivors had been located there at latitude 8° south, longitude 178° 32' east. Twenty minutes later Lieutenant Woodward piloted a plane with Lt. William J. Hall (MC), USNR to Nukufetau to take water, soup, and glucose to Whittaker, DeAngelis, and Reynolds. The survivors in Raft #2 had rowed to the coral island and were being assisted by the coastwatcher and island natives. Help from the U.S. military was on the way.

Doug Haynes (*left*) and Ben Jackson used the old classroom globe and atlas to draw maps of the men's journey.

In the meantime, how could they rescue the third raft still out at sea? Since all survivors had been located, no further search was required during the last hour of daylight, but maintaining visual contact with the last raft would not be possible after dark. The exact location of the USS *Hilo* and PT boats was unknown. How long would it take them to reach the raft? Could the men survive another night in the raft? By daylight, would the raft have drifted, taking hours to find them again? Although the sea was calm, there was a heavy ground swell. Under these conditions, it would require any remaining boat on Funafuti at least five hours to reach the raft. If one of the patrol planes landed for a rescue, even if it did not sustain a casualty, it would be unable to take off again with the additional weight of the survivors.

The Rescue Report told how Lieutenant Eadie, fully aware of the situation and the danger involved, had volunteered to fly back to the raft, land the plane at dusk, and rescue the survivors. He relieved the pilot circling the raft, dropped two flares near the raft at 1930, landed, transferred all occupants to the plane, and began taxiing toward base. After going a few miles, they met PT boat #26 with the PT boat division commander also aboard. Bartek and Rickenbacker were transferred to the PT boat. Colonel Adamson stayed in the plane, with Boutte on the wing. The report stated, "The PT boat, followed by the plane taxiing on the surface, then returned to Funafuti, arriving at 0300 Friday, 13 November, 1942."

While the third raft of men was being rescued, the U.S.S. *Hilo* returned to Funafuti and was instructed to proceed to Nukufetau to pick up the survivors of Raft #2. On Friday 13 November 1942, Reynolds, Whittaker, and DeAngelis were taken aboard the ship and headed back to Funafuti. On account of low visibility, they had to stand outside the north passage, not entering the lagoon until the following morning at 0926 on 14 November 1942. Whittaker and DeAngelis were taken ashore, but Jim Reynolds was in only fair condition and stayed on the U.S.S. *Hilo*.

The sixth graders spent a great deal of time analyzing facts in the Rescue Report and comparing details that they knew from The Book. We had learned the names of the islands. Captain Cherry had used the name Funafuti, which was the atoll island base of the Ellice Islands. We knew the island Nukufetau, where the raft beached, was one of the Ellice Islands. We knew how far it was from Funafuti. We understood the friendly power had a radio station there that was used by coastwatchers, looking for enemy activity. We learned it was PT Boat #21, commanded by Lt. A. P. Cluster, USN, who had picked up Captain Cherry, after Boutte had spotted him. We also knew that the physician flown to Nukufetau to treat the survivors of Raft #2 was not just Lieutenant Hall— he was Lt. William J. Hall, (MC), USNR.

As I had predicted before we started our research, each question answered, led to more questions. Now the sixth graders had these questions:

- *What was the PT Boat #21 commander Cluster's first name?*
- *What had happened to Lieutenants Woodward, Eadie, Forrest, and all the other Kingfisher pilots?*

- *Who were the men on PT Boat #26? Who actually lifted Rickenbacker and Bartek aboard the boat?*
- *Why did Colonel Adamson stay in the plane?*
- *What country was the "friendly power"? And who were the coastwatchers?*
- *What had happened to Toma?*

And then, remembering that one student still wondered if John Bartek had been tied to the left or right wing before he was transferred to the PT boat, I had a question of my own. When Boutte spotted Captain Cherry in the raft, was he looking out the left window or the right window of the Kingfisher? However, we had enough on our plates, and I was not about to suggest this question be added to our list!

As excited as the students were to find factual details about the men's rescue, they were even more excited to communicate with the men on a personal level. Bill Cherry sent letters and photos. The sixth grader's favorite picture was of three generations of Cherry men, including eleven-month-old W. T. Cherry, IV. Enclosed was a message in reference to Captain Cherry's own photograph: "Note the crooked nose. It was broken by a shark while in the raft."

John Bartek wrote personal letters to each student, making each feel quite important. We had sent him a class picture, and he had memorized all the students' names and faces. When a package arrived in the school mail from John, it usually contained photos of his family, questions for the students about things they were doing, and copies of more old newspaper clippings or items for our research.

Jim Reynolds also wrote letters to each student. In a letter to Niki Nilsen, he told about his son. To Jennifer Jones, he wrote about hitting his nose on the radio receiver when they hit the water. He told Cathy Watson that he recently had talked to the other three survivors, after receiving their contact information from us. He shared with David Abelson, "As far as thinking we wouldn't make it, well, the only thing

This is
W. J. Cherry, JR.
WT CHERRY III
& W.T. CHERRY IV
(11 MONTH)
NOW
(NOTE THE CROOKED
NOSE. IT WAS
BROKEN BY A
SHARK WHILE IN
THE RAFT

Captain Cherry thrilled the sixth graders with this photo and reference in his note to the shark that broke his nose.

that kept us alive was the hope that we would be found. With very little to eat and getting very little sleep we had a lot of time to hope." A letter to Ben Jackson said, "Having sent SOS, or I should say being on the key for nine hours, did one thing for me, I can send as well with one hand as well as the other." Jim shared with Doug Haynes, "Most of my fishing is for trout in the Klamath National Forest in Northern California." And in a letter to Travis Senne, Jim wrote, "The first thing I wanted when I got to the hospital at Hickam Field outside of Honolulu was a strawberry shake. However, McDonald's wasn't in existence at that time."

The men knew the general facts about their own rescues, but not many details. Time had also passed. Ultimately, it would be sixth graders from

John Bartek sent a photo of himself in 1985 looking through his scrapbook of newspaper clippings from 1942.

Room 14, Meeker Elementary School in Ames, Iowa, who would tell the men more of their own story than they had ever known.

News reporter Kenneth Pins had interviewed the class and written a feature article that appeared January 20, 1985, in the *Des Moines Register*. He told how the students already knew that Rickenbacker and some others had died, but the students were trying to find members of the men's families and other rescuers. We enjoyed the attention that the media article provided, as students were thrilled to share their project with anyone who would listen. And listen they did.

Chapter Four

SIXTH GRADE
SUPER SLEUTHS

S OON ANOTHER SIXTH GRADER, DAVID JURGENS, received correspondence from Major Lester A. Sliter, USAF, who was Chief of the Inquiries Branch of the Air Force Historical Research Center at Maxwell Air Force Base in Alabama. Major Sliter provided several documents, including a 1942 map of the Pacific, "The Air Transport Command in the Pacific, 1942," and excerpts from *LIFE* magazine. In the January and February 1943 issues, *LIFE* magazine printed Eddie Rickenbacker's story, which later was published in book form. On the front covers of the magazine excerpts was a notice stating this was copyrighted material and "provided only for purposes of private study, scholarship or research." Completely missing the legal caution given, the students were delighted. As one said, "We keep writing that we want stuff for our research project, and they send it to us."

The articles mentioned some of the men's hometowns, including Woodward's and Boutte's. It may seem strange that we did not start with the *LIFE* magazine articles that had been the basis for Rickenbacker's book, *Seven Came Through*, but since the students had a connection with Whittaker's book, we had used it as our primary source. Not only were we looking for more of the story, but we were also searching for information that generally was not published during the war.

However, as we looked through the materials, we found an Iowa connection. Lieutenant Fred Woodward, the pilot with radioman Boutte who spotted Captain Cherry, was originally from Davenport, Iowa. The unsuspecting people of Davenport were about to be deluged with letters from Ames.

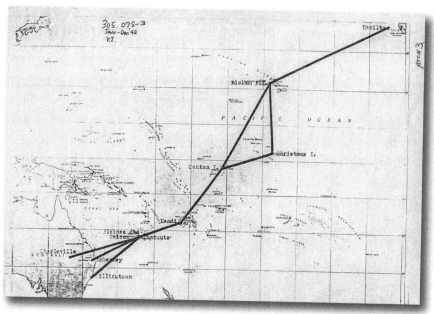

This 1942 map that Maj. Lester Sliter sent the class showed designated locations for the intended journey by Eddie Rickenbacker.

In the biographical data on Les Boutte that was sent to us, we learned he originally had lived in Abbeville, Louisiana. A class letter to the Vermilion Parish Library in Abbeville produced an address. Les Boutte now lived in Metairie, Louisiana. Sixth grader Christy Scott made the contact. We were about to find our first rescuer.

Soon a letter arrived from Boutte, a career military man, now a retired Navy captain. With his letter he sent a small photo of the Kingfisher plane and a note that said, "The aircraft used in the rescue of Rickenbacker and crew."

"Can we keep it?" the class wanted to know. I looked at the small photo that obviously had been pasted in a scrapbook.

"No, we need to return it. But I have an idea," I reassured the class.

My husband was an excellent photographer and had a darkroom in our basement. He agreed to enlarge the photo for our school bulletin board,

Lester Boutte, naval Kingfisher radioman, first spotted "an irregular-shaped object" that turned out to be Capt. Cherry in the doughnut raft.

Les Boutte sent a message with this photo: "The Kingfisher aircraft used in the rescue of Rickenbacker and crew."

make prints for each student, and send the original back to Louisiana. I also sent two enlarged photos to Captain Boutte. He wanted to hang one in his study and autograph the other for me. Increasingly we were reaching beyond curiosity for details of an event in 1942; we were connecting with people in 1985.

In addition to the wealth of research that Major Sliter sent us, he also had a request. Could our class please send news clippings, photos, and other facts about the men and their rescuers to the editor of the *Airman* magazine? This was a very interesting development. Now military personnel were seeking information from us. I now referred to my students as the Sixth Grade Super Sleuths.

One morning the students had an idea. "Mrs. Kelly, let's reunite the men!" I probably looked a little shocked, although I should have seen the signs. These men were becoming progressively important to the students. Why wouldn't they want to meet them?

I moved slowly. "O-kay, " I responded, "and where do you think this reunion should take place?"

"In the middle of the country, so they all will come."

"You know, like from California, Texas, New Jersey, Louisiana— come to the middle."

"Yeah, like in Iowa!"

"Sure. We could have a reunion here! They could all come visit us!"

So in January, with the outside temperature minus twenty degrees and snow piled deep, the students invited the men to a Rescue Reunion in Ames, Iowa, from April 18-20, 1985. I headed for the administrator's office to see my principal. "Lee," I started without much preamble, "I need help." The support he and his wife Abbie supplied over the next few weeks was invaluable. The energy from that first letter to Captain Cherry was erupting literally into an international event. I could not handle it alone.

One day American Airlines contacted the school with confirmation that they would fly the survivors to Des Moines. Captain Cherry had retired as a pilot from American Airlines, and the class had given that airline the first chance at providing free transportation. Deep down I am certain I must have been stifling a grin when the students hit upon this plan during a class meeting. I only remember thinking two things. One, it was clever of them to think that if one airline would not come through, they could simply contact another. And, two, how does a teacher teach subtlety when writing requests? American Airlines was most generous in offering to fly all the men to Iowa.

A second phone call was a complete surprise. Jeanne Coverdale, with the local Gateway Center-Holiday Inn, called to ask if they could please provide free accommodations for the men. In addition, she requested giving a reception for the men, students, a few other guests, and me. We now had free transportation and accommodations for the survivors. We were still trying to find more rescuers to join us.

The Associated Press had picked up the story that had appeared in the *Des Moines Register.* Newspapers across the United States printed versions of the article. We began receiving phone calls from major newspapers across the country wanting personal interviews. Requests came to send press releases, interview the students about their research, visit our school, and observe our classroom. We were busy providing information to others, even as we requested that others do the same for us.

We had not learned much about the B-17. Lieutenant Colonel (Lt. Col.) Ronald W. Shealy (Air Force) had sent David Jurgens a packet. In addition, we did have some information from books, but the students wanted more. Dale Brentnall was my husband's principal at Fellows Elementary. Dale had once installed armament on newer models of B-17s. In World War II he had also been an aerial gunnery instructor in the Navy. Before the Rescue Reunion, Dale came to Meeker one afternoon to share information about the B-17. As sixth grader Niki Nilsen wrote, "Thank you for coming and telling us some facts about the Flying Fortress. We learned a lot!"

In March the sixth grader, who had so much success obtaining the Rescue Report, wrote a letter to PT Boats, Inc., a historical and educational museum in Memphis, Tennessee. David Abelson asked for information on men who would have been on PT Boats. Students had learned that after pilots in planes had spotted the survivors, men in motor torpedo (PT) boats had rescued them. Alyce Guthrie responded with addresses and a description of the "Eddie Rickenbacker Rescue" from their organization's book, *Knights of the Sea.*

We now had an address and first name for the commander of PT Boat #21—Alvin P. Cluster. We also had addresses for other men we had not known about—Edward A. Green, Howard E. Featherling, and W. H. Wepner. These were all men who had been on the PT boats when the men were rescued. Immediately students sent letters requesting that they attend our reunion in April.

The first address was for Al Cluster, the commander of the PT boat that had picked up Captain Cherry. Classmate David Abelson volunteered to write a letter. Yes, this was the same sixth grader who was so frustrated with his first assigned letter. Soon he had a response from Bend, Oregon.

The letter began, "Dear David, How kind of you to invite me to attend the Rickenbacker Survivors Reunion. And what a unique project you and your classmates have undertaken. I am unable to come to Ames at this time and my role in the rescue was a minor one. However, I would like for you to know more about this remarkable young man, Captain Cherry...."

Al Cluster then went on to tell more details about his involvement. The day after Captain Cherry's flight was reported missing, he was taking four motor torpedo boats from Palmyra Island (south of Hawaiian Islands) where they had been based, to Funafuti to protect the Fifth Marine Defense Battalion from which they surmised a Japanese attack would come from the Gilbert Islands to the north. To prevent the enemy from knowing about the occupation on Funafuti, they had been ordered to maintain radio silence. For several days en route they searched for the missing B-17 plane, which they had been told to look for on their trip.

Then, when Captain Cherry's raft was spotted about ten miles north of the base island of Funafuti on November 11, Al Cluster headed out with his PT boat crew. Having been warned of Japanese trickery, and not knowing whether the man was Japanese or American, he ordered his gunner's mate, Sherlie King, to stand on the bow of the PT boat with a gun, just in case there was a problem. "The poor guy in the raft heard me and weakly yelled, 'Don't shoot! Don't shoot!' We realized then he was an American. I maneuvered the boat alongside the raft and lifted him… with *ONE* hand onto the deck….Later I learned he weighed only eighty-five pounds….I took his pulse and it was an unbelievable eighteen. We heated some tomato soup and spooned it into him. His pulse shot up to nearly seventy."

The other three addresses sent to us by Alyce Guthrie were for men on PT Boat #26 that had picked up Rickenbacker, Adamson, and Bartek. One of the Sixth Grade Super Sleuths, Michele Mitchell, wrote to Edward Green in Irving, Texas. He, too, quickly responded, telling us that after the war he began studies for the Roman Catholic priesthood and in 1953 was ordained a Dominican priest. Having lost his own hearing, he was now at St. Albert's Priory, The Dominican Fathers, University of Dallas, ministering to deaf people in the Dallas area. Father Green also shared his recollections with us on the rescue of Rickenbacker and Bartek. As Executive Officer, he was second in command of the PT boat.

After Captain Cherry had been rescued, the patrol planes, PT boats, and the U.S.S. *Hilo* began at dawn to search for the other two rafts. Edward Green wrote, "The day passed with no result, except for eyes that ached from hours of searching an empty ocean." Finally, at sunset a radio message from Kingfisher pilot Bill Eadie to the U.S.S. *Hilo* reported that a raft with Rickenbacker had been spotted. PT #26 was the closest boat to the raft's location, about thirty miles away. They throttled up full speed, heading to the bearing given, the boat "cutting through the moderate swell and pancaking down after passing each wave crest."

After the rescue, Ed Green wrote in a publication, "Chief Motor Mac 'Tex' Featherling [and two others] had a bucket brigade going in the engine room to keep water in the Packards [engines] for their water-jackets were leaking, and to walk between them was like getting doused

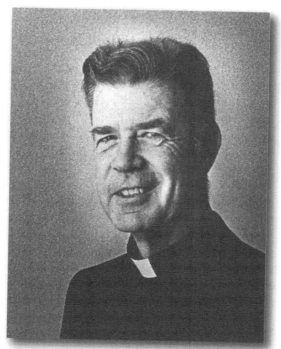

Edward A. Green, a crewman on PT #26, became
Father Austin Green, a Dominican priest, after the war.

in a hot shower." With Adamson in Bill Eadie's plane taxiing behind the
PT boat, they traveled about forty miles to Funafuti. In his first letter to the
class, Father Green wrote, "I remember getting extra blankets to keep John
Bartek warm as he lay on the foredeck of our PT. I also remember telling
the cook to give Rickenbacker hot soup instead of cold pineapple juice—
a better diet for a man who had had almost no food for three weeks."

Later in a letter to me, Father Green wrote so eloquently,

> From the distance of 42 years, I am more keenly aware of
> the coordinated human effort needed to effect the rescue of
> these men and how many seemingly trivial happenings,
> mostly each man's being faithful to his particular job, all

helped to produce the successful rescue. For example, I think of our machinist mates forming a bucket brigade to keep water in our leaky engines while we were running at top speed to rendezvous with the plane that had found the raft.

Sixth grader Amy LeMay wrote to a third PT boat man, Howard "Tex" Featherling, the man Father Green had mentioned. He quickly responded from Sinton, Texas. Although, he too, was unable to come to the reunion, he shared with us by written correspondence. In one letter, he told of saving the knife that had been in the raft with Rickenbacker when he was transferred to their PT boat. He wrote, "It was made by Case, and had bird feathers and dried blood on the blade, so I believed them when they said a bird lit on Capt.'s head...." He later added, "I kept the knife for a long time after the war. Don't know what finally happened to it." I was glad he added that last sentence, or I know the sixth graders would have insisted we track it down.

The fourth address was for William (Bill) H. Wepner, the quartermaster (navigator) on PT #26. This time, classmate Jennifer Jones wrote a letter to Bill Wepner in Ripon, Wisconsin, requesting he come to the reunion. Bill and his wife Marie quickly accepted our invitation. They also sent photos of the PT boat and some young island native boys.

One particular paragraph stood out from the publication Alyce Guthrie sent from the PT boat museum. It said, "Each man of the crew jockeyed for position to be the first to help Mr. Rickenbacker aboard, so he said, 'Just call me Eddie, boys, but get me on that boat!' Helped by Chief GM Blozis, RD Nelson, and QM Wepner, the survivors got aboard and the boat pointed its bow toward Funafuti." We now had another question answered. One of the men who actually helped Rickenbacker aboard the PT boat was Bill Wepner, and he was coming to Meeker Elementary.

While some sixth graders were looking for the "PT boat men," as they called them, others were searching for the Kingfisher pilots, Fred Woodward and Bill Eadie. The media—a newspaper columnist and a

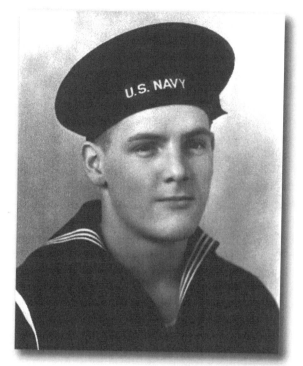

William Wepner, USN, helped lift Eddie Rickenbacker
and John Bartek on board PT #26.

famous radio personality—would assist our next two sleuthing results.

The letters to Davenport, Iowa, about Lt. Fred Woodward started with a request by classmate Amy Murphy to the Davenport Public Library. Mary R. Herr, from the Special Collections Room, suggested locating Woodward through his military records, or through our senators and representatives in Washington. She closed by saying, "Would be interested to know how this turns out."

Amy Murphy followed up with a thank-you to Mary Herr telling her what my students already knew, that due to the Privacy Act of 1974 only the next of kin had access to military records. Amy concluded by saying, "We haven't found Lt. Woodward yet, but we won't give up. Thank you

Photographs from
William Wepner

Boys from
Tuvalu - 1942

A PT Boat

Students began filling their research notebooks with letters and photos from the men. Bill Wepner sent the class 1942 photos he had taken of children on Funafuti and of a PT boat.

for your advice and interest toward our research project." Then she signed her name with a tiny smiley face. I remember thinking how the students had changed. They were less discouraged if they could not navigate one pathway. They simply chose another route. However, before I had time to mail Amy's letter, Mary Herr called the school with another idea—perhaps we could write to Bill Wundram at the *Quad-City Times* in Davenport, suggesting that he might be interested.

Amy's letter to the newspaper columnist was a request. If anyone knew of Woodward or how we could locate him, please let us know. Later the librarian wrote back with a series of articles that Bill Wundram had written for the newspaper. People in the community had responded, and they had located Fred Woodward's widow in Greenwich, Connecticut. Lieutenant (by then Captain) Woodward had stayed in the Navy as a career but died in 1957 near the Aleutian Islands, when his airplane crashed into the sea.

We had material that listed Lt. William Eadie originally from Evanston, Illinois. The class knew by now that a good start would be to contact a library. In this case, it was the Evanston Public Library. A librarian from the Reference Department wrote that no names matched, but she sent phone directory listings of people with the same last name from Evanston, Chicago, and Near North Suburbs. One sixth grader, Brad Arnold, wrote to an address for Samuel L. Eadie. Although not directly related to the Bill Eadie we were trying to find, Sam knew about him. He wrote several pages of anecdotes and history for our class. Brad's thank-you said it all when he wrote how interesting the letter was. "I bet you spent a lot of time writing to us. You wrote a long letter."

In the meantime, phone calls with Les Boutte informed us that Bill Eadie had been killed later in the war. We had thought our involvement with the Eadie family had ended, but we were to be surprised later with unintentional assistance from a famous radio broadcaster.

Chapter Five

PURSUE AND PERSEVERE

T HROUGHOUT THESE SEARCHES, STUDENTS continued their quest for Toma, the native island lad who had spotted Reynolds, DeAngelis, and Whittaker on one of the coral islands. We knew only his first name and a country. Postage was expensive to send correspondence across the Pacific Ocean. Telephone calls were impossible. Thus, each letter written took so much time to send and receive. "Where's Toma?" the students wondered in frustration.

We knew that the Gilbert and Ellice Islands had been under a British Protectorate during World War II. The Ellice Islands had then separated from the Gilbert Islands (now Kiribati) in 1975. On October 1, 1978, they became an independent constitutional monarchy named Tuvalu (pronounced too-VAH-loo), meaning "Eight Standing Together" or "Cluster of Eight," referring to their eight inhabited islands. In reality, Tuvalu is a chain of nine islands, all of coral formation. Of the nine separate islands, six are atolls, consisting of several islets (small islands)—an atoll being a coral island that encircles a lagoon.

In our research reports from the military, we only knew about two of the atolls, Funafuti and Nukufetau. Now, through further research, we learned that Tuvalu's islands are scattered over 1.3 million square kilometers or over 500,000 square miles. But the total landmass for the entire country is only about twenty-six square kilometers, or *ten square miles*. From the northern most island of Nanumea, to the southern most island of Niulakita, the distance is about 370 miles. Nukufetau and Funafuti are in the middle of this northwest to southeast chain. The island of Nukufetau is a rectangular-shaped atoll with a landmass stretched out that would equal about *one square mile*. I remember how this information impacted the students. They were beginning to sense the vastness of the Pacific Ocean and the miniscule landmass on which James Whittaker landed the raft with Jim Reynolds and Johnny DeAngelis. As one student put it, "Mrs. Kelly, they almost didn't make it!"

The more we learned about Tuvalu, the more we wanted to learn. Sixth graders Ben Jackson and Doug Haynes drew maps for us to visualize where events took place. Students poured over maps at the Ames Public and the Iowa State University libraries. Finally, we contacted companies and purchased our own commercial maps. One night I received an apologetic phone call from an ISU librarian informing me that we had more information than they did, and they were sorry to keep disappointing my students, who kept coming there on their own time to learn more about Tuvalu.

We learned that the people of Tuvalu are of the Polynesian culture. They speak two languages, Tuvaluan and English. The sixth graders were thrilled with this information. Although some students wanted to learn Tuvaluan, we decided it was more practical to communicate in English, because of time restraints with the Rescue Reunion coming up!

To find Toma, we applied one of the first guidelines I had given the students. We needed to send out many letters at once. This was especially true when time and distance impeded the efficiency of our research. The class was really working as a cohesive unit. No longer was it functioning as seven independent research groups. Students were sharing materials among groups. Ideas flowed in brainstorming sessions. Finding Toma had become an all-out effort supported by all the Sixth Grade Super Sleuths.

Now, looking back on what happened, it is easier to connect the dots. We have dates when letters were written, but do not have records when letters were received. Therefore, we do not have as good a time line as was given in the Rescue Report. (And we did not have any excuse. We were not in the middle of a war.) What we did have were three distinct pathways of research.

The first pathway involved a friend of Bob's and mine at the University of Hawaii. In early February, I wrote a letter to Dr. Gordon Tsuji. Before

Hazel Jacobson   Suzanne Kelly (left) and Lisa Moore

Retired teacher 'plants a seed' for reunion of men lost at sea

Article in *The Dallas County News*, April 4, 1985. Mrs. Jacobson read Whittaker's book to Suzanne Zobrist, who became Mrs. Kelly and read "The Book" to her student, Lisa Moore. (*Reprinted with permission*)

I taught at Meeker Elementary, my husband and I had been graduate students at Purdue University in Indiana. Our best friends, Gordon and Sharon Tsuji, were neighbors living in the same building unit of married student housing. Later, although I taught at Miami Elementary, Sharon and I both taught in the Lafayette School District in Lafayette, Indiana. We stayed in contact with each other when Gordon took a position with the University of Hawaii, and my husband and I took jobs with the Ames Community School District in Iowa. When Gordon finished his degree and they moved off the mainland, Sharon donated several kitchen metal cooling racks to me, rather than pay shipment back to Hawaii. For years, I had been using these items in my science labs at Meeker Elementary. Students had no idea there was a connection between those cooling racks and a search for Toma.

One of my present colleagues, fourth grade teacher Dr. Dwight Herold, had been in the Peace Corps and alerted us to an East-West Center that deals with the island languages and history. We had tried locating this organization, but we had been unable to find it. Thus, I was requesting Dr. Gordon Tsuji's help. Gordon responded quickly. He had called the East-West Center, a federally funded program of the U.S. Department of State, established for the cultural interchange of peoples of the East and West.

With our written request, Gordon was routed to the Pacific Islands Development Program (PIDP) and spoke to Ms. Titilia Barbour. She came up with our first addresses for Tuvalu—one for the Prime Minister, Dr. Tomasi Puapua, and one for Mr. Amasone Kilei, the Secretary to Government. Students had already used a 1985 World Almanac and found the name of the prime minister, but now they had an address. Classmate Doug Haynes promptly wrote to both addresses. When he wrote "Honorable Dr. Tomasi Puapua, Prime Minister of Tuvalu, Vaiaku, Funafuti, Tuvalu," it was quite momentous. For the first time we sent a letter with U.S.A. added to the return address.

In the meantime, my husband had another idea, which became our second pathway of research. When we first moved to Ames from Indiana, George Beal and his family lived across the street from us, but they later moved to Hawaii. Bob thought George, also, had something to do with the organization that Gordon had described. We quickly found our former neighbor, Dr. George Beal, a research associate with the East-West Communication Institute. He said he knew Titilia Barbour, whom Gordon had talked with, and that her desk was next to Kini Suschnigg, who also was from Fiji. They worked at the PIDP unit. Dr. Beal shared that both units were on the same floor of the center, and he knew these two people well.

On our behalf, Kini wrote to a close friend of hers, Mr. Bikeni Paeniu, who was the Director of Agriculture in the Ministry of Agriculture at Vaiaku, Funafuti Island, Tuvalu. Dr. Beal also wrote a letter to Mr. Paeniu, since they had in common the Ministries of Agriculture, as he was working with Fiji and Western Samoa to improve the effectiveness of their agricultural research. Kini Suschnigg requested Bikeni Paeniu find out if Toma was still in Nukufetau, and, if so, to telex Dr. Beal. If he was no longer there, were there any relatives or friends who could help locate or remember this incident of forty-two years ago?

As I now read copies of these letters, I am touched by the enormous efforts people put forth on our behalf. When our former neighbor wrote to the Director of Agriculture, he said in part, "While I recognize you have many more important things to do...any help you could give would be greatly appreciated." When Kini wrote to her friend, the same Director of Agriculture, she wrote, "Your assistance in this very moving incident will mean *so* much to Ms. Kelly and to her students at Ames Meeker School, Iowa, as well as everyone else involved. We are all keeping our fingers crossed and trust that your investigations will prove fruitful and that we will be hearing some very exciting news from you very soon...We send you our Aloha."

The third pathway stretched in many directions. Super Sleuth Doug Haynes wrote to the British Embassy in Washington, D.C., which directed him to the British Information Services in New York City, and then to the British High Commission in Fiji, which provided an address for the Tuvalu High Commission. Doug had already written a letter to the Tuvalu High Commission with an address in Suva, Fiji. Now he had received the same address with an added "P.O. Box 1495." Doug's letters to people and places were being forwarded from one to the other and sometimes two or more ended at the same location. He wrote letter after letter for four months and then patiently waited for a reply.

All three pathways converged on Monday, April 1, 1985. *We found Toma!* At 6:45 p.m. that evening, my husband took a phone call at our home from Kini Suschnigg, calling from Honolulu. She had sent a telex message on March 20 but did not know why we had not received it, but said she would send another copy of the message, "Toma is alive."

Doug's letter to Prime Minister Tomasi Puapua was given to H. Panapa, Head of the Broadcasting and Information Division of the government. Mr. Panapa wrote, "I am pleased to inform you that the Toma you mentioned is still alive. His full name is Mr. Toma Fakapae. I actually talked to Toma on the telephone and our conversation was recorded. Unfortunately, I cannot send it because it was in Tuvaluan, which I thought you wouldn't understand. Toma remembers very clearly the day he and his crew on a canoe found the three men. He even remembers their names."

In The Book, Whittaker had described Toma as being nineteen years old. Now Mr. Panapa wrote to us that Toma was actually twenty-one years of age when he rescued James Whittaker. And for sixth graders who always want to be taller, they were quite interested to learn, "Toma now is well over 6 ft. 6 inches tall…." Mr. Panapa also enclosed a booklet on Tuvalu and promised to translate a conversation with him and send it to us.

I also received a letter from Kini Suschnigg from the East-West Center. Part of it read, "Dear Ms. Kelly: Just a quick note to enclose a telex received on March 20 from Mr. Tauaasa Taafaki. Thrilled that Mr. Toma is still in Nukufetau Island and that he remembers well event." The telex said, "Attn. Kini from Tauaasa Taafaki, Secretary Ministry Commerce Natural Resources. Your letter addressed Bikeni Paeniu RE. Suzanne Kelly Enquiries Toma of Nukufetau Island. Bikeni has left dept…Toma is still alive and remember well event. Prime Minister's office contacting school concerned in Iowa. Regards."

A third letter arrived from the Tuvalu High Commission, located in Suva, Fiji. The correspondence was addressed to "Master Doug Haynes % Suzanne Kelly, Room 14, Meeker Elementary." It was from the Acting High Commissioner, A. Kilei. (This had to be from Mr. Amasone Kilei, the second address provided by the East-West Center. Doug had written to the Prime Minister and to the Secretary to Government, Mr. Kilei.) Somehow, all three pathways had linked. Mr. Kilei wrote, "As you requested we have managed to get confirmation from Tuvalu that Toma is alive and living on his home island of Nukufetau. He is however unable to walk for paralysis in both legs." He went on to say that he had sent two official documents on Tuvalu for us to use. He closed by saying, humbly, "We hope you will accept them."

As soon as we knew Toma was alive, my husband went into action to facilitate help from the U.S. Embassy in Fiji, requesting visa assistance for Toma in the event he could travel. Although that was impossible, we were still glad to hear from him. Another telex sent to Kini and passed on to us read, "RE Toma Fakapae…[I] have contacted him but regret he cannot travel to USA as his both legs are paralysed and too sick to travel. He would like to thank for the invitation and apologise for not able to make it and Toma also wish to see them."

The sixth grade students were ecstatic with their investigative research. Even if it was April Fools' Day, it was no joke. The next day the Super Sleuths proudly made a sign and posted it on the classroom door. "WE FOUND TOMA!" Most of the school population had no idea what the sign meant, but it was the 1985 version of high-fiving—multiplied to the nth degree!

Our class procedure was that once someone corresponded with us, we immediately wrote thank-yous. Students wrote one and I wrote one. Predictably, Doug's thank-you to the prime minister's office was also filled with more questions. He also requested that besides the English translation of their conversation, could we please have the one in Tuvaluan? Then Doug added, "Since we have done a lot of research we would be interested in learning how you found Toma." The students now were becoming curious, not only about the destination, but about the journey.

Not all the letters the students sent were answered with an envelope of colorful stamps from a far-off country. Some of the letters were returned undelivered. Yet, students continued to write. They might not "reach," but they still wanted to "reach out."

Four days after we found Toma, I received a beautifully written letter on my desk. It began, "Dear Mrs. Kelly, I would like to inform you I would write the longest letter you want me to. My invention is done and I know what happens in my books…." It was signed by Super Sleuth

Nicki Moreland. There were no more writing assignments, only adventures. And there was nothing like success to motivate more searches.

The reunion was two and a half weeks away. The days before the Rescue Reunion were hectic with the press and media. Sometimes news organizations, many from the men's hometowns, called and wanted interviews. As much as possible, I had students do the interviews. They were well versed in the project and knew the facts. Speaking to reporters was excellent experience with communication skills. One day we had been particularly inundated with requests. I remember continuing our lesson, and each time someone came to the door I would ask what they wanted, turn, and say to the class, "Who has not given an interview today?" Then I would send those students off to tell their story. After school, a network crew contacted me with a request to follow me around all day in the classroom. Would I object? I talked to my principal, and Lee had no objections, if I did not.

In preparation for all this publicity, my husband thoughtfully asked if I wanted a new dress for the Rescue Reunion or any of the television appearances I was making. I assured him I did not, but I then decided that I could use a new slip—a shorter one would keep me from worrying that it was showing. (How times change. I have not worn a slip in years.) That night I was running late after school because of a telephone interview with a newspaper in Texas. (The reporter had said, "Ya, know? We're right fond of Captain Cherry in this neck of the woods.") But I decided a clothing store would still be open and headed downtown.

In the store I hurriedly picked out a slip and took it to the counter to purchase. I became aware that two older women were whispering nearby.

"You ask her, " the first one said.

"No, *you* ask her," the second one argued.

The first one stepped forward, cleared her throat, and said, "Excuse me, but are you a teacher?" At first, I wondered if I had chalk dust on my face or some other sign of my profession. But I nodded.

She then turned to her friend. "I just knew it. Mabel, I told you it was *her*. Could we please have your autograph, Mrs. Kelly?"

I remember shaking my head all the way home. I had a new understanding for people who are in the news, however fleetingly.

The next day was a busy one. A network crew had arranged to meet before school, conduct an interview, and then tape classes all day. I had insisted I did not have time to talk to the media when I was teaching. Thus, I planned to meet them before school.

At home, before I left, everything went wrong. The outfit I wanted to wear was dirty. The second choice was in the washer, but needed more time to be dried. The third choice, a dress, had a red and white figured top with a plain red skirt, but the skirt's hem was ripped. I quickly dressed in choice number three, grabbed a spool of thread and a needle, and drove to Meeker Elementary.

The television crew was waiting in the parking lot. I unlocked the school and suggested they set up equipment, while I went to fix my hem. The cameraman assured me he would not show my hem. "But you'll show my face, and I'll know my hem was dragging," I insisted. After I was back in the classroom and finished the interview, the soundman approached me with a battery-packed microphone.

"Just lift up the edge of your blouse and put this pack around your waist so it won't be seen."

"But I'm not wearing a blouse. This is a dress."

"You have to be wearing a blouse." The soundman looked uncomfortable.

"No problem. I'll just lift up my dress, and you can attach it. Wait. The bell is about to ring. Here, come to my closet and help me."

Now the man was extremely distraught. "I can't do that. I'm married."

"Oh, for goodness sake. I'm married, too. What does that have to do with anything?" I headed for my large storage closet and turned on the light, practically pulling him inside and partway closing the door.

I lifted the skirt part of my dress, and he placed the battery pack in the center of my back. Then, just for orneriness, I whispered, "I'm so glad somebody gets to see my new slip."

At noon, my husband rushed over to Meeker during noon break to see how I was handling the media. "Anything I can do to help?"

I looked at the television crew and at my class waiting to go to lunch. "Could you please walk the students to the lunchroom and supervise until I get there? I need my battery recharged, but only this guy can do that." With that comment, we almost needed to call the school nurse to resuscitate the soundman!

The media was everywhere. We had done interviews with major city newspapers where all the men were located. We had provided "the rest of the story" for Paul Harvey's radio show and stories for National Public Radio Broadcasting. All three major television networks—ABC, CBS, and NBC—had sent crews to cover our research project. Each time the telephone rang in the office, a secretary had to bring a message to the classroom. We were disrupting the school, although I was trying hard to keep distractions at a minimum.

Sometimes I had so much to handle I did not know what to do first; however, I certainly had "To Do" lists. One day I had a stack of messages from the office with people wanting me to return phone calls to them. With time differences on both the East and West Coast, I prioritized the list, trying to juggle everything at once, and not doing a very good job of it.

Sixth grader Erik Smedal's mother, Sharon, was a substitute teacher. She had often subbed for me when I needed to be gone. One day she showed up at the door with a message for Erik and casually asked if she could help. I looked at the clock and admitted I needed to call someone back. Could she please supervise the class while they read? "No problem," she said. "In fact, if you want, I'll just use your plans and continue the lesson."

The students were dealing with the media attention like pros. Initially, they were antsy and excited. Now they viewed the press as a necessity to get the story out, so we could find more clues. Sometimes we had so many pathways we were searching, I found it difficult to remember which student had sent a request and to whom. One day the school secretary came for a student to talk to the State Department. An hour later, a sixth grader had a call from the National Archives in Washington, D.C. The third interruption was a call from the Pentagon. I was very confused and in the midst of the science lab asked, "Okay, class. Who's wanted by the Pentagon?" which brought a round of laughter from the students.

We had a Rescue Reunion to prepare. The students wanted to give some gifts to the men, and I wanted the students to complete their poetry and prose unit. Combining both ideas, we decided to write about the men and make booklets of their creative writing to give as presents. One morning I told the class we needed to finish the books. Did they want the booklets stapled or spiral-bound? In unison they responded, "Spiral-bound." What color did they want for the covers? Suggestions were given. Opinions were stated. Sides were chosen. Each student seemed to be out-shouting the next one. Within seconds, the entire class had erupted into a very disrespectful shouting-match. Some students were standing nose to nose, loudly repeating their choices over the differing opinions of their classmates. What had happened to this class of students that had been working cooperatively together for several months?

"Enough!" I commanded above the ruckus. Then I glared. "That is inappropriate. We will decide in an orderly fashion. Now raise your hands and I will list choices on the chalkboard before we vote."

They wanted to know why. They had all agreed that the cover should be chartreuse. I stared in bewilderment. Every head nodded in agreement. I have no idea how that compromise happened, although years later one boy, now a young man, laughingly surmised, "Aw, Mrs. Kelly. We were just messing with your mind."

The sixth graders worked hard on their individual creative writings. For example, we had studied diamante as a form of poetry shaped like a diamond, which starts with one subject and flows into an opposite one. Student Brad Arnold wrote this diamante poem:

Salt-Water
Salty, Yucky
Stinging, Hurting, Disgusting
Dirty, Bad, Good, Cool
Enjoying, Eating, Tasting
Red, Thick
Strawberry-Shakes

James Whittaker had described the men's intense hunger for strawberry malts, suggesting that the red sunsets across the ocean made them hungry for that flavor. However, in *Seven Came Through,* Rickenbacker had written about their intense desire for chocolate ice cream.

As part of our language arts studies, I read several pieces to the class. We analyzed the use of sensory detail, development of plot, and writing style. Usually the class understood that an author writes from experience, and though the men had a shared experience, they assimilated it from their own perspectives.

However, concerning the malts, the class would not be swayed. The flavor had been strawberry, not chocolate. I remember pausing and asking the class, "But *you* weren't there. How do you *know?*"

I thought they would concede. No. The class was insistent. *We just know it was strawberry!* So, for treats the afternoon the men visited Room 14, I asked Erik's mother, Sharon Smedal, to go to Boyd's Dairy and bring back strawberry malts. Brad Arnold's poem had convinced me that this fact was too important to ignore.

Besides the poetry books, the class wanted to provide more presents. Since there was no money budgeted for gifts, we had to think of something that was not costly, but unique and special. I asked my mother her advice. "I could sew pillows," she suggested. Whittaker had written how the vivid sunsets had reminded the men of fruit juices—orange, strawberry, lemon, grape. This had particularly intrigued the students. We decided to give the men pillows with the front side made of colorful fabric squares, the colors of sunsets, and each square signed by a student. The backside was to be a blue fabric representing the ocean, with a personal inscription written by Christy Scott for each survivor.

We also wanted a drawing of a B-17 plane. Who was a good artist? The students all pointed to classmate Chad Watson. I asked him what he liked to draw. "Airplanes," he replied.

But what were we going to *do* when the men came to visit? The students had several ideas. Mostly, they wanted time with the men in the classroom and some time in a "fun" activity. Before we had made definite

Chad Watson drew a B-17 Flying Fortress for the class.

plans, I had a phone call from David Abelson's mother, Sallie, the same mother who had purchased that erasable ink pen. "Suzanne," she began, "the story about your class was picked up by the Associated Press. You're going to have to think big." I did not know exactly what that meant, but I soon learned.

Sallie had a business called "Contemporary Designs" that made and marketed specialty items. She designed and donated Rescue Reunion pins for all of us and contributed items for gift baskets that the students put together to be placed in the men's hotel rooms.

Next, I had a phone call from the Associated Press. Exactly where would the press conference be held? I made a phone call. "Lee, I know it's late at night," I apologized to my principal, "but I need help. This thing is getting awfully big."

Besides time with the men at school and a casual, fun event, we needed to have an opportunity for the public to greet the men and hear their story of survival and rescue. That meant an evening presentation in a large auditorium. We soon arranged for my photographer husband to come to Meeker and take a picture of the class. Bob's skills were much appreciated. He also charged the right price for his services! The class photo would be on the program cover the students designed to pass out at "An Evening with Our Friends."

Central administration called and informed me they were preparing packets about the city and the school district for the media. I checked the language arts objectives—"Identify fact versus opinion." We knew the facts. We could write our own press releases as we waited to see the men.

Chapter Six

THE RESCUE REUNION

I T WAS RESCUE REUNION WEEK! Everything was ready except for the classroom. On Saturday, I headed for school to take care of Room 14. Our beloved school custodian, Arnie Munson, had the building in top condition, just like always. He always kept the floors polished, the windows shined, and the drinking fountains cleaned. However, I needed to clear off a couple of counters and dust my desk. Although we daily kept up with our research journals and maps, I also wanted to display them better for visitors to view.

When I returned home that afternoon, Bob informed me that I missed a phone call from some general, who was a little upset that we were having a reunion without him. General? I did not know any general. At least, I did not think I did. I called the man back in Harlingen, Texas. George Good had been the commander in charge of planning and coordinating the men's rescue on Funafuti. Ah! Now I knew who he was. His signature was on the Rescue Report that we had used to find so many details of both the rescue and rescuers. Now, George Good was eighty-three years old and a retired lieutenant general. I expressed to him how much we had used the report he had written, the same report that my Sixth Grade Super Sleuths believed had become declassified because of them. He had no copy of the operational report, because that was not possible during the war. "No problem," I assured him. "I'll send you copies for your grandchildren."

On Wednesday, William Wepner, formerly from PT #26, arrived at school from Ripon, Wisconsin. Bill, a retired dairy farmer, and his wife

Marie drove to Ames a day early, because they wanted special time with the students. As a teacher, I was glad they came first. Their arrival gave the excited sixth graders a chance to meet their first rescuer and gave me an opportunity to manage adults, students, and the press on a smaller scale, before the full reunion began. The Wepners brought surprises. They had contacted the Ripon Chamber of Commerce and businesses and put together gym bags for each student. The bags were filled with all kinds of goodies and mementos. I recall most vividly the packages of cookies and the numerous ink pens.

In all the excitement of digging into their bags and unwrapping the gifts—"*Yes, Travis, you may eat your cookies if you want....*" "*Cathy, do you want to make introductions...?*" "*Lisa, grab the camera off my desk and take some pictures for us, please....*"—Marie Wepner touched my arm. I remember we were in the southwest corner of the room, and I sensed that she wanted to tell me something in private in this most improbable place. I looked at her expectantly and was not prepared for what she shared. "I have bone cancer," she said gently, but matter-of-factly. "Bill and I always wanted to go to Europe. We worked hard all our lives and promised ourselves that someday we would take a trip to Europe. We will never take that trip." I know tears were filling my eyes. "It's okay," she said. "What I wanted you to know, Mrs. Kelly, is that this trip is so much better. Thank you." As I gave her a quick hug, I heard, "*Hey, Mrs. Wepner, thanks for all the stuff! It's like having Christmas in April!*"

The next day, Thursday, the rest of our guests were to arrive at the Des Moines Airport. Sixth grader Nicki Moreland's parents, Jana and Arnie Moreland, had chartered a bus for the students to ride to the airport. This generous donation solved many logistic problems. I wanted to have the students greet the men as they came off the plane, but I also did not know how to get all of them to the airport, and then all the students, men, and guests back to Ames, about thirty miles away. (Where is a cargo plane when you need one?)

Left to right: Erik Smedal, David Jurgens, Amy Larson, and Lisa Moore displayed their Rescue Reunion pins, before leaving for the airport to meet the men. (*Photo Bob Kelly*)

Another concern I had was one of safety for the students. About this time, there had been two missing boys from the Midwest, which had made national headlines because of their assumed kidnappings. All of a sudden, I had a cold fear that I had placed students in danger. Again, I went to my principal, Lee Himan. "What do you need?" he asked.

"I need Ruth Walker."

Ruth was my colleague next door. For fourteen years, she and I had been educational neighbors. For the last few years, we had taught in a semi-departmentalized arrangement. Miss Walker was the students' math teacher. Throughout the year, Ruth had listened to me for hours as I alternately shared excitement and frustration about my class's progress. They were her students, too. "Lee, I *really* need Ruth Walker to go along and help with the students." He agreed.

Was there anything else I needed? Yes. "Could you contact central administration and ask if they would pay for a half-day substitute for my husband? I think we need him to take photos for us." Again, Lee agreed.

Then he added, "By the way, my wife and I drove down to the airport and scheduled a room for your press conference." Somehow, for growing up not wanting to talk in public, I was quickly over my head in public speaking requirements.

Thursday morning of Rescue Reunion week we had exchanges of classes as usual. After an early lunch, the students gathered back in the classroom with antsy enthusiasm. Everybody was all over the place, chattering at once. Bob came from Fellows Elementary to ride on the bus with the Wepners and the class. Then the office signaled that I had a phone call. I left Bob and Ruth in charge, as I hurried to the office.

When I picked up the phone, a lady said, "Mrs. Kelly, my name is Diane Smith. I am calling from Walla Walla, Washington. My son Matthew said he heard about you on the radio with Paul Harvey talking about his grandfather."

"Who is his grandfather?" I asked.

"Bill Eadie," she replied.

I remember catching my breath. This was the same Lt. William Eadie who had landed his Kingfisher at dusk to save John Bartek, the man I was about to meet at the Des Moines Airport.

"My father died when I was eleven-months-old," she said quietly. "I never knew my father." I grabbed a notepad and scribbled her address and phone number, promising I would get back to her soon. We had found pilot Lt. Fred Woodward with the help of a newspaper columnist. Now we had found Lt. Bill Eadie with the help of a radio program.

Back in Room 14, I corralled the students into barely contained order, dishing out instructions and reminders, much like all adults do when they want children to behave themselves in public. "Are there any questions before we leave?" I asked.

One student, Derrick Boden, raised his hand. "What if we don't like the men?"

"What do you mean?" I needed him to elaborate.

"What if they're...you know...not nice?"

I remember looking at him strangely. The thought had never occurred to me. In the months we had been exchanging letters and phone calls, it had never crossed my mind to think that these men were anything but top-notch, wonderful people.

I gave what I hoped was a reassuring smile. "Think about it. We wrote to these men in the middle of winter. The temperature was freezing. We asked them to come to Iowa to spend time with our class. And they quickly said yes; they wanted to come, mostly to be with all of you sixth graders. Now, what does that tell you about the men?"

Derrick, who had recently moved to Iowa from sunny California, looked around at his buddies, full of mischievous energy simmering just beneath the surface, and answered in two words. "Oh, help," he said with a grin.

We all boarded the bus for the airport. A chartered bus is luxurious compared to a normal school bus. It has a rest room, every teacher's dream. In addition to students, the Wepners, parent chaperones, and school personnel, we also had members of the press. One of those with a press pass was Richard (Dick) A. Blair, Sgt. USAF, and a Media Relations Specialist from the U.S. Air Force Academy in Colorado Springs. Dick Blair had been a sixth grader in my very first class at West Elementary, Storm Lake, Iowa. He was the first of my students to hear The Book. It was fitting that he should join us in this next chapter of excitement.

When we arrived at the airport, I gave one final direction to the class reminding them to stay together. As I stepped off the bus and turned to watch the students exit, I glimpsed some of that mischievous energy spilling over. Many of the boys had donned sunglasses and adapted an "I'm cool" swagger I had never seen them display.

"Excuse me," I said to one of the parents. "I think I need to pass on a few more reminders." That reminder speech consisted of recognizing their pride in accomplishments, understanding their fascination with the press,

Bill and Marie Wepner rode the bus with the sixth graders to meet the men at the airport. (*Photo Bob Kelly*)

and appreciating their youthful energy. However, they were representing their state, their school, their parents, and most of all, themselves, and a little more humility would be in order when we were in public. The shades were pocketed, and the students filed off the bus, still smiling, ready to meet their heroes.

An earlier phone call from Les Boutte had confirmed that his flight from New Orleans through St. Louis to Des Moines would arrive a couple hours before the other men. They were all flying into and then out of Dallas to arrive in Des Moines together on one special American Airline flight. I was concerned that Captain Boutte would be alone in the airport. "Don't worry about me," he said, "I'm used to airports. I'll just sit around and watch the girls go by!"

We first met Les Boutte near an airline counter. I do not remember much of our conversation, only that I was glad to give him a hug. He was using a

At the airport sixth graders Doug Haynes (*left*) and Amy Murphy greeted Les Boutte, the radioman who spotted Capt. Cherry. (*Photo Bob Kelly*)

cane and was joined by sixth grader Amy Murphy, who was recently sporting crutches. They immediately struck up a conversation and talked all the way to the main area, where we caught the escalators to the second floor.

We arrived at the terminal area before the other men's plane landed. There to greet us were my parents, Edith and Herman Zobrist; my former sixth grade teacher and her husband, Hazel and Herb Jacobson; and—a surprise—my former second grade teacher, Mrs. Wilma McManus. Friends, community members, and people we did not know had all crowded into a small area to wait for the men.

Along with these faces were others that were now familiar. They belonged to the three major networks, local television affiliates, and numerous people from the media who had interviewed and visited us in our classroom. As I passed through one section, I recognized a familiar television crew and could not help but turn to the soundman and ask, "Been to a closet lately?" Hoping for a quote, people with notepads and pencils clamored around him to ask what I had said. He simply shook his head. I

This was our first glance at the three survivors who came to the Rescue Reunion. *Left to right*: William T. Cherry, Jr. (pilot), James W. Reynolds (radio operator), and John Bartek (engineer). (*Photo Bob Kelly*)

grinned, realizing that I truly understood some of that mischievous energy when it simmers beneath the surface.

Sixth graders Nicki Moreland and Amy Larson danced up and down with anticipation as the plane landed and taxied to the gate. Super Sleuth Ben Jackson had written to the Iowa Air National Guard, and Bob had helped coordinate having an Honor Guard for the men. The Honor Guard rolled out the red carpet and stood at attention with their white-gloved hands ready to salute. As we strained our heads to look past the roped barrier, we waited with not much patience to catch our first glimpse of the men. The airlines had other people debark first. I always wondered what those passengers thought as they entered the terminal to be greeted by a crowd of people and media everywhere with boom mikes ready. We waited, and then…nobody else came.

As we waited to greet the men, John Bartek took this photo of the sixth graders. (*Photo John Bartek*)

Finally, an airline official sent word to have two students come and greet the men first. I heard the surrounding chorus of voices, "Pick me! Pick me!" I could not choose. A selection this important to the students needed to be an impartial decision. I turned to my second grade teacher. "Mrs. McManus, would you please choose one boy and one girl?"

Soon my husband took his place at the end of the red carpet to snap the first photograph of the survivors—William T. Cherry, Jr. jauntily waving on the left, John Bartek brimmed with exuberant expectation on the right, and James W. Reynolds, smiling with quiet confidence in the middle. Immediately after Bob took his photo, John Bartek took one of Bob and the

Amidst the mob at the airport, the Sixth Grade Super Sleuths finally had the opportunity to meet the men. (*Photo Bob Kelly*)

Niki Nilsen (*left*) was interviewed by the news media at the airport. (*Photo Bob Kelly*)

Captain Cherry held Christy Scott's hand as though he did not want to let go. On the extreme right was Mrs. Jacobson who first read The Book to her sixth graders in 1955. (*Photo Bob Kelly*)

sixth graders. Then John turned and tried to guess all the students' names from pictures we had sent him.

What a moment! I ushered students through throngs of people to introduce them, as well as myself, to the men. Suddenly, Les Boutte was in front of me, and John Bartek was at my side. These men had not set eyes on one another for forty-two years—not since Les had lifted John from a raft and strapped him onto the wing of an airplane. Reporters strained to catch their first words of greeting. John laughed and said, "Well, put on a little weight, haven't you?" Then he thanked the former radioman for saving his life.

Next, we went to the airport area that formerly had been a famous restaurant, called the Cloud Room. When I was a young child, my father

The sixth graders and the men posed for a photo during the reception. *Top Row*: Lee Himan (principal), Chad Watson, Brad Arnold, Michele Mitchell, Christy Scott, Cathy Watson, Lisa Moore, Jennifer Jones, Amy LeMay, Derrick Boden, and Amy Murphy. *Middle Row*: John Bartek, James W. Reynolds, Hazel Jacobson, Suzanne Kelly (teacher), William T. Cherry, Jr., William Wepner, and Lester Boutte. *Front Row*: David Abelson, Doug Haynes, David Jurgens, Erik Smedal, Ben Jackson, Travis Senne, Amy Larson, Nicki Moreland, and Niki Nilsen. (*Photo Bob Kelly*)

sometimes took my mother, brother, and me there from the farm to have Sunday dinner and to watch the airplanes. Of course, my dad had no idea that my brother Dale would later retire as an engineer from The Boeing Company that had made the B-17 or that I would be standing where he had eaten Sunday dinner, to give—of all things—a press conference about an incident with a B-17.

I had seen press conferences on television. There were microphones lined up on a podium, and someone stretched above them, answering questions right and left. I was a teacher, and I wanted more control. I thought perhaps "raise your hands and I'll call on you" would sound a

At the evening reception: (*Left to right*) Lester Boutte, William Wepner, John Bartek, Herman and Edith Zobrist (the author's parents), Suzanne Kelly, William T. Cherry, Jr., and James W. Reynolds. (*Photo Bob Kelly*)

little condescending, so I simply greeted the media, introduced the students and the men, and asked each survivor and rescuer to say a few words. And there, standing nearby, watching the students and keeping them safely in sight, was my colleague Ruth Walker.

I remember Captain Cherry advising, "No matter what you're doing, you've got to be prepared to do it. And you've got to be prepared for help from up above."

I remember Jim Reynolds saying, "I'd like to thank one man, for one heck of a good landing, or I wouldn't be here."

Then I announced, "I'll call on *The Iowa State Daily* for the first question." The college journalist told me later what a thrill it was to be singled out for that honor. It was my tribute to the Iowa State University telecommunications classes I had taken twenty years earlier, which had helped me survive my present situation.

The bus trip back to Ames was a more relaxed experience. Some press people rode along and interviewed the men as we visited across the bus aisles. My most vivid memory is Jim Reynolds's observation that we had gone from inner city to farmland. He was not used to the stretches of fields and rural areas that we have between Des Moines and the smaller city of Ames. We left the men at the Gateway Hotel to become settled and then drove back to school. Our Rescue Reunion was just beginning.

The reception for the men and the students that evening was a more formal affair, with opportunity to practice some social skills of handshaking, making introductions, and joining in conversation. Students Derrick Boden, Brad Arnold, Michele Mitchell, and Nicki Moreland acted as official class hosts and hostesses at the reception. Sixth graders Cathy Watson and Lisa Moore presented Mrs. Jacobson with a corsage from the class in honor of her having read The Book to her students. Her husband Herb beamed proudly beside her.

We had also invited my parents, Herman and Edith Zobrist. Dad had donated boxes of Drew's Chocolates as gifts for the men. Mom had taught at Dexter, Iowa, where the hand-dipped chocolates are made. Chocolate was symbolic for another reason. When the men were in the rafts, they should have had chocolate bars, fishhooks and lines, and other equipment. However, Whittaker wrote how these items had been pilfered from the jungle packs zippered into the cushions of the parachutes. He told how he wished that whoever had taken their items might someday be as hungry as he was. I had always paused at this point and led a discussion with students about how seemingly little decisions we make, can have such big consequences.

Two more guests, whom I requested, were our neighbors, Ruth and Randy Matson. Randy had been in World War II and had followed daily the story of our class's research. While serving in Italy, Randy had lost a leg in battle. When our son was quite young, Randy asked me if he could show his prosthesis to Ryan and talk about it, rather than have him ask questions at an inopportune time without the teaching that could accompany an explanation. I informed Ryan that Randy wanted to talk to him about something and that Randy had fought in the war. Ryan had wanted to know what that meant. I had thought quickly how to make a comparison that a preschooler might understand. I asked, "Remember how you wanted to be Superman for Halloween? And how Superman fought for 'truth, justice, and the American way'? Well, that's what Randy did in the war."

Ryan had been rather quiet when he returned from the Matsons. However, the next morning, as Randy prepared to mow his lawn, Ryan stood on our front porch and yelled a boisterous, friendly greeting across the street, "Hey, Randy, how's your prosthesis?"

Almost every night I scooted across the street to give the Matsons a quick update on our project. They donated stamps for our project, along with seed corn caps for the men. I really appreciated the stamps but not the caps. The men liked them so much they wore them to several events, and they appear in many photos and videos. Randy also wanted to do something special for the class. With his encouragement, the class received a congratulatory letter from Caspar Weinberger, the current United States Secretary of Defense. Between World War II and our Rescue Reunion, titles of government cabinets had changed. The Secretary of War had contacted Rickenbacker. The Secretary of Defense had contacted us.

In addition to these guests at the reception, we had several family members that Captain Cherry had bought along for the event. We were excited to meet his son, William T. Cherry, III, and his wife Glenda; Captain Cherry's daughters Paula Cherry and Diane Stacy; and two granddaughters, Terry Alexander and Elizabeth Stacy.

At the reception, the students also gave me a corsage and a lovely gold bracelet engraved with "Super Sleuths." (I wore the bracelet every teaching day from then on until I transferred to fifth grade in 1994.)

Corsages were not the only flowers that evening. Mrs. Jacobson provided a lovely bouquet. Another bouquet arrived for the class from the family of Fred Woodward. A mailgram from Western Union to Bill Wundram at the *Quad-City Times* arrived the day of the reunion. Part of it read, "Thank you for your interest and dedication in endeavoring to honor him [Fred]....If he were alive today as he is in our hearts we would know he would be here with us."

John Bartek brought the little New Testament that he had on the raft and from which the men read and prayed, while adrift in the ocean. Whittaker wrote much about this khaki bound object, currently housed in the Freehold Museum in New Jersey. John told how the men had gathered their rafts together nightly with Captain Cherry leading prayers to the Old Master. Students were fascinated to touch the object that had actually been

John Bartek showed the students the New Testament he had on the raft in the Pacific. (*Photo Bob Kelly*)

in the Pacific on the rafts with the men. John Bartek, who was a forensic photographer with the New Jersey State Police, also brought another surprise for each of us. When the state police heard about the class's investigative work, they sent along tie tack pins of their organization for each of us to have. One student remarked, "Mrs. Kelly, I think the New Jersey State Police pin is even better than a badge!"

Friday morning we arranged for the men and guests to be chauffeured to Meeker School at 9:45 a.m., allowing them first some time to have breakfast and visit over coffee. The class, however, was to start its day as usual. Just before I left for school, I received a phone call from Captain Cherry. His granddaughter Elizabeth, just a year older than the sixth graders, didn't want to sit around the hotel that long, and he asked could she please come to school? I met her at the hotel and took her to Room 14 to help me put up new photos Bob had just processed in his darkroom after the reception. A news crew met us, and filmed Elizabeth and other sixth graders, never knowing we had an adopted addition to the class.

When it was time for the caravan of parent chauffeurs to arrive with the men, we went to the parking lot to greet them. Classes of primary

Captain Cherry fit right in with the sixth graders in Room 14. His granddaughter Elizabeth (*top row, fourth from left*) became Mrs. Kelly's adopted student. (*Photo Bob Kelly*)

students, kindergarten through second grade, saw us from their windows and came to join us in welcoming the men to Meeker Elementary. This greeting was so different from the airport one. We were still surrounded by the press, but boom mikes were at a distance, and no reporter interrupted the moment, letting the students greet the men freely. There were no formal handshakes, only hugs. Gone were the introductions; only energetic chatter remained. Those nice men were already our friends, and we welcomed them accordingly.

In Room 14, the students had one request of James W. Reynolds, the B-17 radio operator, now retired from the telephone company. He granted it. Under Jim's leadership, all the sixth graders used their desks and deliberately tapped out SOS. An image flashed through my mind of my brother. Dale had survived a difficult bout with polio and learned Morse code in the hospital. I had grown up with his messages being sent next to my bedroom, as he communicated around the world with his ham radio operator friends. Had anyone ever picked up Jim's SOS that fateful day?

About mid-morning, several parents drove the sixth graders and men across town to Welch Junior High to see the auditorium stage for the evening presentation. The Armory at Iowa State had provided flags of different branches of the service, and a political organization had donated the flag-colored bunting. In addition, the Meeker art teacher had made a large sign for the podium. The music teacher came along to set up microphones. We arranged round tables, with open areas facing the audience. To the side and back of the stage was space for our class piano.

I had saved the piano from the junkyard. Even though the piano could not be tuned, it had character. One of its special features was a door that opened to view the hammers inside hitting the strings. My first class of sixth graders at Meeker Elementary had painted the piano red, white, and blue. We often used it to play for opening exercises or for pleasure during indoor recesses when Iowa winters were too cold to go outside. My principal, Lee Himan, expressed concern about the piano being used for the public event. However, I persisted. All my past sixth graders were special to me, and the piano represented time with many of them. Tunable or not, it had served us well. "Besides," I told Lee, "the way I play the piano won't make any difference if we have one in tune or not." I do not think that is what persuaded my artistic principal. The colorful piano would look quite patriotic on stage, so we agreed to use it.

We finished checking out the junior high in time to head back to the Meeker lunchroom. Judy Hopson, the kitchen manager, and the cooks I called the "Culinary Queens" had prepared special line garnishes—the island of Nukufetau formed from peanut butter, bulgur (cracked wheat), and endive; palm trees from carrots and green peppers; the Pacific Ocean from blue gelatin; and rafts from three pear halves. And most delightful of all to the sixth graders, the shark that broke Bill Cherry's nose by flipping its tail in the raft was made from a cucumber.

The men picked up their lunches, including "hero sandwiches" and ate with other faculty members in the same room where we had first talked by phone with Captain Cherry. Then the cooks handed me a bowl of halved oranges. As I offered the extra oranges to the men, sentimentally I had

Top: The Super Sleuths and their guests enjoyed malts that had to be strawberry! *Left to right*: John Bartek, Jim Reynolds, Bill Wepner, Bill Cherry, and Les Boutte.

Middle: At the Meeker Media Center presentation, Jim Reynolds lightened the mood with a joke about Capt. Cherry. To Suzanne Kelly, the men sounded as endearing as sixth graders.

Bottom: Les Boutte (*left*) smiled as Suzanne Kelly served Bill Cherry oranges—as many as he wanted!   (*All photos Bob Kelly*)

tears in my eyes, thinking of the anemic oranges they had rationed to survive. Captain Cherry started to decline, saw my face, and then, with an understanding smile, took an orange

After lunch, the men and guests toured the school and made brief visits to other classrooms. Early in the afternoon, we met in the media center with other sixth grade classrooms, including Bob's class from Fellows Elementary. Super Sleuth Amy Larson's letter inviting the classes had said, "Since you have read the book and are familiar with the men, we would like you to come meet them." One parent had persuaded the publishing company of Whittaker's book to grant us permission to reproduce a few passages. These excerpts we had typed as a small souvenir for the visiting sixth graders.

While the men shared their experiences, what I most remember was the heat. We had asked the men to come when it was cold. Now Iowa had unusually warm weather. We had not been prepared for the hot, stuffy afternoon. Our custodian, Arnie Munson, and our media assistant, Judy Ferguson, brought pitchers of ice water to the men as they talked. I poured glasses of cold water for the men. How symbolic was that?

Then it was time for the men to join the Super Sleuths in Room 14. First, we all enjoyed those strawberry malts. Next, we presented the gifts of pillows to the survivors; locally made Iowa coffee mugs to the rescuers; and certificates, stationery, and writing booklets for all the guests. During our classroom time with the men, the school maintenance crew arrived to move that out-of-tune, heavy, old piano. They loaded it onto a truck and took it to the junior high where it would be waiting for our evening program.

Individual families of classmates had volunteered to host guests for a meal in their homes and to transport the men to the auditorium. By now the parents and students felt very comfortable with each other, and the families that participated provided an Iowa warmth and hospitality that was typical of our school district and our state.

Approximately 700 people filled the junior high auditorium to hear the men's story of survival and rescue, and the students' story of their

Ryan Kelly, son of Bob and Suzanne Kelly, was thrilled to meet John Bartek after the evening presentation. (*Photo John Bartek*)

research. The huge bouquet of flowers from Fred Woodward's family stood in center front of the stage. To the side was our room's piano with the bouquet from Mrs. Jacobson.

"An Evening with Our Friends" began with sixth grader Amy LeMay inviting the audience to join us in singing the "National Anthem" and saying the "Pledge of Allegiance." The students had worked hard to tell what they had learned. Now they had an opportunity to do so.

Although Alvin Cluster, the lieutenant who had picked up Captain Cherry, could not attend the reunion, I shared some information about him. Cluster later had been a commander of young Lieutenant John F. Kennedy, before Kennedy became President of the United States. Remember the movie, *PT-109?* I also read part of a letter Lt. Al Cluster had sent to David Abelson. "And he [Captain Cherry] said several times,

The students chose the design and engraving for the plaques presented to the survivors. (*Photo Bob Kelly*)

'God Bless The Navy!' I told him I would remind him of that some day so you can do that for me."

During the program, each student spoke about part of the research done by the class. It was a marvelous experience for sixth graders, and I hoped they were more comfortable than I had been at that age. Besides telling our story of research, personal recognition was given to Mrs. Jacobson. Students also presented the men with Iowa walnut wood plaques, engraved with their names, the date, and a special inscription.

By Saturday morning, all the press had gone home. Student Chad Watson's parents organized a potluck picnic for noon at Inis Grove, a local park. The weather was perfect, and the students and their families had a great time. Our kindergartener son Ryan was especially attached to the big sixth graders. I do not recall the activity, but I do remember

At the Saturday picnic with the students' families, Bill Cherry joked with Suzanne Kelly. Notice the special gold bracelet on her left hand. (*Photo Bob Kelly*)

him asking, "Captain Cherry, will you be the captain of my team?" I saw Bill Cherry head over to play.

For some reason, I needed to go back to school to get something—probably ice—and Captain Cherry's daughter Paula rode along. I asked her, "Did you know all this about your Dad?" She soberly looked at me and shook her head.

"We didn't know hardly *anything* until the letter arrived at our brother's house. Dad was visiting, so we asked him what it was all about. We had no idea. I guess that's why it was really special we all could come and share this with him." My own father once had taught veterans. The Servicemen's Readjustment Act of 1944 provided vocational education to returning veterans, commonly called G. I.s. Through this G. I. Bill,

Jennifer Jones hugged Bill Wepner good-bye at the picnic. The men had moved from strangers to friends, and now they seemed like family. (*Photo Bob Kelly*)

Dad had taught agriculture to several men in the community. After the war, he knew many young men like this—men who did their jobs and then quietly came home to do their jobs.

Following the potluck picnic, Lee Himan opened up the school, so we could use a television in the media center and together watch some of the network news spots about our reunion. During one reporter's interview with me, I had told about Lt. Bill Eadie's daughter contacting us, as we were ready to head to the airport. Captain Cherry pulled me aside. "Mrs. Kelly, you're not going to believe this. Bill Eadie was my roommate at flight school." And where was that, I wanted to know? "In Texas—at *Kelly* Field."

Then it was time for more of those fun activities. Some of the men invited students to go swimming with them in the motel pool, others played golf with Captain Cherry, and all of us ended our evening at the local roller skating rink. The men and I stood around the outer railing, ready to slap-hands with any sixth grader skating by.

Captain Cherry came up and stood beside me. This was the first time during the Rescue Reunion that I was not supervising a student, playing hostess, being interviewed by the press, or organizing some activity. It was *my time* with Bill Cherry. What could I ask him that I would remember the rest of my life? Although we had thought we would ask detailed questions when the men came, we had not. We had simply enjoyed being with them. But I knew what I wanted him to share with me—*that moment when the B-17 was going down...*

"Captain Cherry," I began, "I can't imagine the responsibility you must have felt when you were going to crash into the ocean."

"Excuse me, Mrs. Kelly, but I did not *crash* into the ocean. A crash is an uncontrolled landing. I *ditched* the plane into the ocean." I understood. He certainly controlled that landing, or we would not be with the men today at this noisy place.

I started again. "I mean, I can't imagine how you felt, knowing you were responsible for eight lives."

In his rapid-fire Texas accent, he corrected me once more. "At that moment I wasn't scared."

I must have shown my bewilderment, as I looked into his direct, blue eyes. My hero came close to falling off his white horse for telling a lie, before he quickly continued. "I was not scared then, but I sure was forty-five minutes earlier until I figured out what to do. Once I had a plan, I knew what I should do. I would do it. I figured the rest was not up to me. It was up to the Man upstairs." And just like that, my Army Air Corps knight was back in the saddle, sitting tall and upright, with skating rink lights shining on his head.

The Cherry family had rented a car and had been in contact with my mother, who was certain they would like to visit an Iowa farm. Early

Captain Cherry said good-bye to Suzanne Kelly, telling her, "I'll be back to see my kids." (*Photo Bob Kelly*)

Sunday morning, before their plane was scheduled to leave, they drove to the Zobrist farm in Dallas County, about fifty miles from Ames. The promise of Mom's homemade cinnamon rolls was too tempting to miss. Captain Cherry told me, "The chance to see a real Iowa red barn and spring asparagus growing in the garden was too good to pass up." I later learned that a school district central administrator had requested Captain Cherry play golf with him, but Bill had turned him down. I really do not think it was the barn or asparagus. Mom was a retired home economics teacher. I know it was her cinnamon rolls!

Then it was Sunday afternoon. Parents had taken the other guests when they needed to make flight connections. Now Bob and I drove to the airport to say good-bye to Captain Cherry. I reached out and hugged him. "I'll be back," he promised, as he waved.

Chapter Seven

PEOPLE RESPOND

F OLLOWING THE RESCUE REUNION, I SENT A LETTER to the faculty and staff at Meeker Elementary. They had contributed much to make the reunion meaningful to all of us. I also thanked them for being the Super Sleuths' former teachers and encouraging their curiosity and search for knowledge. The primary teachers had taught the students their first lessons in reading and writing. The staff had already worked with the parents. I was able to build on those positive first experiences. In one television interview, I was asked if this was the end to our research and time with the men. I had replied, "It's just the beginning." However, I did not know how true that statement was.

With initial coverage of the Rescue Reunion, we immediately received responses. One early phone contact was from Harry Elliott, photographer for the Public Affairs Division of the United States Air Force Museum at Wright-Patterson Air Force Base in Ohio. Mr. Elliott had read an Associated Press article about us and called to say how disappointed they were not to have heard about the reunion earlier, so they could have sent people. Without thinking, I blurted out, "Oh, we had people, but would you have sent planes?" The students and I really wanted to see a B-17 Flying Fortress.

Mr. Elliott did send us the article that alerted him to call us. We found it interesting, because he had underlined clues in the article to track us down, much like we did to find information we wanted. In addition, he mailed each student a photograph of Eddie Rickenbacker's orders for his assignment from the War Department. Not all the order could be read because of deterioration of the document. However, the museum photographer

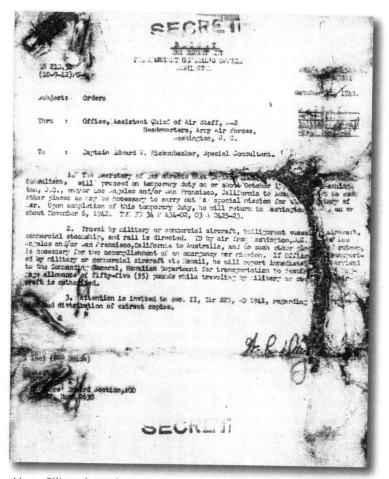

Harry Elliott, from the United States Air Force Museum at Wright-Patterson Air Force Base in Ohio, sent each student a photo of Eddie Rickenbacker's 1942 orders. (*United States Air Force Museum*)

explained that the orders had been recovered with infrared. He added, "The marks on the left side are from a rusted paper clip and the black marks on the right side are actual holes in the paper." Part of the orders caught my eye. "Upon completion of this temporary duty, he [Rickenbacker] will return to Washington, D.C., on or about November 6, 1942." We knew Eddie Rickenbacker did not make it on time, but he did make it.

The museum also sent B-17 photos, books, and pamphlets for all the students. These were greatly appreciated. However, I admit I was not so positive about the public affairs specialist's request, "If you do something like this next year, please keep in mind to let us know in advance so we can be there!" I was so tired, the year was not over, and I did not intend to get so involved in anything next year. Little did I know how involved I was to be yet this year with my Super Sleuths.

Another early phone call from Solana Beach, California, was from Robert Eadie, brother of Bill Eadie. He had seen our story in the San Diego edition of the *Los Angeles Times*. I told him we had talked with Bill Eadie's daughter, and relayed how she had also found us through a national radio broadcast. He told us he had an eight-page report that his brother had written—some in his own handwriting—about his involvement with the rescues in 1942. Three days later Bob Eadie sent a letter with his brother's report. "Perhaps your students would like to incorporate it into their recent project," he wrote. Would we! Now, we had even more information about the Kingfisher pilots and radiomen.

Two weeks later, we received a letter from Diane Eadie Smith, thanking us for information about her father. Captain Cherry had called her. (He later made a video about Bill Eadie and took it to Diane and her children, Matthew and Kathy. He wanted them to know more about their grandfather.) My next letter to Diane said, "I have sent a package to each of your children because I remember how much fun it was to receive my own mail." When I had a note from Matthew, also a sixth grader, I showed it to the class. One boy thought Matthew should be in our class, and then he could write some of our thank-you letters.

We also heard from Phyllis Eadie, Diane's mother. Few photos were taken during the war. However, when Les Boutte, the Kingfisher radioman, came to the Rescue Reunion, he brought a small photo of himself with Bill Eadie. My husband enlarged it, and we were able to send it to Bill's widow. She later wrote, "Thanks again to you and the great sixth grade class detectives. Greetings to Mrs. Jacobson who started it all."

Dr. William Fisher Eadie, II, a college professor in California and Lt. Bill Eadie's nephew, had seen the CBS and ABC news reports. He wrote,

Lieutenant William Eadie, USN, was the Kingfisher pilot who picked up Rickenbacker, Bartek, and Adamson. *(Photo courtesy Les Boutte)*

"As you probably know by now, my uncle was killed in a jeep accident in 1945, the year before I was born." He shared with the class that he grew up in a family that was very proud of his uncle's part in the rescue. He added this thought, "Not many of us get to be heroes like the men in the story, but appreciating heroism helps all of us to be better prepared to perform the little heroic acts we are called on to do every day." Dr. Eadie then concluded, "As one who does research on a regular basis, I hope that working on the project showed you how exciting and rewarding research can be."

What started before the reunion as a search through a public library, phone directories, and letters to people in Evanston, Illinois, to find Lt. Bill Eadie had become a realization that this pilot had died during the war. After the Rescue Reunion, we heard from his brother, wife, daughter, granddaughter, grandson, and nephew. As meaningful as it was to correspond with all of them, it was also special because we learned more about the pilot who had helped rescue two rafts of men. Students realized that while some men had been rescued, some of those rescuers later had died. No one had been able to rescue them.

We previously had been unsuccessful in finding any relatives of Alex Kaczmarczyk (pronounced Kaz' MAR' zack), the young man who had died at sea on November 1, 1942. Before the flight, he had recently been released from the hospital where he was treated for an appendicitis and yellow jaundice. The class had been quite moved by "the one they left behind" and had Alex's picture from an old newspaper clipping displayed in the corner of the classroom by the American flag.

Classmate Ben Jackson had written a letter to the Torrington Public Library in late January, but we had not had any results in finding relatives. After the reunion coverage in April, however, we received a letter from Lillian Olmstead from Thomaston, Connecticut. She began, "I would just like to add a couple of anecdotes about this story to your very thorough research." When she had been in the sixth grade in the mid-1950s, a short story had appeared in a basal reading text about the World War II event. It had impressed her because Alex had been from a neighboring town, her teacher had known him, and her sister-in-law was one of his teachers. Alex's teacher later had become her seventh grade teacher. Mrs. Olmstead related that years later she had become a teacher in the same school system, had come across the same basal reading text, and had read the story to her students. Then in 1975, her husband met a relative of Alex's in law school, and he had dined with them in their home.

I immediately wrote Mrs. Olmstead and asked if she could still contact this relative of Alex's from law school. I must have been at home and ready to pack a lunch for school, because my notes from her were scribbled on a brown paper sack with names, addresses, and phone numbers for Alex's sister-in-law and a brother. We later made connections with the family.

Vera Bathurst from California provided the first clue for us in tracing Col. Hans Adamson's relatives. She, too, had just seen us on television and called to offer us an autographed book about the wartime event. Vera had been a very close friend to Col. Adamson's wife Helen, when they both lived in the same building in San Francisco. Following the phone call, Vera sent a letter saying, "She [Helen] gave the knife that saved the raft to Hans as she bid him good bye the day he left…" Colonel Adamson had written in his book, *Rickenbacker*, that when they were struggling to leave the ditched plane, John Bartek had used a small penknife on his key ring to cut the strong cord that held the inflated rubber raft to the plane.

In that same letter to our class, Vera Bathurst had enclosed addresses for two of Col. Adamson's nieces and the announcement of a surprise she was sending us. "I went to my storage room and pulled out one item that I knew right where it was and it will soon be en route to your school.

Colonel Hans Adamson, U.S. Army Air Corps, served as a military aid to accompany Eddie Rickenbacker on his mission for the War Department. (*Courtesy Auburn University Libraries Special Collections and Archives*)

I hope it will be of some value to the class."

We soon heard from both nieces living in Massachusetts. Janet Crosby confirmed that her aunt had lived on Nob Hill in San Francisco for nineteen years where Vera Bathurst was the concierge. Janet ended by saying, "My uncle would have been interested in your class...."

Then her sister, Natalie Christopher, wrote that their uncle had been born in Denmark and came to the United States just before World War I, where he had developed a friendship with Rickenbacker when they were both flyers in that war. Before World War II, Col. Adamson was with the Museum of Natural History in New York City and authored several books. Natalie further told the class, "Colonel Adamson died in 1968, a semi-invalid as a result of the crash [injured back], but leading a productive life with great courage and fortitude."

The week before school was out for the summer, Arnie Munson, our school custodian, brought a large package to Room 14 from Vera Bathurst. She had sent the surprise as promised. We opened the extensive wrapping to find an award, the size of a large painting, which had been presented to Colonel Adamson by the Circumnavigators Club. Students researched that a requirement of the organization was that the person had to have crossed all meridians of longitude, thus completing a global circumnavigation. *Mrs. Kelly, we know about longitude!* Evidently, Vera had contacted family members at the time of Adamson's death, and nobody had claimed the award, so it had been in storage. She wrote to the class, "Thank you for wanting and liking it."

We were also given another large item to hang in the classroom. Dr. Lee E. Rosebrook, the physician who had found the tumor on my neck, had been a group flight surgeon with the Army Medical Corps in 1942. He gave the class a large framed photograph of a B-17.

Most other letters from the public contained requests for addresses of the men, information on how to obtain Whittaker's out-of-print book, or a personal story of how the rescue of the men had affected them during the war.

Then a letter arrived from Peg Kahn of Cincinnati, Ohio, that made us chuckle. She had worked for American Airlines at the ticket counter at La Guardia Field in New York City, a job that was more complicated with priority passengers. Peg explained in her letter that sales were either by cash or government voucher, called a 1030, with ticket agents, like herself, accountable for all monies and any discrepancies deducted from their salaries. The day Colonel Adamson appeared to arrange a flight for himself and Eddie Rickenbacker, Peg had to fill out tickets for each leg of the flight, each ticket about two feet long. They waited for Rickenbacker to come with the 1030 forms to pay almost $400 for the round trips to San Francisco. When he arrived about ten minutes before the scheduled takeoff, he did not have the required 1030 for himself or Adamson. Peg adamantly refused to give them the tickets until her superior signed the sheet. She then wrote to us, "If they had listened to me they would not have been on that raft in the South Pacific!"

As the students had more opportunity to work with television and radio crews, they became quite adept at analyzing their own performances. We had worked on speaking skills. For my part, I have always been slightly embarrassed by one interview I gave to ABC television. The reporter, Al Dale, asked me if there was anyone else we wanted to find. We had found Toma, but we had never found anyone connected to James Whittaker, the author of *We Thought We Heard the Angels Sing*. I mumbled something about how important it was to us to find him, because "if he hadn't written the book we couldn't have read it." The sixth graders analyzed my interview. "*Duh, Mrs. Kelly!*"

The students' search for the Whittaker family had been extensive. In one letter, sixth grader Chad Watson wrote to one organization, "In the past we tried to find James Whittaker, but he died. We decided to follow up on his relatives, so we could find more about the man and his family."

However, as the story unfolded across the airwaves, members of the Whittaker family began contacting us. No resource had worked until Al Dale, the correspondent for ABC News, put out a television plea to the public during our reunion.

David Green, ABC Bureau Chief from Denver, called me the night we were giving our community program, "An Evening with Our Friends," to tell me that Anne Alexander, Whittaker's sister, had phoned and wanted me to contact her. Later, a letter from her to the class requested information. She wrote, "I wish desperately that I had seen the Channel 7 news broadcast of your classroom project…A neighbor who did see the news broadcast stated that there were pillows presented to the survivors who were there. Would you please let me know what was written on them?" I described the pillows for her. After all, I knew what it was like to have simple curiosity and the excitement of waiting for the answer in the mail.

We also heard from Marge Hughes, the author's first cousin. A neighbor of hers, also, had watched the broadcast. Marge's daughter called Channel 9 news, was directed to Chicago, then routed to New York, and then finally Denver. There she talked to David Green, the same network bureau chief Whittaker's sister had contacted, and he had provided my address. We were able to send her copies of the program, clippings, and other information about the Rescue Reunion.

Shortly after school was dismissed, I received a phone call from Captain Cherry, requesting that I contact Mrs. Thomas Whittaker in San Mateo, California. The author's son, Tom, was deceased, but Captain Cherry had contacted his widow and wanted us to send her a package about the reunion. Her thank-you note said in part, "Your package arrived today. I've been spellbound!"

James Whittaker's second wife, Irene, told us that after Jim retired from the lecture circuit, he had gone back to his former occupation of building contractor and automobile sales, retiring in 1964. She reported that he died in 1975.

Also, after the television report, Shirley Whittaker Hurd (Jim Whittaker's daughter) had contacted Jim Reynolds in California with information that her father, mother, and brother were no longer living. Shirley then sent us her father's scrapbook so we could copy any pages. This was a complete surprise. We had not visited about it or even knew the scrapbook existed. Shirley simply wanted to share with the students. We were excited to read newspaper clippings about Whittaker's raft ordeal, his rescue, and the many public events he participated in after his rescue.

James Whittaker had kept a diary while floating on the raft and later used it to write The Book. The first entry said, "Lost & down at sea. Crash landing—10-21-42— 16:30 H.W.T." (But this sixth grade teacher knows better. It was a *ditched* landing!) The entry continued, "Canton wouldn't furnish us bearings to there." I am still amazed at Shirley's generosity in sending her personal artifacts for us to view.

The students wrote thank-yous to Shirley Hurd, but, of course, had more questions. Sixth grader Jennifer Jones wrote to her, "Do you have the outrigger?" and Michele Mitchell asked, "Do you have the canoe that Toma gave to Mr. Whittaker?" In The Book, Whittaker had described in detail how Toma had carved a model outrigger canoe and given it to him with his name on it and the name of the island. Students knew the author was no longer living, but they wanted relatives to tell them what had happened to that little outrigger canoe model. Shirley wrote back, "Lt. Whittaker's oldest grandson now has the outrigger at his home in Oregon." Her letter arrived the day school was out, but I wrote back, "...thrilled to know that the outrigger canoe model given to your father by Toma is in good condition and still cherished...We are still waiting for the tape from Toma to be translated and sent to us." In about a week, we had heard from Whittaker's sister, cousin, daughter-in-law, second wife, and daughter.

Later in the summer, we had another letter from Shirley Hurd who lived in California. She sent us a June 1985 copy of the *Island Business*, a magazine from Fiji. The doctor she worked for had just returned from a vacation there, where he bought a copy of the magazine. It had a story

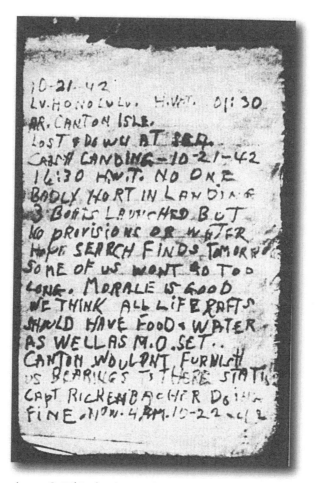

James C. Whittaker kept a diary on the raft. This photo is of the first entry, dated October 21, 1942. (*Courtesy Whittaker Family*)

about Shirley's father and us. Part of the article said, "Forty-one years later, the children of an American school encountered the book and embarked on some detective work." This was one of many little connections in the years to come. But for now, I was thinking how much fun "detective work" was, when no danger was involved, and those "children of an American school" were my Sixth Grade Super Sleuths.

A major publication that we put together at the end of the year was a Souvenir Booklet with information about the Rescue Reunion and photos that Bob had taken of the events. For the cover of the booklet, we used titles that had appeared in newspapers about our class.

Our purpose at the time was to compile some basic remembrances for the class and the men. However, we had extra copies printed and soon learned that many people wanted the souvenir booklet. It was a great thank-you for many of the people who sent us information about the raft event.

By now, we had received mail from over forty states and several countries—and a box from Lima, Ohio. Mr. Gerald D. O'Connor,

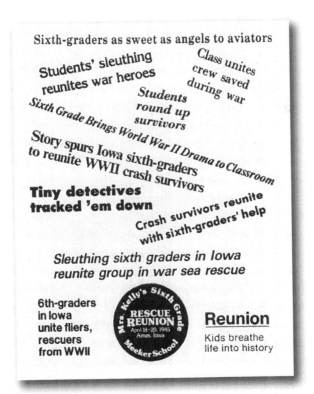

Cover of the Souvenir Booklet featuring headlines from various newspapers that had written stories about the class.

president of the Range Kleen Manufacturing Company, had read an article about us in his local paper. He was a World War II veteran and proud of what the class had done with the reunion. He wanted to do something for the students, so he sent key chains, shaped like a #1, from his business and inscribed, "You're No. 1 with Us." Travis Senne, the student who insisted we track down the survivors of the raft ordeal, exclaimed, "Oh, cool. How did he know I collect key chains?" After all the mail and attention the students had received, I was amazed how excited they were over a little plastic item. But again, I should have known. They were still sixth graders for a little while, and sixth graders are such a rare breed.

This was also demonstrated towards the end of the year when students were in math class next door. Through the back wall, I distinctly heard repeated SOS being tapped out. I was almost certain which two students were responsible. When classes exchanged, I overheard one student say to the other, "I wonder if she heard us?"

After they put their books away and were heading outdoors for recess, I asked nonchalantly as they passed by, "Still lost or are you found?" to which they whooped in success that their message had been received.

Chapter Eight

A REAL CASE SOLVED...
AND MORE

A FEW DAYS AFTER THE RESCUE REUNION THAT SPRING, we received a special request from a woman in Lawndale, California. The letter was dated April 25, and the envelope post-marked April 30, which was a Tuesday. We had no school on Friday, because of a holiday for students to participate in a local celebration, VEISHEA (see page 152), organized by Iowa State University students. For two days the next week the students were at an overnight environmental camp-out. Thus, it was probably Thursday, May 9, before I actually read the letter to the students. The last day of classes for the school year was scheduled for May 30.

Betty Carter, the woman from California, wrote, "Dear Teacher Suzanne Kelly and Class, We heard on TV and in our paper of how you found those men after so many years. We got to thinking you probably have ways of going about finding almost anyone." She told the story of her husband, John Goodwin Carter, who, at the age of two, was placed in the Iowa Soldiers Orphans Home in Davenport, Iowa. Around the age of five, John Goodwin was adopted and given the last name Carter.

Two years before writing us John had requested the Iowa governor's help to get court-ordered adoption records for medical reasons. Through these records, John learned he was the youngest of several children, with information about two brothers, Robert and Albert, and a sister, Mary Ann, who had also been adopted out of an orphanage in Toledo, Iowa.

With these several clues, John and Betty had placed requests in newspapers and phoned people to find John's lost siblings, but they had been unsuccessful. Betty then wrote to the class, "If you feel you would like to see if you can help or have any ideas, you'll never know how much it would mean to us."

I recall discussing the request with my sixth graders. "Class, you have no obligation to do this." It was the end of the school year with activities to complete—science labs, music concerts, field days, end-of-the-year assessments, orientation to the junior high, an all-school skating party— the list seemed extensive. And, as much as I loved investigative research, I needed a break. I looked at my Sixth Grade Super Sleuths and remembered one television interview where I was asked what I wanted for my students. I had answered, "For them truly to care about individuals."

"You're not expected to be adult investigators," I said.

"What are we expected to be?" one student asked.

"Sixth graders—almost seventh graders. You're expected to continue learning to read…write…be the best students you can be…" But I knew, as my brother would say, "my goose was cooked!" The very reasons I had always given them for the importance of language arts skills were the same arguments they now tossed back at me. But being sixth graders, they did not just toss. With those beloved smirky grins on their faces, they began brainstorming ideas.

"Is that orphanage still there? It's Davenport, Iowa. Get the research book, and find the librarian we wrote to who helped us find the Kingfisher pilot Fred Woodward."

"Betty wrote that John was born in Benton, Iowa. Use the atlas. Where's Benton? Oh, Ringgold County."

"One brother was adopted out of a home in Toledo, Iowa. Hey, can we use that atlas?"

"You guys, John thinks his sister was adopted by a lady in Dexter, Iowa."

"Dexter? That's the town where Mrs. Kelly's mom used to teach. You know, the place where they make the chocolates we gave the men."

"Let me see that letter from Betty and John Carter again. Yep, it says Garner, Iowa. One brother was placed on a farm near Garner. We get the atlas next."

As I watched the students organize their research, analyze the clues they had, and pursue ways to find John Carter's older siblings, I thought how much they had grown this past year. What had started as finding men because we were curious was now leading to a real-life investigation. I had a room full of Nancy Drews and Hardy Boys, and they were on the case.

When I talked to my parents by phone to share the latest development of Room 14, I relayed that John Carter thought his sister Mary Ann had been adopted by a lady in Dexter. My father never passed up a possibility of buying some Drew's Chocolates, so he and Mom drove to Dexter. They first contacted a man with the local historical society and the alumni association for the high school, where Mom had once taught. Although we were provided with names, addresses, and phone numbers that tracked all the way to Bogart, Georgia, the woman we thought had adopted Mary Ann evidently had not. At least we never could confirm this information.

In the meantime, classmate Michele Mitchell wrote a letter to the Garner Public Library, "Would you please help us find Albert Goodwin?" On May 22, Michele received a letter from Gail Linahon from Garner, Iowa. Gail explained that the librarian, who was new to the community, had contacted her because of her involvement with a local genealogy group. Around 1958, Gail had known Albert Goodwin, a truck driver, who was employed by a livestock trucking company. Gail talked to the company's owner, now retired, who volunteered to look through his employment records. She was also following another lead. She talked to the lady from whom Albert Goodwin had rented a room. Gail concluded her letter by saying, "We may not be able to complete this before school is out, but whatever information I find, I will send to your teacher. Have a nice summer."

Just as school adjourned, I received another letter from Gail Linahon. She wrote, "Possibly it was fate or something, but I knew Albert Goodwin." Then she wrote something I had not thought about. "It is possible that the three older children were aware of the existence of each other and have been in contact with each other. If Mr. Carter locates one, he may find the others." I did not know how prophetic that would be.

Eventually, we were able to obtain an Iowa address for Albert Goodwin. On July 1, I wrote him a letter with our story and requested that if he were the Mr. Goodwin we were trying to reach, please write or call me collect. On July 6, I received a phone call from Mr. Goodwin—but it was not Albert. It was his brother, George. I wished we had still been in school. I could just imagine how the sixth graders would have reacted. *"George! We don't know about a George! Wow! We can even find people we're not trying to find!"*

George said that Albert was on a trip, so he was looking after his brother's mail. When my letter arrived, he had called his brother, because it was a personal letter, and Albert had instructed him to open it. Thus, George called me collect, as per my instructions, and confirmed that our facts were probably correct, and that we did have the right person. There were eight children, and they had been placed out of two different adoption agencies. Albert and George found each other by accident. They also had a brother, Robert, who was retired but still living in Iowa. The sister, Mary Ann, whom we were trying to locate in Dexter, had died about three years previously. As I wrote to Gail Linahon to update her on the search, "George seemed pleased that the lost brother is now found. He was going to call John in California today. Wouldn't it have been exciting to have heard that conversation?"

On July 9, the Carters wrote to me to fill in missing family information, with names and history of all the siblings that George had told them about when he called. Betty wrote, "We are so grateful to you for all your help...How did you find this one brother, George?" As Gail Linahon had suggested, finding one led to the finding of others.

I recalled my childhood Nancy Drew phase and visit to the Lindeman's farmhouse at dusk. A notepad and pencil had been my tools to record clues. Now I thought of the volumes of material we had gathered, not only about the Carters, but also about the World War II event. I had copies of hundreds of letters the students and I had written. Mostly, I thought of the joy of bringing people together. The path of curiosity had led to a journey of connections.

Although school was out and my Sixth Grade Super Sleuths were now officially seventh graders, I still had contact with them during the summer. With their usual high-level-we-have-a-great-idea energy, they had suggested that we have a slumber party in the school gymnasium as a way of celebrating all the great things we had shared this school year. I was dubious. We had only had positive publicity, and I did not want a "joint slumber party" to be questioned. Also, the gym was the holding place for moving furniture as rooms were cleaned, and I did not want to cause our custodian Arnie any extra work.

My husband suggested that we have two separate parties, one for the girls and one for the boys, and have them in our home. No parent objected, and with slight reservation, I issued the invitations. The girls' overnight was first. Our young son was delighted with all the excitement of girls staying all night and promptly pulled his sleeping bag from the closet to join them in the living room for a little while in the evening.

The boys' overnight was very different. I later wrote to Bill Eadie's sixth grade grandson Matthew, that I wished he were here to join the boys in their slumber party, where they planned to make a video tape like a science fiction movie, starring guess who. I think they thought I would make the perfect outer space alien. I joked, "Now you know why I'm sending them all to junior high! It should be a fun time with lots of noise and food. Do you think I will survive?" I survived, only by finally going to bed completely dressed, while Bob chaperoned the boys in the last wee hours of the morning. I only remember that they not only produced a creative video, they brought me breakfast in bed.

The students were now responding to requested speaking engagements. Several service organizations asked them to tell the story of their research. When I received a phone call from a particular group, I took the class list and began soliciting volunteers. Students were busy with ball games, family vacations, and other activities. (For example, Chad

Watson's parents had taken him to see the Air Force Museum in Ohio.) But usually I could round up a few willing participants. In August, I agreed to speak to the Ames Noon Kiwanis Club. Super Sleuths Erik Smedal, Niki Nilsen, and Amy Murphy were also presenting. During the program, I was handed a note. "Please call before you leave. No major problem. Bob." After we finished our presentation, I phoned my husband. His first words were, "You'll never guess who's sitting in our driveway."

Instead of taking the students to their homes, we headed to meet John and Betty Carter. Along with two of their daughters, two grandchildren, and a friend, they had come from California to meet the relatives we had located for them in the Midwest.

John told us how emotional he had been when he had answered the phone and heard a voice say, "I think I'm your brother." Betty told us that he was so overwhelmed, he had handed her the phone.

John had searched for years to find his siblings. They were so appreciative of the students' help. John admitted, "Then I didn't have any more questions about who I am. There wasn't any more emptiness in my life. I felt like I was home."

The Carters brought California T-shirts for all the sixth graders and two gifts for me. One was a coffee mug that said "#1 Teacher" in bold red letters. The second was something John had made. It was a model plane, constructed from a beer can, complete with wheels and rotating propellers. John hugged me, and then I choked with emotion when he said in his gravelly voice, "Mrs. Kelly, I wanted to give you something I knew you would like—and I knew you liked airplanes." I still treasure my little plane.

Bob recalls that he first fixed them cold lemonade and then called the local media. When asked which investigation she liked best—the Rescue Reunion or the Carters—classmate Amy Murphy replied, "This one. Because this one is family." I thought how our family of friends was growing.

When I jotted a note to Gail Linahon with an update on the Carters, I said, "Do keep in touch. It's nice to have a new friend in Garner, Iowa." I hoped Gail and I might keep in touch, but another class came to know her, too.

A collage of photos taken when Super Sleuths Erik Smedal, Niki Nilsen, and Amy Murphy met John and Betty Carter who surprised the author with a visit from California. *Lower Right:* In the background are Randy Matson (neighbor) and the Carter's granddaughter, Maritza, and daughter, RoxAnn.

The next fall Gail's husband was killed, and her rural home was lost in a tragic gas explosion. Our school's Parent Teacher Association had provided our class with money to purchase group games for use during indoor recesses. Since one of my language arts activities was to have students produce their own board games, our class really did not need this money. It was far more educational that the students do their own research, write sequential directions, and design their own activities, than to purchase them. So the students agreed to send their PTA money to Gail. As I quoted one student in my letter to her, "She helped the other sixth graders find John Carter's relatives. She helped many people. Now let us help her." Gail used the money to buy a slow cooker and wrote to the class in her thank-you, "When I use it, I will remember what good friends you are."

Another major event happened the summer following the Rescue Reunion. I learned to swim. Kathy, mother of Super Sleuth David Jurgens, gave swimming lessons in their family pool. I admitted to her that I was forty-two years old and had always wanted to swim. She had given lessons to our son Ryan at the start of the summer, and I wanted to be able to swim with him. Kathy was matter-of-fact and encouraging, "Of course I can teach you to swim." Finally, I gathered my courage, thinking that if the men could survive three weeks in a raft, I could certainly survive in Kathy's lovely pool. One afternoon after I had practiced a few laps, I decided to dive off the low diving board. Just before I hit the water, I heard a loud shout from David's upstairs room overlooking the pool. "Save the whale!" It was only a three-word phrase, but I know it was shouted with a smirky grin!

After the Rescue Reunion, I was asked by Debra Gibson, an Information Specialist with the Iowa State University Alumni Association, to share our story with readers in their publication *The Iowa Stater*. I gladly did so, and the article was published. In September, I received a letter from Noriko Ito, a woman living in Toyama City, Japan.

Noriko wrote, "You are the honorable alumnus of ISU. [Our teacher] is an alumnus of ISU, too. She is my teacher of English class." Noriko explained that she had been given the article about us in *The Iowa Stater* as a way of learning to read and write English.

We immediately became pen pals and corresponded for years. She once asked, "Has Ryan ever made a snowman? If not, I would like to teach him how to make a snowman with my two children in the rice field behind my house." As with the Japanese culture, Noriko had great respect for my parents and sent them many gifts over the years. In a round about way, because I graduated from Iowa State, I was participating in someone's learning in Asia. How strange that a result of reuniting the survivors and their rescuers of World War II should include meeting a very lovely woman from Japan.

After the Rescue Reunion, Mr. H. Panapa, Broadcasting and Information Officer with the Prime Minister's Office of Tuvalu, wrote to classmate Doug Haynes. He sent Toma's address, the *Tuvalu Fact Sheet*, and information about their school system. They have only one secondary school, and the principal was a good friend of his, so he also enclosed an address for the principal at the Motufoua Secondary School on Vaitupu Island, in Tuvalu. Mr. Panapa also added, "I have known Toma for many years because his son was a classmate of mine. Toma is known throughout Tuvalu because he was a crew of a Missionary Ship that cruised within the Pacific Islands after the war." I remembered how the Meeker students had wondered what had happened to Toma and if he ever had left his island home.

Another letter came to me in mid-June. Donna Ryherd, from a town in Iowa, about forty miles from Ames, was first alerted to our class project because it isn't every day the *Des Moines Register* mentions the country of Tuvalu to its readers! The Ryherds, Dan and Donna, had been in Tuvalu two years earlier, serving in the Peace Corps. Although they had been on the Tuvaluan island of Nui, about eighty-five miles northwest of Nukufetau, they had two friends in the Peace Corps who did live on Nukufetau and knew Toma. In fact, one of them had sent her a copy of the *Tuvalu Echoes,* what Donna described as "their closest thing to a newspaper." Donna enclosed the article to us, describing my sixth graders' research from the Tuvaluans' point of view. It seemed surreal to read, "A student from the Ames Meeker School wrote to the Prime Minister of Tuvalu seeking information regarding a native believed to be a Tuvaluan who rescued the three Americans who survived a plane crash…" and how they had tracked down "Mr. Fakapae [commonly known as Toma]."

Then Donna offered, "Should you or your class ever have a desire to see pictures or slides of Tuvalu and see how tiny the islands are in the middle of the Pacific Ocean, we'd be happy to share these with you." Was she kidding? We wanted to learn so much about Tuvalu.

I wrote to Donna in mid-July that we still wanted a picture of Toma, direct correspondence from him, and a detailed map of Nukufetau. I thought perhaps Donna's Peace Corps contacts could help.

In August, Donna wrote back that she had sent a letter to a friend, Scott Erickson, who had been a Peace Corps volunteer in 1980-82 and was visiting Tuvalu again this summer. She explained that there are very few cameras on Tuvalu and film has to be sent away for development. She also indicated that communication in Tuvalu is much different from here, since mail goes by ship from Funafuti, the capitol island, to Nukufetau only every six weeks or so. The map, however, she thought would be easy. She had requested Scott buy a government one for us for about $1.50, Australian currency. Scott was due back within the month, so we should have some answers. In the meantime, how about coming to their home to view some slides?

Scott Erickson's letter to the Ryherds on August 15, 1985, was copied to me. Scheduling had worked out perfectly. Siniela, a fellow working at the Lands and Survey Office, had given Scott a map of Nukufetau free, when he heard what it was for. Then, the inter-island ship *Nivanga* had spent the day (August 12) on Nukufetau, allowing Scott plenty of time to take Toma's picture and interview him for us.

Then Scott recounted some of the details Toma provided about the rescue in 1942. The U.S. forces on Funafuti had alerted both the people of Nukufetau and the New Zealand coastwatchers (the friendly power) that a plane had gone down in the area and any survivors were believed to be in green and yellow lifeboats. Toma and two or three others left in a canoe to do some chores and check around the islets outside the village. Then Scott wrote that Toma said, "While passing along Motulalo islet at the area called Kavika (see the faint 'x' drawn on map), he came across a single man, a European." At this point in the letter, I looked at the map and saw the exact spot where the men had been rescued. From Whittaker's book, where the island was unnamed, to the exact spot where he had been rescued, had taken us less than a year to find.

Scott's account of his interview continued. Toma told how Whittaker had been frightened and suspicious, wanting to know the name of the island, who was there, etc. Toma was the only islander who could speak a little English to answer these questions. Finally, Whittaker decided to trust him and led them a short distance away to the other two men who had been in the same lifeboat.

Scott then wrote, "Toma explained to me that he (Jim Reynolds) had sand all over his face and in his eyes, ears, and nose (possibly to guard from the sun), and the only way Toma could tell that he was alive was by observing his tongue move slightly through his partially-opened mouth." I remembered at our airport press conference the description Captain Cherry had used to describe Jim Reynolds at the time of their rescue, "If you ever saw a dead man walking…"

What had happened to Toma after the war? Toma told Scott in their island interview that from 1954 until 1961 he had worked on the church mission boat *John Williams* and travelled all over the Pacific. He then became involved in local politics, serving as the Island Council President of Nukufetau for several years, and an additional role as local magistrate. He had retired from the latter position earlier in 1985.

Scott also learned that Toma's wife passed away in 1969. They had seven children, five boys and two girls. He now has fourteen grandchildren. Scott concluded by saying that he would send pictures as soon as they were developed.

The photos arrived in November. Dan and Donna Ryherd had collected the film from Scott and had it processed for us. We now had a photo of Toma in 1985—and an added surprise—a photo of Nukufetau. The Ryherds had sent an aerial shot of the tiny, tiny, tiny strip of land on which Whittaker had beached the raft. I recalled the Super Sleuth who had visualized what I was seeing in a photograph. He had said, "They almost didn't make it." More than ever I wondered, *"How did they ever make it?"*

In late August, Betty and Jim Sommerhauser wrote to me from Mission Viego, California. Betty had several connections with our story—John Bartek, Tuvalu, the state of Iowa, Iowa State University, and Bill Cherry. She was a good friend of Joyce and Bob Horne, who had recently come to visit her. They started talking about our Meeker project. Joyce was the person who had first contacted me and given a clue that helped us find the survivor, John Bartek. Betty's second connection was Tuvalu and Toma. Her son John was a Peace Corps volunteer in Tuvalu in 1977-79 and had stayed in that part of the world after leaving the Peace Corps. Betty's husband was born in Iowa, and his brother was an Iowa Stater. But to me, her most fun connection was her story about going to the library a week after Joyce's visit. As Betty was checking out materials about the rescue of Rickenbacker, the crew, and Tuvalu, another librarian overheard her requests and took over immediately. This librarian had been a former American Airlines stewardess who had served with Captain Cherry! Betty's closing in her letter touched me. "Suzanne, we feel quite honored to perhaps be a small link in this great big, beautiful chain you and your students have formed around the world."

With all those connections, Betty Sommerhauser wanted to do something for the Meeker class. In February she wrote, "Jim and I have wanted to send you something for your classroom for a long time and have finally found what we think is a lovely globe...Please tell us you could put this globe to use and it will be on its way."

I looked at the rusty metal globe in our classroom. Its two halves had been put together at the equator, practically obscuring the region we

In 1985 Toma Fakapae visited with a former Peace Corps volunteer, so the sixth graders could have this photo from Nukufetau, Tuvalu. (*Photo Scott Erickson*)

always wanted to see. The new globe arrived with a light bulb inside. When plugged in, the globe lit up, with special dots for the capitals of countries. "*Quick! Find Tuvalu!*" The students were extremely impressed that this updated globe identified Tuvalu, instead of Ellice Islands. We immediately thanked the Sommerhausers for their generosity and used the globe at Meeker for the rest of my teaching career.

In mid-September we arranged an evening at Meeker Elementary with the Ryherds to share their pictures and experiences in Tuvalu, when they were Peace Corps volunteers on the Tuvaluan island of Nui. The seventh

An aerial view of the southeastern corner of Nukufetau showed where James Whittaker, John DeAngelis, and James W. Reynolds were rescued. A spot on the narrow strip of land between the Pacific Ocean on the left and the atoll's lagoon on the right is the Kavika area on Motulalo Islet where Toma found the men. (*Photo Dan Ryherd*)

graders, who had found Toma, chose to sit in the back of their former classroom, and the new class of sixth graders sat in the front, as they learned about the people of Tuvalu. It was truly an evening of passing the torch. The Super Sleuths, who had grown so much in their investigative skills, were already involved in the pre-adolescent phase of junior high culture. They were ready for different, unique, exciting adventures. My new class of sixth graders was in awe of the big seventh graders. I adored the class

Donna and Dan Ryherd were Peace Corps volunteers on
Tuvalu two years before the Rescue Reunion. (*Photo courtesy
Dan and Donna Ryherd*)

that had accomplished so much with their research. But after all, once you
watch them take those baby steps, you guide them to walk carefully—and
before you know it—they are off and running. That evening I almost felt
like I was waving good-bye to the Super Sleuths that they had been, but I
was grateful to reach out to the young men and women they would become.

After our story first appeared in the *Des Moines Register*, Robert W.
McMullen from Sacramento, California, began corresponding with us.
A friend had sent him the article before the Associated Press picked up

the story. Mr. McMullen had been a meteorologist with a Navy squadron on Funafuti, early in 1944, over a year after the rescue of our men. In his own account of his military experiences, Mr. McMullen had described his three months on the island. "My first impression of Funafuti was that it didn't amount to much and it was a lasting impression. Take away the palm trees and what would you have? Coral reefs, that's what." From a meteorological standpoint, he explained that the lagoon at Funafuti was well protected from trade winds from the east, but when those winds did not blow, there was a problem. The unprotected western boundary of the lagoon was subjected to frequent and unexpected strong west winds. These winds and the long westerly fetch (how far the wave has traveled) caused waves of such magnitude that they created a hazard for takeoffs and landings of seaplanes. This happened during intrusions of Northern Hemisphere air across the equator.

Mr. McMullen recalled the interest on Funafuti when he was there, because of the considerable publicity that had been associated with Eddie Rickenbacker's rescue, although the island had not been identified at the time. The Meeker students were intrigued with his connection with Tuvalu and grateful for his help with our research, particularly in finding maps of the island for us. In one letter to him, Michele Mitchell had written, "Every time we send you a letter you send us back a letter with a lot of information which we think is neat."

After the Rescue Reunion, Mr. McMullen wisely wrote to one classmate, "It won't be much longer before your class will cease to exist as a class...It was a nice thing that your teacher and the class did. The best thing about it is that in addition to what you did for the survivors, you inevitably did a great deal for yourselves."

Chapter Nine

_____

MEEKER AND MOTUFOUA

A FTER THE RESCUE REUNION, PEOPLE IN the community often asked me how I could top last year's group. To me, there was never a question of comparing one class to another. Each group was unique. However, people were now curious about what I was going to do next with students. As much publicity as I had endured, I knew that often the best teaching was done in private, one-on-one. When teachers finally help a student make a connection, there is that "Aha!" moment. It is magical. You do not need the world watching what you are doing. You just need to know how to make more of those moments happen.

One way is to motivate children. Particularly now, I realized how vital that self-motivation is. Fundamental skills are necessary for a sturdy educational foundation. But I had also learned that problem-solving activities applied to life situations are powerful learning tools. The value of the research project last year had been the journey, while reaching shorter goals had provided a great sense of accomplishment.

Although I did not have the perspective before, I realize now that this was a turning point for me as a teacher. New classes would search out new pathways to travel, but I would revisit some of the pathways we had already found. For a decade, as a sixth grade teacher, I would use the World War II event as a catalyst for children's learning. And for the rest of our lives, I would cross paths and reconnect with the people I had first met on the journey to help Travis "find the men."

My next group of sixth graders could hardly wait to hear The Book. They, too, were interested in the men, Toma, and Tuvalu. But they did not want to be last year's class or do the same things. And each fall I could not just pick up where I left off. The beginning of a particular grade is, and certainly should be, quite different from the ending of a school year. A new year and new students meant, in a way, starting over. There are always individual student needs, but there are also specific class needs.

What should I do to continue the research project? Students did not want me constantly explaining what last year's class had done. *This class* wanted to do something. And one thing this class wanted to do was correspond with the children of Tuvalu.

When we were originally trying to locate Toma, classmate Ben Jackson had written to the headmaster of the Primary School on Funafuti. Ben wrote, "We have written several letters to your government but we haven't had any answers yet. We were hoping your students might be able to help us find Toma. We thought your students might enjoy trying to find him or any of his relatives."

What we did not know was that there are primary schools on all the islands for children, starting at the age of six. In Tuvalu, selected children at ages eleven to thirteen transfer to the only secondary school for the country, the Motufoua Secondary School on Vaitupu. Therefore, Ben's letter had to be transferred from a primary to the secondary school, and from Funafuti to Vaitupu, about eighty miles away. To us, the secondary school would be Ames High School, about a half-mile from Meeker Elementary. We had caused a great deal of confusion and extra effort for the Tuvaluans to answer our request.

There were other differences, too. A boat travelled among the islands with a six-week trip needed to deliver mail and supplies. Besides the time it took for any mail to cross the Pacific Ocean to Funafuti, it took more time to go from Funafuti to Vaitupu.

School sessions were also opposite between our countries. When the children of Tuvalu were on vacation, we were in school, and vice versa. The teachers at Motufoua also received different classes each year, and with each group of students, they also needed to explain why we were corresponding and the history of the exchanges. Then they wanted time to help their students prepare letters so they were meaningful to the recipients.

At the end of May 1985, I had written to the principal at Motufoua. Upon the advice of Mr. H. Panapa, a great friend of his, I had explained that we had become very interested in Tuvalu. I wrote, "Would it be possible for us to work together so that the students of our schools could learn more about each other?"

The exchanges would take not only time, but also money. In early July, I received a letter from Mr. Pafini Nouata, the Principal at Motufoua. He expressed a great deal of admiration for our efforts to locate Toma and our interest in their country. Then he indicated that it was a privilege to post introductory letters to us, but after that, the teachers would be responsible for replying to letters. I had assumed the cost for my students, but I had been insensitive to what I was asking my counterparts in Tuvalu to do.

After Dan and Donna Ryherd had talked to the class about their Peace Corps experiences in Tuvalu, the sixth graders expressed interest in learning the Tuvaluan language. With a few guidelines from the Ryherds, I purchased two references for the class: *Tuvaluan Lexicon* and *Ttou Tauloto Te Ggana Tuuvalu* (*A Course in the Tuvaluan Language*). The author had compiled both books in 1981 for the United States Peace Corps. To begin, I typed a one-page sheet for the students to use with some of these guidelines:

The language of Tuvalu has these **consonant** sounds:
F, NG, (H), K, L, M, N, P, S, T, and V

The language of Tuvalu has these **vowel** sounds:
A (vowel sound as in "hot")
E (vowel sound as in "late")
I (vowel sound as in "feet")
O (vowel sound as in "vote")
U (vowel sound as in "food" or "tube")

Of course, students wanted to know some basic words and numbers, so I added the following:

Words to Learn:

talofa — "hello" — similar to Hawaiian "Aloha"

tofa — "goodbye"

faafetae — "thank you"

tamiliki — "child"

fale — "house"

vaka — "canoe"

vakalele — "airplane" (word means "flying canoe")

ika — "fish"

futi — "banana"

Numbers are:

1 — tasi

2 — lua

3 — tolu

4 — fa

5 — lima

6 — ono

7 — fitu

8 — valu

9 — iva

10 — sefulu

Students soon realized they could put the numbers together as the Ryherds had taught them. One student quickly caught on. "Mrs. Kelly, did you know that *lua sefulu fitu* means 'twenty-seven'?"

I was not sure the cost of ordering the large language books was appropriate. The language would be very complicated to learn. But the expense of the references was worth it to me the day one boy came to my desk and announced, "*Au e fano ki tai.*" The literal translation is, "I am going in the direction of the lagoon," which is also a very polite way of saying you are going to the restroom. I do love those sixth graders.

In October, I wrote to Mr. Pafini Nouata again and shared with him how my class had celebrated Tuvalu's Independence Day. We knew that Tuvalu became an independent constitutional monarchy, with Britain's reigning monarch as its head, on October 1, 1978. So on October 1, 1985, we wore white clothing that is standard celebration dress in Tuvalu, made a celebration poster, and spoke the few phrases we knew in Tuvaluan. I was not sure how repeated phrases of "hello, how are you, what is your name, my name is, good-bye, and numerous numbers" directly tied into an Independence Day celebration. In any case, the students were learning about a different country and culture, and I knew that was good. I also sent photos to the Motufoua School principal of my class eating coconut cupcakes and playing a game of batting a ball (in our case made of heavy folded paper) over our heads—a game that a student had researched and thought would be a traditional activity in Tuvalu.

The following March, I received a letter from Dennis and Elizabeth Fowler, two missionary teachers from England, who taught at the school on Vaitupu. Elizabeth had appreciated the photos we sent and had gone to great lengths to send us some in return. She wrote, "All the students in Form 2 are included in the photos we have managed to take with our Polaroid camera. The film we bought in Fiji seems to have been affected by the heat. The film we brought from England on our annual leave is much clearer, but, unfortunately, it has run out. If we used ordinary film, we would have to wait for months for it to be developed overseas. We do not leave the island during the school year, so we have to make do with what we have." We were grateful to have photos of our pen pals. And I was much more appreciative of my husband's photography and darkroom right in our own basement.

In my late-April correspondence with the Fowlers, I identified items that I had sent them, which I thought they might enjoy. We had found some copies of *We Thought We Heard the Angels Sing* and newspaper clippings that mentioned Toma and Tuvalu. We also ordered a *National Geographic World* magazine subscription for their school.

In late June 1986, Elizabeth Fowler wrote and thanked us for the items we had sent. She said they had old copies of *Time* and *Newsweek* but no children's magazines for their library. Mrs. Fowler closed her letter with, "Thanks again for the book. Toma's great-niece is one of the pen-friends writing to your students—Esealofa—and our Chief Education officer remembers the rescue when he was a boy on Nukufetau." When I first heard Mrs. Jacobson read The Book, I remember thinking what a big world it is, but now I believe as the Disney song says, "It's a Small World After All."

Soon pen pal letters arrived from the Motufoua students in Tuvalu. And we did hear from Ese, as Mrs. Fowler had said we would. In her letter Ese wrote, "I have read a story about the men who rescue by Toma. Toma is related to me. He is my grandmother's cousin."

A second pen pal, Silafaga, wrote about living in dormitories and that the houses were named after members of Parliament in Tuvalu. Another student, Seela, explained more in a letter. "The name of my house is Naisali. I think you may know the man called Henry Faati Naisali. He is the Minister of Finance in Tuvalu." Seela closed the letter with, "Please, I would like you to send me some photographs of yourselves, and to become not only my pen-pal but my friend, as well."

Molipi told about getting up in the morning and going to have a bath in the sea. Ouddus wrote, "Every morning when I wake up, I wash my face then I had my bath. I always went to have my bath at the sea. Our school was near the sea and I think you never see the sea." Lea's letter explained to the land-locked Iowans, "I can tell you about the sea. The sea is like a lake but very big and salty. There are rough waves." These Tuvaluan students knew of the sea but had no knowledge of lakes, rivers, ponds, or streams. I thought of the lake at Storm Lake, Iowa, where I first taught school and its significance in my life, and the Raccoon River in Dallas County, and even little Panther Creek that ran nearby our farm. These children had a great deal of salt water on their island homeland, but they had no fresh water except the rain that came from the skies.

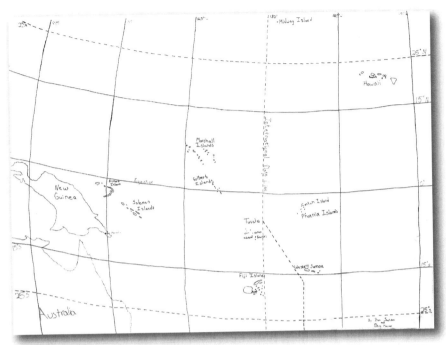

Ben Jackson and Doug Haynes made a map that future sixth grade classes used for their research. (*Photo Bob Kelly*)

One student wrote, "My life is good, because we have food in school, and one thing I worry about food. Breakfast we have biscuits. At lunch we have rice, fish, or stew." There was only one secondary school for the nation. Children were selected to attend, based on passing examinations. I wondered if this child's home life on another island was difficult and school provided a sanctuary from some of life's hardships, just as it did for some children at Meeker Elementary.

A letter from one boy Paape explained, "Here when you have no knife or a broom, you'll be down for fatigue. When someone has been put down for fatigue he must do and dig old [coconut] trunks." The day that letter arrived I had to send a student to the principal's office. Although this was fifteen years before 9/11 and our country's concern for homeland security, our school already had a policy against bringing knives to school. However, the principal and I believed this student really had forgotten that he had the small pocketknife in his jacket that he had used when he and his grandfather had gone fishing over the weekend. So the principal simply kept the knife in the school office until dismissal, and then the boy took it home. At Motufoua, the children were taught that for survival their knife was important, and they must have it with them. At Meeker, the children were taught that for safety they should leave a knife at home. Although it seemed our cultures were quite different, I viewed them as quite similar—both schools wanted to teach and practice safety.

Lama told us, "There is only one ship in Tuvalu. There are many kinds of boats. But we usually go fishing on our outrigger canoe." Another student wrote, "At my Christmas time at my home island I was happy... I went with my daddy Moeaa on the outrigger canoe for fishing that time. I think I will die time. The big wave pulled the canoe very hard, the canoe upside down, and I am carried by the waves. I fell on a big stone, but I'm lucky I just have a broken arm and I looked for my daddy he was swimming toward me." His father reached him beyond the waves. Again, I always thought of the men. *That time...that I think I will die time.*

The Fowlers had arranged for students the following year to be our pen pals, also. In the next term Milikini wrote, "My home island is Nukufetau. Nukufetau has two sides. They are Aaulotu and Maneapa. My parent's live at a big islet call Motulalo. There are many people live on Motulalo."

Another student, Letasi, described it this way, "My house island is called Nukufetau. It is very small and it has a population of altogether about 400 people. If you look at your map, your country is very different from my island. My island is like a dot."

Our classroom was now filled with maps. I had also purchased one where the Pacific Ocean is positioned in the center, with Asia and the United States on either side. It was much easier for us to find locations mentioned in our World War II research. But when you looked at 8° 31' S and 179° 13' E, it really is a dot. But that dot held people who had greatly enriched our lives.

One letter from Matele caught my attention. Obviously, it had been discussed that we knew little about island life from our location in the center of Iowa. She wrote, "The name of my island is Vaitupu. Vaitupu is the biggest island in Tuvalu. There are nine islands in Tuvalu. I think you can tell me your island. And your parent's name. And your name. And how old are you? I think you tell me some things on your island. Ha! Ha! Ha!" It was the sixth grade-ish humor that endeared me to Matele.

Before we started exchanging photographs, letters that students sent often included physical descriptions of themselves, such as color of eyes, length of hair, and height. The Tuvaluan children often mentioned they had "brown skin," and the girls told that a school rule was for them to have "short hair." When we later enclosed photographs with our letters, the children from Motufoua School were extremely complimentary, often saying how handsome the sixth graders looked, including students who were very fair skinned with blond hair. But one year a Meeker sixth grader in my class wrote to his Tuvaluan pen pal that he knew about an island, because he had been born in Puerto Rico. His pen pal Siliona wrote back, "I looked at your photograph and you looked handsome. And you looked like a Tuvaluan student."

Some students wrote short descriptions of things they shared. Others started on one theme and wrote about it in detail. Still others were filled with questions. Most letters contained the common threads of having the same birth dates, liking the same sports, and not liking chores—or in the Tuvaluan case, the "work parties."

Later correspondence included trading audio cassette tapes of students singing. The songs the children of Tuvalu sent were recordings of their Children's Day "fatele," or local dancing. In return, we sent songs that the Meeker music teacher recorded from his classes. Room 14 chose "God Bless America," "You're a Grand Old Flag," "Star-Spangled Banner," and the "Iowa Corn Song."

Throughout this period, we had been trying to find a film on Tuvalu. Historically, for the Rescue Reunion we used video tape recorders, but teachers still used 16mm educational films that were available for science

Teachers Elizabeth and Dennis Fowler at the Motufoua
School in Vaitupu, Tuvalu, took this photo of our 1986
pen pals. (*Photo Elizabeth and Dennis Fowler*)

and social studies classes. Since the school district did not have any films
on Tuvalu, we searched other sources. We learned that a film, *Change in
Tuvalu,* had been produced in 1983 to document Her Majesty Queen
Elizabeth II's visit to this new Pacific nation. Our Peace Corps friends,
the Ryherds, heard from a friend in Tuvalu who wrote, "It is interesting
to note that some people in your part of the world are interested in our
tiny country. I append hereunder the full address of the Australian team
that filmed the documentary you enquired for."

I next wrote to the Australian Consulate-General in San Francisco,
California, explaining our interest in Tuvalu and requesting help in either
obtaining or renting a copy of the film. It was not long before I received
a note from a school secretary that said, "The film came called Change
into Value." The invoice enclosed, indicating there would be no charge

for us, actually said, CHANGE IN TU VALU. Since the secretary had not been at Meeker for the Rescue Reunion, the country's name had no meaning for her, so she had written the note to me that made sense to her. When I returned the film, I also thanked the Australian Consulate-General with my sincere appreciation for the loan of *Change in Tuvalu*.

We invited the Ryherds to view the film with us. They knew the people and places depicted in the film and told us other stories, which made the experience even more meaningful. We saw the inter-island supply ship, *Nivanga*, the same ship that carried our letters to the children at Vaitupu. We saw the children having lessons at Motufoua Secondary School, the men fishing on outrigger canoes, and the old World War II airstrip built by the Naval Construction Battalion and from which the men had left the island. We even saw the Broadcasting and Information room, about the size of our room's storage closet, where Radio Tuvalu carried a story about our class's celebration of Tuvalu's Independence Day. Maybe the school secretary had been correct; we had a "change in our values." This small country, the third smallest nation in the world, was important to us, because we were learning to know its people.

Although most of that second year of research involved corresponding with students at Motufoua, we continued to follow-up on research originally started with the Super Sleuths. No longer were letters sent only with specific requests for information. Now we were also interested in personal letters with stories connecting people.

After awhile of doing research, we had a system that worked. We documented everything. When writing letters, the sixth graders usually followed a pattern—summarizing the class project, telling what we knew, explaining why we were contacting this person, requesting specific information, and thanking them for any help they could provide. The students had also learned the difference between a business letter and a friendly letter. The copies we made of our business-letter format, with inside addresses and dates, provided the paper trail we needed to document our research. Phone calls, too, were detailed and recorded.

One letter that was first written by a Super Sleuth initiated correspondence with three servicemen and spanned a decade of connecting us with Toma. What started as a clue with one group took many years to complete.

When the newspaper article featuring our class appeared in the paper, Alden Harrison from Ames called me on January 24, 1985. After his phone call, I typed notes from the conversation and added directions for the students to follow-up. Mr. Harrison was the stepfather of Paul Heil, who had been a science student of mine ten years earlier. Mr. Harrison recalled that during the war, a member of his company was transferred to an island near the equator and knew Toma or one of the men who rescued Rickenbacker. This story was told to Mr. Harrison on a ship headed back to the States in May 1945. Then, two years ago, Mr. Harrison had seen this same man, John Guthrie, and now provided us with his address.

My follow-up notes to students on John Guthrie were: "He is now an attorney, working for the government. Write to him. Recall the story that Mr. Harrison told us. Let him know we are interested in any information that would help us find Toma, or any of the other men in the service who helped rescue the men in the rafts." By now our story was getting much harder to summarize, so students usually enclosed newspaper clippings to explain our continuing project.

Earlier Super Sleuth Amy LeMay had written to John Guthrie in Knoxville, Tennessee. Mr. Guthrie quickly answered and told of being a cook and mess sergeant for ten men and two officers who occupied Funafuti in the Ellice Islands in 1943. "Our group was there to maintain a short-wave radio station so that stray planes would know the island was in friendly hands if they needed to land." Although Mr. Guthrie had not been there a few months before, when the men were rescued, he had met Toma and described him to us. "He was a very handsome boy, tall and well built with a beautiful Polynesian complexion. All of the native girls were crazy about him!" Then Mr. Guthrie suggested that since the islands were a New Zealand Protectorate, we might want to write to the New Zealand State Department.

Although that lead produced no results, we had gone on to locate Toma. Now in July, after the Rescue Reunion, Alden Harrison stopped by my house and delivered photos of John Guthrie—and Toma! A recent military reunion had put together Alden Harrison, John Guthrie, and a third person, Orie W. Kahn. Mr. Harrison had looked through his war photos but was unable to locate any of Toma. But Orie Kahn had, and he sent the photograph to us. The photo, taken in 1943, showed Toma, flanked by two servicemen, standing in front of an outrigger canoe. My husband immediately captured Toma's face, enlarged the image, and gave us our first look at this native islander who had been the focus of so many of our investigations.

I was overwhelmed. How could these men possibly know what their generosity meant to us? My thank-you to Alden Harrison included this message, "Not only are we grateful for what you people did during World War II and for our American heritage, but we are also grateful for the 'reaching out' with our unique class project." But I could not resist a request in my thank-you to Orie Kahn. "If it wouldn't be too inconvenient for you, we would really appreciate you sharing more with us. In the photo, are you standing to the right of Toma? Do you know the other person in the picture? Do you know if that outrigger was the one used to rescue Jim Reynolds in November 1942?"

In late July, I also wrote another letter to John Guthrie to update him on our project and to let him know I appreciated the photos of him that Alden Harrison had taken at their recent reunion. I also sent a souvenir booklet and other items I thought he might enjoy reading. An August letter from Mr. Guthrie expressed such pleasure with the materials we had sent. He wrote, "I am reading every word in the booklet…it brings back lots of memories of my army days." He then shared how he recalled how much he had enjoyed talking with the Natives. They held torches made of coconut branches over their heads to fish in the lagoon at night. Mr. Guthrie added, "We also would dynamite fish for them but the New Zealand government would not let us do that but one day per week for they did not want them to lose the art of fishing by themselves."

In early January 1986, my husband took a phone call and message for me. I was to call Orie Kahn in Everett, Washington, after 6:00 p.m. Washington time. When I reached him that evening, Mr. Kahn said he was mailing me a letter with more information, and I would receive a surprise in the mail. I know I must have sounded like an impatient sixth grader when I begged him to tell me what it was. He only responded, "I wanted to send it to someone I knew would appreciate it. I want you to have it." That only made me more curious. What could it possibly be?

Very shortly, a package arrived. Inside, was a wooden model of an outrigger canoe. Orie Kahn wrote, "This one was given to me by Toma's father." And now he had given the model to me. I think he had the vision of how much it would be shared with hundreds of people who would eventually hear our presentations and learn the story of Toma and the men.

Mr. Kahn also drew maps of the lagoon and told the location of military areas that had been established there the year after the men's rescue. He also answered my three questions. The men in the photo were Commander Barber, U.S. Navy on the left, Toma in the center, and he, Orie Kahn, U.S. Army, was on the right. He also wrote, "I would believe the outrigger in the picture could very well be the one used to rescue Jim Reynolds in 1942." That was enough for us. We had not only located Toma; we just *knew* we had also located a photo of the outrigger canoe that once had saved the men.

Mr. Kahn later sent us hot pads that were made for him by someone in Toma's family. He had found them while going through his old footlocker. He sent these to us in 1987 to add to our collection. Several times when we communicated, I told him the latest adventures of the model of the outrigger canoe he had given me. Once, Mrs. Jacobson, my former teacher, borrowed it for a community talk. Students used it as a visual aid for speech presentations about other cultures. My class had developed a display for our local public library and had used the outrigger as part of a scene. Then, I sent a letter that was returned, unopened.

In April 1995, I received a letter from Victoria Kahn Mercado. She started her note to me, "Dear Suzanne—I've just spent an incredible couple hours reading of you and your special class back in 1985. My father was Orie Kahn—the gentleman who sent you the outrigger and pot warmers from Toma's father. Both my parents passed away in 1989-90 and it's

Original photo (*top*) given to sixth graders by Orie Kahn, and an enlargement to make it easier to identify the men in the photo. *Left to right:* Commander Barber (U.S. Navy), Toma Fakapae, and Orie Kahn (U.S. Army) posed in front of outrigger canoe that Toma used to rescue Whittaker, DeAngelis and Reynolds. (*Photo courtesy Orie Kahn*)

Orie Kahn sent the class this model of an outrigger canoe, given to him by Toma's father during WWII. (*Photo Bob Kelly*)

taken this long to reach the point where I can go thru albums and boxes of 'stuff' to organize." She wondered about a couple of things and requested I help her find them. Victoria ended her letter with, "When going thru my parent's home I wondered where the outrigger had gone. I am so glad he sent it to you."

Victoria and I corresponded a few more times, sending photos, information, and items back and forth. In one letter she wrote, "I was so fascinated with all the articles of your project. He never mentioned it was all going on and I saw them at least once a week! I have a question. How did you locate him or hear about his involvement in all this? I'd love to know!" She ended by saying, "I feel like I'm on my own sleuthing mission."

It had been ten years since this part of our research started, and although Orie Kahn and I had never met, there was a shared history between us. Each time I look at the model of the outrigger canoe, I not only think of Toma, I remember a wonderful man from Washington.

Chapter Ten

ALBERT AND KELLY ENTERPRISES

ROM THE BEGINNING OF THE SIXTH GRADERS' research, we knew that Eddie Rickenbacker had passed away in 1973. However, the students still wanted to learn more about him. Since he was the most famous of those on the "raft adventure," it was not difficult learning about his many careers and accomplishments. But the class wanted to find his family.

The students started with the public library in Columbus, Ohio, where we knew Rickenbacker had lived. Our local library had addresses for libraries in the United States, so classmate Brad Arnold contacted the reference department of the Public Library of Columbus and Franklin County. He requested help in locating Rickenbacker's two sons, David E. and William F.

Librarian Sam Roshon quickly responded, not only with information, but also with many helpful hints. First, he suggested books about Edward V. Rickenbacker and how we might obtain these through an interlibrary loan system, which I had not thought about. Secondly, he informed us that Eddie's son David and his brother Louis were no longer living. Next, he supplied possible addresses for Rickenbacker relatives—son William Frost Rickenbacker, niece Mrs. Ralph Darby, and brother Albert Rickenbacker. For Albert, the brother of Edward, Mr. Roshon also added this note, "Age 84—Write soon!" He also indicated he had called Rickenbacker's niece, Mrs. Ralph Darby, who lived there in Columbus, and she had reported she would write to us. Mr. Roshon indicated he had been unable to find phone numbers for other relatives, but suggested that we try public libraries in nearby areas and search city directories, adding, "If you locate any of them, please let us know."

Classmate Michele Mitchell contacted William Frost Rickenbacker in New Hampshire. In February he responded, "Your project looks fascinating, and I'm sure you'll have an amazing coup if you can convene the four survivors of 'the Pacific fishing expedition,' as it was known in my family."

Super Sleuth Lisa Moore contacted Eddie's surviving brother Albert Rickenbacker, in Los Angeles, California. Lisa explained the class project and enclosed a clipping about it from the *Des Moines Register.* Lisa also indicated in her letter that we were reading Eddie's book, *Seven Came Through.*

Albert's response started, "It was with great surprise and pleasure to receive your letter of the 11th yesterday and I hasten to answer same with kindest St. Valentine good wishes." Since he remembered Valentine's Day, he had immediately bonded with my sixth graders. He told us he gave all his memorabilia to Eddie to use in writing his book. Then he suggested we contact Eddie's son, William F., at the address he enclosed. This really thrilled the students. It was the same address we had already used. Albert had also mailed, as a gift to the class, one of Eddie's books that covered his experiences in World War I.

In my thank-you to Albert, I explained how excited the students were to have him write and send the book. I wrote, "They were particularly pleased that you autographed it and all wanted a photocopy of your message to them!" I had then added, "They wanted to send you a class picture. We hope you enjoy it. They look much quieter than they are— especially when they receive special letters or packages in the mail."

Mrs. Ralph L. Darby, Eddie Rickenbacker's niece, responded to classmate Brad Arnold's letter. She enclosed pictures of Eddie's burial place there in Columbus and of a memorial marker at the Rickenbacker Air Force Base south of Columbus. She also mentioned a movie that was made of his life in the 1945 period called, *Captain Eddie.* (I remembered seeing it in high school on late-night viewing, while babysitting at a neighboring farmstead.) She also told how she had traced the family back to the Fifteenth Century in Switzerland. (Both my father's parents had come to America from Switzerland, and I envied her knowledge of so much family history.) Mrs. Darby concluded with, "One does not live without leaving many traces. Just one good lead and lots of patience and perseverance can take you into new worlds of research adventure. Best wishes on your project. It was a pleasure to know that you are interested in these times and in the lives of these men."

After the Rescue Reunion and throughout the summer, I had continued to correspond with Albert Rickenbacker in California, sending him materials about our research. In August he wrote, "I have read and reread every page several times...Many thanks again for your kindness in letting me know of all your doings." He also requested, that if we had a spare copy would I send our souvenir booklet to his nephew, William C. Rickenbacker, in Michigan. (This was not the same relative, William Frost Rickenbacker, we had contacted in New Hampshire.)

In September 1985, William C. Rickenbacker wrote to thank me for the memorabilia. He also wrote a postscript. "The enclosed photograph is Captain Eddie Rickenbacker taken at the end of World War I. The Hall of Fame Brochure is self-explanatory. These items are for you or to be used as you wish." What a treasure! The large portrait-sized photograph depicted Eddie in his World War I uniform. I explained what we would do with this treasure in my thank-you to William. "The photograph will be on the ledge above the windows, by our red, white, and blue piano. Each morning as we sing a patriotic song, we will enjoy the photograph, too." I concluded my letter, "We have decided that more than one member of the Rickenbacker family is very special. Thank you for sharing with us in such a beautiful way."

I continued to correspond with Marian (Mrs. Ralph) Darby. In September she thanked me for the autographed copies of our evening program, souvenir booklet, and photos of the Rescue Reunion. She had made copies of the materials we had sent her and provided them to the

Eddie Rickenbacker, World War I Flying Ace, in 1918.
(*Courtesy National Museum of the U.S. Air Force*)

Columbus Public Library, for the same librarian, Sam Roshon, who had originally tracked down the Rickenbackers for us. Marian wrote that the librarian was thrilled to have followed our story on the network news and to have these materials.

Although I did not intend to try to "top" the learning experiences of the Super Sleuth Sixth Grade class, I was next given an opportunity I had not anticipated. The following August, Albert Rickenbacker had offered to donate something to our group, but I indicated to him it was not necessary. I wrote, "We are just so appreciative of the many people who have helped us and shared with us. It was a marvelous learning and teaching experience. Our lives are certainly richer because of the outreach from so many people like yourself."

However, in September 1985, a couple weeks after I started school with my next group of sixth graders, I received a letter from Albert that said, "In regard to my suggestion please accept the enclosed. Knowing you as the Captain you will have many ideas to use same." And in the letter was a check for $1,000. How could someone who did not even know us, care so much, and share so much?

When I read the letter and the amount of money to the class, their response was immediate and overwhelming. *"A pizza party! Let's have a huge pizza party!"*

No way were we going to consume the money with a pizza party! The check had my name on it, and I had a different idea. We knew that Albert Rickenbacker was a businessman. He had told us that he had been interested in accounting and had later joined a Wall Street firm to learn the financial business. I decided that a good use of the check he sent would be two-fold—provide economic learning experiences for the students and contribute to some organizations that had helped us with our research.

I first deposited the check at the bank in a money market account in my name, but called "The Rickenbacker Account," to keep it straight from personal finances. We then held a class meeting and formed an unofficial corporation titled, Kelly Enterprises. Students elected five classmates to serve on their Board of Directors and an appointed student as Chairman of the Board.

The Board of Directors met and discussed possibilities for investments in the categories of:

- Room 14 classroom items
- Meeker Elementary School donation
- Ames Community School District donation
- Ames community donation
- Children of Tuvalu donation

The Board of Directors announced that decisions would be made to use some money as financial contributions and some money for further investments.

I knew very little about investments, so I contacted a stockbroker, Corbett Griffin, from Piper, Jaffrey, and Hopwood, Inc. here in Ames. He had heard of last year's project and was willing to help us with this new venture. In January 1986, he came to Room 14 to discuss the stock market and investment possibilities. After a period of questions from the class, Mr. Griffin outlined in more detail the specific choices we might consider with some of the money.

In late January, the Board of Directors narrowed both the financial contribution options and the investment options and gave a ballot to each sixth grader as a shareholder in the company. Votes were cast, and ballots were tabulated. For Room 14, they chose to purchase an activity for the classroom. For Meeker Elementary, they wanted to construct a rock wall for geology study. For the school district, they voted to contribute money for a new bus fund for student environmental field trips. Since there was a tie between support for the Ames Public Library and the newly consolidated junior high, we decided we could support both. And for the children of Tuvalu, they wanted to purchase a subscription of *National Geographic World* and send it to the Secondary School in Vaitupu for our new pen-pal friends.

For the class investment, students chose to place $300 in a mutual fund. Its yield average over time had been 12.5%, but in 1985 it was around 32%. Then the students asked, "You mean we really are going to invest with real money?" I thought that was understood, but obviously not. Some students believed it was just a mathematical exercise. I assured them I would arrange with Mr. Griffin, and we really would invest the money. Since the school district legally could not make a profit, it was decided I would make the investment in my name. Whether it made or lost money, we would sell the mutual funds at the end of their senior year in high school and decide how to use the hoped-for profits. "How will we find out how much money we made?" they wanted to know.

I was waiting for this question. "Because you all will be coming to my house—for a pizza party!" I received many comments from adults who thought I was trying to teach children that sometimes you could not always have instant gratification. Yes, but that was only part of it. I already knew how much fun it would be to have a reason to see these young people again in six years.

We had learned about investments and studied some rudimentary ideas on economics. The students had listened and voted. But I wanted them to have a more active part in Kelly Enterprises. I had an idea. After preparing a letter for parents explaining this next project, I withdrew crisp new five-dollar bills from the Rickenbacker Account at the bank — one bill for each student.

The next day I explained the project to the sixth graders. Each student would receive five dollars. The goal was to use the money as an individual investment, which over the next few weeks would yield a profit. If they did not make a profit, hopefully they still would learn something. If they did make a profit, they could decide how much money to donate to the over-all class project. Choices would be theirs.

After a discussion on "supply and demand," we talked about their interests. Hopefully, someday they would have a job in which they were interested. Until then, I wanted them to use their own talents, skills, expertise, and interests to create a product or business. At the end of the experience, they were to share what they decided to do, why, how it worked out, and what they learned. I was fascinated with the results.

One boy bought a baseball card and sold it at a profit. What did he learn? "Sell it before the other person finds out how much money you paid for it!"

Another student lost his money before he got it home. He reported, "I learned whenever you get money, put it in a safe place."

One girl went to a local chocolate business. Her mother purchased the molds and flavorings she could use, so her daughter could use her investment money for chocolate. Next, the student constructed boxes made of discontinued wallpaper books that she obtained free. She added, "This cut down on my overhead." She then explained how much she had charged and how much profit she had made, adding, "My biggest buyer was Mrs. Kelly."

Another girl made cinnamon applesauce which she then rolled out like dough and cut into shapes of bears and hearts. After drying the items and stringing them, she had created aromatic decorations. This student had increased her original investment to $13.25. "I learned that money can go a long way if you want it to," she wrote.

One boy reported that he had a plan, but he became too busy with his paper route and jobs around the house. He returned the original money with this comment, "If you want to do business you can't be lazy about it."

Another student, who was a very good artist, loved to make pencil drawings of animals. For her project, she sold them in colorful folders and made $14.00. Then she added, "That's because my mom and grandparents bought them for more money than I was selling them for." Then she added, "I'm not sure if I learned anything about business or not, but it was fun and I will turn in the $14.00."

One boy made cookies with his mother for Christmas and Valentine's Day. He subtracted his costs and donated $32.00 to the project, adding, "I learned it's hard to be a salesperson."

Another boy made fruit pizzas with cookie dough and cherry pie filling topping that he sold to people who worked for his dad. He reported he learned to take orders and make change.

A third student made Trivia Fortune Cookies. He kept meticulous records of supplies. Inside the cookies he placed trivia questions about politics and sports. He reported, "From my business I learned you have to keep the price low so the consumer will buy it, but high enough to make a profit."

One sixth grader decided to interview the city treasurer, who suggested putting the money in a savings account. By adding $5.00 of her own money, she collected 6.5% interest, or a profit of ten cents. She said she learned, "how to put money in my account and that the city treasurer isn't all business," which was her interpretation of the adult's interest in her project.

Another hard-working student used his investment money to purchase a shovel. Throughout the time we had allotted, Iowa had a great deal of snow, and this student made money. He summarized, "I learned that you must keep working to make a profit. I also learned that you must have will power to keep your money and not spend it. Also, I learned you are in charge of what happens to your money." He had asked me if he had to turn all of it in for the project, and I reminded him there were no rules. He could decide. Perhaps since he had used so much labor, he would want to keep some for himself. He turned in all $17.00.

One girl decided to babysit, and she used her original money to purchase some books and games to take with her to entertain the children. She further decided that she would charge less if the children could feed themselves and if they were toilet-trained. She donated her entire $17.50 to the project.

Another girl organized a business called, "Neighborhood Movie Theater." She checked out free movies from the public library and borrowed a movie projector free from her church. She reported, "We watched different kinds of movies: sad, happy, funny, and dippy." From advertisements to events, her income and debits were carefully recorded. Pictures of her project showed some siblings and other classmates involved. She also added that her father and brothers helped by staying away. She learned that "Saturdays are some of the best days to have parties," and that "if you have treats on a project to earn money, you will get a whole lot more!"

One girl chose to do work that did not involve additional costs for materials. She did lawn work, cleaned a patio, and washed the family car—jobs for which her mother paid her. "Sometimes it's a lot of fun and sometimes it's a lot of hard work and not that easy," she wrote, "but there are many different ways to make money."

Several students must have decided on the same investment plan, although I do not know if they discussed it with parents or among themselves. However, their reactions to the same experience were quite different.

One girl purchased a troy ounce of silver at a coin shop for $6.77. She reported that silver did not cost that much at the time, but the store had charged her retail. Each night she watched the news to see if the price of silver had increased. Before she could sell it, the person she was going to sell it to was placed in jail. She then reported, "So I decided to keep the silver to give to my grandchildren, and give Mrs. Kelly $8.00 I have made babysitting."

A boy had a similar experience. He used the original five-dollar bill, plus additional cash of his own, to purchase a piece of silver. Then the owner was jailed for fraud. He concluded, "So I still have my silver in the freezer at home because no robbers will look there and it keeps cool cash."

Another boy tried the same approach, decided the price might go up, so he still had not cashed it in. He summarized, "I learned that everything that you invest in won't always make money but sometimes you make something. I don't like to invest unless it is a sure thing."

The students obviously learned some facts about finances. I also learned about my students. And for the class investment project, we gained a profit of $221.30.

In our science classes, we studied geology. This group was particularly interested in rocks and had been fascinated to learn the formation and identification of specific rocks—sedimentary, igneous, and metamorphic. They wanted to contribute some lasting project to Meeker Elementary School. We brainstormed and came up with a plan. How about cementing larger rocks together to make a bench for the fifth and sixth grade playground area?

I contacted a local contractor, Eugene Babcock, who agreed to come and help us mix cement and make a rock bench. The administration advised we could place it in a little alcove near the recess door, under the shade of a tree. It was a perfect spot. Next, the sixth graders solicited the support of other students to contribute rocks from vacations or other family outings. Especially the kindergarten class became involved and brought us their rock treasures for the project. Geodes, the state rock of Iowa, were especially featured in the structure. Mr. Babcock's note to me that said, "Enjoyed the kids helping," confirmed that I had selected the right person with expertise. Six years later, those kindergarteners connected, not only with The Book, but also the Rickenbacker Rock Bench. "I remember doing that! I just thought it was about rocks. I didn't know it was about people."

Students finished details for the Rickenbacker Rock Bench as Mrs. Kelly and WWII veteran Randy Matson checked their progress.

Installed within the rocks was a commemorative plaque in honor of Rickenbacker—not Eddie—but Albert. He had shared with us that he had never married or had children, so the students adopted him. Immediately the bench was a special spot. Children read on it, visited on it, and jumped off it. Albert wrote, "Enjoyed pictures with your comments and the one Rickenbacker Rock Bench brings much pleasure and happiness to all. May your investments do likewise."

In mid-May we had an Investment Reception and presented checks to people representing organizations. My favorite response was from a School Board member, Carolyn Jons. She started her letter with "*Talofa*," the Tuvaluan greeting. Mrs. Jons captured the essence of our project when she praised the class for practicing skills, doing research, developing awareness of other countries, and learning free enterprise principles—through projects that are real and exciting. She closed her note by telling the class the School Board gratefully accepted its gift for the new ECO bus, and "*Faafetae!*" the Tuvaluan word for "thank you."

In April, Kenneth Pins wrote another news story about this class, entitled, "6th-graders forgo pizza, make investment in future," which was published in the *Des Moines Register*. The reporter told the story of last year's sixth graders reuniting the survivors and rescuers, which led to Albert Rickenbacker's check and this year's investment project. I remember explaining, "I didn't want to think of last year's project as an ending. I wanted to look at it as a beginning."

After reading the article, Fred and Barb Miller contacted me. Mr. Miller owned a local pizza franchise. They supported our projects and wanted to provide the class with a complimentary pizza party. Their generosity and encouragement for our educational endeavors was a wonderful way to end the school year. To me, an investment did not mean only with money. It also meant time in teaching students.

For the next six years, we watched our mutual fund. In February 1992, I tracked down those former sixth graders, now high school seniors, and wrote them a letter. "You may recall that when you left sixth grade, I promised you a party! It is now time to collect!" Many of them came to our home in April to eat pizza, laugh over elementary memories, and share future plans. The original investment of $300 had grown to $625.55. I noted that the former sixth graders had grown, too! On April 20, they appeared at the School Board meeting to present two checks to Charlie Ricketts, the Board president. Half the money was to go to the high school environmental committee, and half was to go to Meeker Elementary to be used for more "Rescue Reunion" projects by sixth graders. The older students valued their experiences and wanted to mentor future sixth graders. What an example of how learning and teaching are forever entwined.

Chapter Eleven

THE JOURNEY CONTINUES

L IEUTENANT FRED WOODWARD, THE KINGFISHER PILOT who happened to be flying from the southwest to the northeast in the exact position for Les Boutte to spot Captain Cherry, was about to form another link in our research chain. He had made a career in the Navy and had been lost in a tragic 1957 Christmas Eve accident off the Aleutian Islands. Fred Woodward's body had never been recovered.

Though we had communicated with family members now in Connecticut and sent them photos and clippings, something more was about to happen because of the Sixth Grade Super Sleuths. After we requested assistance to find Lt. Woodward's relatives, Bill Wundram, columnist for the *Quad-City Times*, and the people of Davenport and Bettendorf, Iowa, plus the readers in nearby Moline and Rock Island, Illinois, became involved.

People in this area, along the Eastern edge of Iowa, were quite familiar with the Rock Island National Cemetery—a national resting place for veterans—located just outside Davenport on what had been an arsenal on an island in the Mississippi River. Originally established as a place for the remains of American Civil War Union Army soldiers, it now had thousands of interments. After hearing the story of Fred Woodward, a technical assistant at the Rock Island National Cemetery, Joann Munson, had an idea. Why don't the people of Davenport obtain a cemetery marker for Captain Fred Woodward?

In June 1985, Bill Wundram wrote to me about an artist from the Rock Island Arsenal doing a painting of Fred Woodward. I thought it was quite an understatement when Bill added, "Gosh, we certainly stirred a lot of memories in this episode."

I sent a letter to Joann Munson in July, telling her how pleased I was of her efforts to initiate the monument to Fred Woodward. Her response in August identified Dorothy Pate as the local artist doing the painting of Woodward with the American flag and the memorial marker. The painting was to be displayed in the Veterans Administration office there at the Rock Island National Cemetery.

Joann also invited the Super Sleuths to their Veterans' Day tribute on Nov. 11, 1985. Getting all the former sixth graders there would have been difficult. But I did arrange for a carload to go, stay overnight, and participate in the dedication of Captain Woodward's marker. However, at the last minute I became ill with a horrible cold, and since the weather was a typical Iowa surprise, complete with several inches of snow, it was necessary to cancel our trip.

In February 1987, I wrote to Joann Munson with a request. We had never been able to locate a photograph of Lt. Woodward and really wanted one for our research records. We knew a picture had been used in the Davenport newspaper columns, but we did not know its source. We had intended to write to Mrs. Humberstone (Woodward's widow), but we had learned she had passed away. Now we were hesitant to ask her children for one. Joann contacted Dorothy Pate who graciously lent us her photo of Fred Woodward. Side by side—photograph and painting—it was easy to see the remarkable artistic talent Ms. Pate had shared with all of us.

Finally, in June 1988, our family was able to tour the Rock Island National Cemetery. When Bob, Ryan, and I walked into the office for directions to Fred Woodward's marker, a lady looked at me and said, "You're Mrs. Kelly." Joann Munson had recognized me from pictures we had sent of the Rescue Reunion. The Sixth Grade Super Sleuths had linked the people of the Quad-Cities with one of their own—and at last, we all had paid tribute to this Iowa serviceman.

In 1985, when I first corresponded with Mr. H. Panapa, the Broadcasting and Information Officer in Tuvalu, I confessed, "Our biggest wish is that we could obtain a photograph, a letter, a signature,

Dorothy Pate with portrait of Fred Woodward she
painted for the Rock Island National Cemetery.
(Used with permission of the family)

or a tape from Toma." And since I learned from sixth graders, I added,
"We know that Mr. Reynolds and the other men landed on an islet of
Nukufetau. Would it be possible for us to learn where that piece of land
was in relationship to Toma's village?"

Our wishes were about to be granted. In July 1985, I received a
package from Mr. H. Panapa that included a booklet that was prepared
for heads of the Pacific region and contained relevant information about
Tuvalu. He also included some post cards, so we could see the ship
Nivanga that carried our correspondence to the various islands and the
main government offices in Funafuti. On a map of the islands, Mr.
Panapa marked exact spots to show where the secondary school is on

Vaitupu, and three places on Nukufetau—Toma's village, which was the main settlement on Nukufetau; the place where an American base was during the war (actually built in 1943, after the men were rescued); and the exact spot, Kavika, on the islet where Toma found the survivors. This information helped us understand why Toma took the men in rafts to go to a village for soup. Whether by open sea or lagoon, Nukufetau has far more water than land.

There was another special item in the package—an audio cassette tape of Toma, telling the story in his native Tuvaluan language. Mr. Panapa had also enclosed an English transcription of the tape, describing the rescue of James Whittaker, Jim Reynolds, and Johnny DeAngelis.

Toma Fakapae

I was born in 1921, so I was 21 years old when I found these survivors.

There were four of us on my canoe. We could see at a distance, in the direction of one islet of Nukufetau, a dark speck bobbling up and down in the sea. When we got closer to it we recognised it to be a boat [the raft]. We could see one man [Whittaker] getting into it. He looked very sun-tanned. We were rather scared because we could not figure out whether he was a Japanese or an American. So at times we would paddle away from the approaching boat. The wind was blowing from the east and was carrying the boat in the direction of both the village and our canoe. I was somehow convinced that this was the boat we were looking for since the boat was painted green and yellow, just as we had been told before we set out. So I asked my crew to paddle for it.

When we got closer, we saw a man trying rather tiredly to sit up in the boat. He then called us. He looked scared, no doubt, of us. He did not however, realise that we were also scared of him. He asked if any of us spoke English.

"Yes," I replied.

"Which island is this?" he asked again.

"Nukufetau Island," I replied.

He apparently did not know Nukufetau, so I continued: "It is part of the Gilbert and Ellice Islands Colony."

He seemed to understand now for he was nodding his head.

"Which country rules these islands," he continued asking.

"Britain," I answered.

"What religion do you belong to?" he asked again.

"We are Christians. We belong to the London Missionary Society," I answered again.

"Are there any white people here?"

"There are three New Zealand soldiers here [the coastwatchers]*."*

"Where is your village?"

"To the west."

"Who is the captain of your canoe?"

"I am," meaning of course the canoe was mine.

He then told me that he had two companions ashore on the islet.

"Let's go to them," I said. "We can get some drinks for you and your companions, rest a little, for an hour perhaps, and then we will take you all to the village."

"It's fine with me. You decide," he said.

I then gave orders to the members of my crew:

"Aleki, you carry Jim Whittaker, the oldest of the survivors, ashore. Tavo, you fix up the anchor and I will look after the canoe." We found another white man ashore exhausted and crying. When he saw us, he stood up, took a faltering step towards us and then, I suppose, because of sheer exhaustion, he fell over. Popu (another member of my crew) and I helped him. His eyes and mouth were full of sand. As Popu helped him get rid of these, I climbed some drinking nuts. As he drank one of these nuts I did my best to comfort and reassure him.

"Do not be afraid," I said. "You have been rescued now and we will do our best to look after you."

It was only when he finished drinking that he was able to utter his first words to us.

"Thank you very much. I feel much alive now," he said.

I then carried him [Jim Reynolds] down to the water's edge where the other white men and my crew were. The white man Popu was looking after [Johnny DeAngelis] asked for some cigarettes. He was crying. He told us that he had only been married a year before and he was longing to see his wife again. But the oldest of the white men [James Whittaker] asked me not to give him any cigarettes yet- not just yet for he was too weak to indulge in that.

I then prepared food for them. This was the meat of the green coconuts they had just drunk. They appeared to really enjoy this. One of them asked me if it was porridge.

By then the other canoes which had also set out to look for these men had arrived. So we all decided to return to the village before nightfall. There were four canoes altogether, including mine.

As we approached the village I raised a makeshift flag on a makeshift mast on my canoe to indicate to the people ashore that we had indeed found the survivors. At the village we found a lot of willing helpers who had come to carry the survivors ashore.

It was five o'clock in the afternoon when we reached the village. An hour later, a doctor [Doc Hall] had arrived from Funafuti to help the survivors.

On their third day on Nukufetau, a battleship [U.S.S. Hilo] arrived to pick up the survivors. However, before they left Nukufetau, one of them [Whittaker] asked me to make a model of an Ellice canoe, one that he could take with him as a souvenir. I willingly obliged and had my name TOMA FAKAPAE and the name of the island NUKUFETAU carved on the canoe.

Toma had written more—but this was part of the story Whittaker had told, but from Toma's viewpoint. I could hardly wait to send copies to all the seventh graders. Mr. H. Panapa had put so much time and effort into getting these items to us. We wondered how we ever could repay him, but he provided us with an idea. He wrote, "Before I close down, may I ask you if you would send me a copy of the book *We Thought We Heard the Angels Sing*? There is no copy of it on the islands. Many people have asked me for

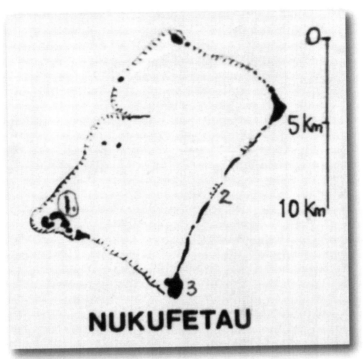

Map sent to the class by Mr. H. Panapa, the Broadcasting and Information Officer in Tuvalu. *On Nukufetau:* 1. Toma's village, the main settlement. 2. Kavika, the islet area where Toma found the survivors. 3. Location of the American base, developed more after 1942.

the book when they heard me broadcasting the news about the detective work your class has done." I mailed him a copy of the book that same day.

A month later Mr. Panapa sent me another treasure. This was a letter to me from Toma, written in his own handwriting. The translated copy told how much he had wanted to come and meet the students and me. He had appreciated the photographs we sent. He wrote, "I casted my thoughts back to the time...Now my hair is all grey and I sorry for those who have died. My crew have all died." Then he told about his family—children and grandchildren.

Savave, Nukufetau, Tuvalu Group
13th July 1985

Fakafetai lasi kooti ne maua ne au taulua tusi ne faitau ne au mo toku fiafia lasi kae vikia te alofa o te Atua ko mafia tatou o fetaui i laupepa penei.

Fakatoese atu e tusa mo toku se oko atu ki toutou fekau ona eiloa ko au ko se maua o sasale mao ako toku fia fanatu se fakatau mai eiloa. Toku fia fetaui mo tamaliki ote akoga kae sili atu a te toku fia fetaui mo koutou oku taugasoa kola ne maua ne au i konei. Ne kilo oku mata ki olotou ata ne maligi oku loimata i taku kilo atu ako kilo au ki taimi ne maua ei ne au kati e [kautaua?] eiloa matou tela kote 21 tausaga o toku olaga kae nei ko kena a motou ulu i te sina. Ko moe atu a mata o nisi o matou taugasoa toku faoa pela foki mo toeaina faoa o te poti. Fakafetai kite Atua ko avatu tou taugasoa koi toe mai tatou.

Aku tama e toko fitu – toko lima tagata kae toko lua fafine. Tamaliki tagata matua e nofo nei i Niusila. Ko toko lua tagata foki e galue nei i Tarawa. Toko tolu e nofo maua. Toko fa e fakatoka nei o fano ki vaka i tua. Toko lima e akoga faka pailate nei i Ausitalia. A ko tamaliki fafine ko avaga katoa. Taku avaga ne mate ite 1968 ke oko mai ki taimi nei nofo loa au mo aku tama. E toko lua tamaliki seki avaga ko taku toe ki tua mo tamaliki tela e pito atu ki ei. A ko tamaliki kola ko avaga e afu katoa tela la toku kaiga se fakatau loa i toku uke.

Fakamoe ke fetaui tatou i ne aso fakam ne ia oko mai kati ka fiafia lasi au o feta atu mo koutou katoa. Tofa tofa,

Toma Fakapae

Savave Islet, Nukufetau, Tuvalu Group
13th July 1985

Thank you very much for your letter which I read with great happiness, and I thank the Lord that we are able to meet this way via letter.

I apologize for my inability to make it to your event. I am unable to walk very far these days, although I really want to be there. I would really like to meet the students and I would especially like to meet the friends that I made when they were here. When I looked at their photos it brought tears to my eyes and brought me back to the days of the war when I was 21 – and now here we are with heads of white due to the gray in our hair. Some of our friends from those days have passed away from my crew and the crew of the boat. Praise God for those of us who still remain.

I have seven children – five boys and two girls. My oldest son lives in New Zealand. The second son works in Tarawa (Kiribati). I am living with my third son. The fourth is preparing to go abroad to work on a ship. The fifth son is studying to be a pilot in Australia. My daughters are both married. My wife died in 1968 and since that time I have lived with my children. My two youngest kids are not yet married. Those that are married all have children so my extended family is very large.

I hope that we may meet sometime in the future. If any of the students or one of my friends is able to make it here, I would be very happy to meet with them. I'll end this letter and say farewell in the name of Jesus Christ with great affection to you all – good bye.

Toma Fakapae

First page of the handwritten letter from Toma Fakapae to Suzanne Kelly and class, July 11, 1985. Below it is a version typewritten in Tuvaluan. Below that is the English translation provided by Scott Erickson.

After our celebration of Tuvalu's independence on October 1, I wrote to Mr. Panapa. I was also able to send him photo reprints of Toma from 1942 that had been shared with us. He wrote back, "The bit in your letter about you and students celebrating Tuvalu's Independence Day was broadcasted on the day I received your letter. You can see then, the Tuvalu people are well informed of your project since we first writing to each other. My best wishes to you, your family, and students."

Eight months after the Rescue Reunion, my mother was diagnosed with cancer. Mother always said that two things from the Rescue Reunion helped her through the difficult surgery, chemotherapy, and radiation. One was a practical item, and the second was a reminder to have faith. Bill Wepner, the PT boat rescuer from Wisconsin, sent us soft blue turbans for Mom to wear. They had been his wife Marie's, and he thought Mom would feel better to have something comforting and warm to wear on her head. And secondly, we had a video recording of Captain Cherry at the press conference. Mom later told me sometimes she would play it repeatedly, "No matter what you're doing, you've got to be prepared to do it. And you've got to be prepared for help from up above." I knew Mom would do what she had to do to get well and that strong arms of "the Master" would wrap her in His care.

By March, Mom was doing better, but my father was not. While waiting with him in the doctor's office, he went into cardiac arrest, was resuscitated, and was then taken by Life Flight helicopter to a Des Moines hospital. After a week in intensive care where he was fitted with a pacemaker, he was ready to cheer the Iowa State Cyclones in the basketball regional playoffs.

Surprisingly, both my parents enjoyed many more years of the ripples of the Rescue Reunion. In fact, they often met visitors we had found in our research and hosted them at their farm in Dallas County, Iowa.

In April, one year after the Rescue Reunion, I was summoned to the school office for a phone call. It was *Newsweek* calling. The magazine was doing a special June edition of "100 Unsung Heroes." They had selected the Sixth Grade Super Sleuths and me to be part of that celebration. By now, classmate Doug Haynes had moved to Illinois, but we wanted him to be in the magazine's photo of the class, so we used some of the Albert Rickenbacker money to share his bus fare. The people from *Newsweek* asked how this experience had impacted our lives. I explained that our friendships could be measured by how the men closed their letters. They had gone from "Sincerely yours," to the latest—"All my love."

We were pleased again to have an opportunity to tell our story, and the publication opened new doors for people to find us. As Jim Reynolds laughingly said when he called from California, "Suzanne, you had no idea what you were starting!" to which I replied, "Technically, James W., it was YOU who started this!"

In May 1986, Captain Cherry arrived to take, what he called, "his kids" out for pizza and a roller skating party. He stayed a few days and attended our college spring celebration called VEISHEA*. Besides watching the parade with us, Captain Cherry took our son Ryan to central campus to view a parachute jump demonstration. Ryan was excited to explain how the parachutist landed "in the circle." Captain Cherry seemed more interested in the airplane, shading his eyes to look into the sky.

In June, Jim and Margaret Reynolds came for a couple of weeks from California. A highlight of their visit was their treat of taking the former sixth graders and their parents out for pizza. This fun time, however, seemed a little calmer without some of the sixth grade-ish unbridled energy. My Super Sleuths were growing up.

---

*VEISHEA was an annual week-long celebration held each spring by the students of Iowa State University. The acronym stood for the original colleges—Veterinary, Engineering, Industrial Science, Home Economics, and Agriculture. The celebration featured an annual parade and many open-house demonstrations of the university facilities and departments. VEISHEA was the largest student run festival in the nation, bringing in tens of thousands of visitors to the campus each year. It was permanantly discontinued in 2014.

Captain Cherry and Ryan Kelly attended VEISHEA at Iowa State University a year after the Rescue Reunion. Captain Cherry had come back "to see his kids." (*Photo Bob Kelly*)

In the summer following the Rescue Reunion, Captain Cherry called and asked me to send a souvenir booklet to an address in Corona, California, for Coreen and Elmer Schwenk. Coreen had called Captain Cherry after his trip to Iowa and told him she was the girl who had been engaged to Alex Kaczmarczyk, the young man who had died at sea.

I wrote to Coreen: "I am sorry for any sorrow that you had to endure forty-two years ago. My students shared that sorrow. Before our public presentation, they asked if they could have a moment of silent tribute for

During their visit to Iowa, Margaret and Jim Reynolds treated former Super Sleuths to a pizza dinner. *Left to right*: Erik Smedal, Travis Senne, Chad Watson, Ben Jackson, Derrick Boden, Brad Arnold, and David Jurgens, along with Ryan Kelly. (*Photo Bob Kelly*)

Alex." One sixth grader, Lisa Moore, wrote a poem about him in the gift booklets we gave the men who came to the reunion.

Coreen had been watching KABC news one night of reunion coverage and had realized Captain Cherry was from Southern California. When she was able to visit with him, he told her he had tried to get in touch with her after he had recovered from his ordeal in the Pacific, but he had been unable to do so, probably because by then she had joined the WAVES and stayed in until the end of the war. Then Coreen wrote to me, "Sgt. Alex was a fine person and we loved each other very much. We planned to marry after the war but it didn't turn out that way. Life teaches us so many lessons as we go along our way and also gives us many beautiful memories. As you get older and look back at your life, you realize that there really were reasons for the experiences you had and a true Master Plan through it all. I have a very happy life with my second husband, children, and grandchildren."

A year later Coreen wrote they would be traveling across the country and would like to meet us. I invited them to visit. When Coreen wrote to say when they would arrive, she added, "We are just plain people. Elmer is very quiet and usually only speaks when he has something important to say. With me, *everything* is important!" During our visit, she expressed gratitude for our reuniting the survivors and rescuers. She said, "When Captain Cherry came to visit me, he told me things Alex had said before he died. At last, I was able to close that chapter in my life. Thank you, Suzanne."

Although time did not permit the Schwenks to stay longer and visit the class this trip, they did begin corresponding with them. In a September letter to the present sixth graders, Coreen and Elmer had signed it, "Your adopted grandparents." This third group of sixth grade researchers immediately latched onto that title. As one student expressed it, "I have grandparents, but I've never had *adopted* grandparents before!" And just that quickly we started a yearlong exchange of what Coreen called "priceless letters" between Iowa and California.

In 1942 after all the men were rescued, except Alex, a newspaper reporter had interviewed Coreen and Alex's parents. A photographer had taken their picture looking through scrapbooks and remembering, "the one they left behind." Coreen had kept that tiny photo but now sent it to Bob who enlarged it and sent it back to Coreen to give to Alex's family. In December, Coreen wrote, "We gave the picture of Alex's parents to his sister Vicky when we were in Connecticut. She was so pleased."

In December two packages arrived from the Schwenks. Coreen wrote to me, "Since your Dad will celebrate his 80th birthday on Christmas Day, and since he likes boysenberry jam, we sent him a larger jar!" The second package was for the class, so I took it to school to open. Inside the box was a large container of cookies. The students loved those treats that we portioned out each day before vacation. They also asked to make a videotape for their adopted grandparents. This was fine with me. It was a different form of communication and part of our language arts curriculum. So students each prepared their presentations and taped them. Coreen wrote back, "I think the idea of the tape with the children talking to us was a wonderfully unique idea. We sat here watching it last night, grinning like two Cheshire cats, we were so pleased."

By August, I had again said good-bye to another class, but wrote to Coreen about our son, "Ryan celebrated his ninth birthday with a swimming pool party. Considering that I'm not a fish in water (more a beached whale!) we really had a good time...We look forward to your visit on Monday."

We also organized a potluck picnic for the students and their adopted grandparents, so families were able to meet the Schwenks. Included also were Mrs. Jacobson (former teacher) and her husband, my parents, and our neighbors, Ruth and Randy Matson. Randy by now had nicknamed me "Update" because of my daily jaunts across the street to tell him the latest news. We also had a special breakfast with Lee and Abbie Himan, my former principal and his wife.

Coreen and Elmer were to visit us many times. Sometimes they stayed with us and sometimes on my parents' farm. Although their long trips eventually ceased, the correspondence continued for over twenty-five years.

By mid-November 1986, with that third year of researchers, we were contacted by Jack Fincher, a writer from Oregon, who wanted to do a feature on the original Sixth Grade Super Sleuths for *Reader's Digest.* It was not that I had any objections to the story, but I wondered how I could make the experience meaningful to this year's class. I finally agreed to the story on the condition that Jack would teach my language arts class for the week he was here. He agreed, and we were off on another adventure.

During the day, Jack read the volumes of research we had accumulated and taught writing to my present sixth graders. It was a marvelous opportunity for the students to follow how a feature article is written from notes to publication. I gained insights to help students progress from their rough drafts to polished writings. At night, Jack interviewed the Super

Elmer and Coreen Schwenk during one of their many visits over the years. In 1942 Coreen was engaged to Alex Kaczmarczyk, the one lost at sea. (*Photo Bob Kelly*)

Sleuths in our home. I remember David Jurgens, now an eighth grader, shared his experience about the Rescue Reunion in a 4-H State Fair award-winning scrapbook. Then in the midst of an Iowa snowstorm, Jack had checked out of his hotel, but we persuaded him to stay at our home until the blizzard stopped.

Five months later, Jack called to say the article was in its final stages of preparation for a July 1987 publication. He wrote, "I hope all of you are as pleased with the end result as the magazine and I are. As I said on the phone, Suzanne, my editor hailed the story as my 'masterpiece,' the best thing I've ever done. And much of the credit for that goes to you and your breezy but meticulous record-keeping on letters, clippings, etc. I hope we meet again." Enclosed with the letter were his submitted draft, magazine cuts, recommended changes, transcribed tapes, and research notes.

Olinda Woods, Research Editor for *Reader's Digest*, contacted us in April to check every minute detail of the story. After the article was

Jack Fincher and the author. Jack wrote an article on the class for the *Reader's Digest*. He also taught writing to the sixth graders the week he stayed in Ames, Iowa. (*Photo Bob Kelly*)

published, she sent copies of the magazine to us that were printed in other languages—Chinese, Korean, Hindu, Spanish—and even Braille. With an elementary classroom in a university town, I sometimes had students from other countries as my students. I particularly remember a little girl who arrived from Korea and spoke little English. When I handed her a copy of the magazine with our story in it, she latched onto it immediately.

When Olinda mentioned by phone that she would be interested in knowing some of the responses to the article, I gave her an update about those who had attended the Rescue Reunion.

Marie Wepner had lived to attend her daughter's wedding. She had been pleased to see her name mentioned in the *Reader's Digest* article—a highlight for the Wepners that had contributed some joy to their last days together.

Former radioman Les Boutte had just finished hip surgery, was doing fine and ready for therapy. He, too, had enjoyed the article.

John Bartek had asked me for copies of letters written to me and decided he wanted to respond to many of them personally. I knew the people would be thrilled.

Jim Reynolds was going fishing—if the California forest fires were under control. He had just sent "Oakland A" caps to us this week. I wore mine to school.

Captain Cherry was playing golf in Scotland. He was having a ball—no pun intended!

But I also told Olinda about other journeys with our research. A lady wrote to us from El Paso, Texas, wondering if our school could have been named after her grandfather, Warren H. Meeker. We told her it had been. Professor Meeker was on staff at Iowa State University for fifty-five years and had been former head of the Department of Mechanical Engineering. He had served thirty-three years on the Ames Board of Education, until March 1945. When the men were on the rafts, he had been guiding the education of the children in Ames. My husband, of course, took a picture of the photo that was hanging in our school lobby and sent it to her. Now the great-grandchildren of Warren Meeker have photos of him, which they never even knew existed.

Another update I shared with Olinda was about a contact from an Ames man requesting my help for a man from Culpeper, Virginia. Could I please help J.B. Hudson, Jr. locate a member of his former B-29 crew from WWII? I was able to find the man, and the crew was soon having a reunion.

Over the next several years, Olinda continued to correspond with me, sending the class books as gifts from the magazine and enclosing personal notes. One gift was *The Reader's Digest Atlas of the World*. My husband suggested an activity that students could use with the atlas. First, they thought of riddles, then used the atlas to match places with latitude/longitude coordinates. For example, "What is an inner area of a B-17? (19° N, 73° E)." By using the atlas and finding those coordinates, they had their answer. An inner area of a B-17 is a bomb bay, and the coordinates locate Bombay (India). We were given a globe before and now a new atlas. Our references were growing, and so were our connections around the world.

Chapter Twelve

DOC HALL AND THE
MEDICAL CORPSMEN

B Y NOW, I HAD A PROCESS TO EXTEND THE original research and still make the experiences unique for a new class. After reading them The Book, I made a list of possible categories to research. I questioned one group of sixth graders, "What would you like to find out this year?" The overwhelming response was, "Doc Hall!" Jim Reynolds always referred to the physician who had started glucose and plasma treatments that had saved his life as "Doc Hall," and that is the title the students always used. We had three clues to find him—doctor, rank of lieutenant at time of rescue, and a very common last name.

Original Super Sleuth, Christy Scott, had written to the Superintendent of the U.S. Naval Academy at Annapolis in February 1985, requesting information about any of the rescuers. Frederick S. Harrod, Chairman, Department of History, referred her letter to Robert William Love, Jr., Associate Professor of History, for further research. Prof. Love looked through the U.S. Naval Academy "Register of Alumni" lists, but he could find none of these officers as graduates of the Naval Academy. He indicated he was turning our correspondence over to Dr. Dean Allard, Director of the Operational Archives, Naval Historical Center, Navy Yard, Washington, D.C. He also suggested that if we could acquire Lieutenant Hall's Christian name, then we could check with the American Medical Association for prewar or postwar records of membership. The same week Prof. Love sent Christy's letter to Dr. Allard—Dr. Allard received a letter from classmate David Abelson, requesting similar information. Our requests were traveling, being read, and then being passed on to other experts. It was Dr. Allard who then sent David the declassified Rescue Report which we used so much—the one that also contained Lieutenant Hall's name, William J. Hall, (MC), USNR.

Time was limited before we held the Rescue Reunion, and we certainly wanted Doc Hall to join us. Christy sent an urgent request to the American Medical Association in Chicago, Illinois. Could they help us find Lt. William J. Hall, M.D.? The staff assistant in the Department of Data Release Services forwarded our request to Micaela Sullivan in the Division of Library and Archival Services.

Ms. Sullivan, historian for the American Medical Association, called Meeker School, but we were having class. During recess, classmates Christy and Jennifer went with me to the office to return Ms. Sullivan's phone call. She had wanted us to know she found an address for the doctor in Mexico. Christy sent a letter to Mexico, but it was never answered.

Now in November 1986, a different class was picking up the trail after the Rescue Reunion. One sixth grader wrote to Ambassador John Gavin at the U.S. Embassy in Mexico City, asking for assistance in locating Dr. William J. Hall. David L. Stone, Vice Consul, wrote that the Office of Citizen Services and the Embassy were unable to locate a U.S. citizen by that name in Mexico. Mr. Stone indicated that most Americans residing in Mexico register either with the embassy or one of the U.S. consulates, and he had checked both registries.

In their next letter to David Stone at the American Embassy in Mexico, the sixth graders thanked him for writing back and trying to assist us. Almost as an after-thought, the students added they might have a possible address because they had a postal number for a city, but no other address. And then, because sixth graders do not give up, they decided to try out the address used by the class two years earlier. As they explained to me, "That letter *could* have gotten lost in the mail!"

On December 12, 1986, Dr. Hall wrote to the class, "You are pretty good researchers to be able to track me down to San Miguel Allende, Mexico." And two weeks later we received another letter from David Stone saying, "Thank you for your letter providing additional information...As

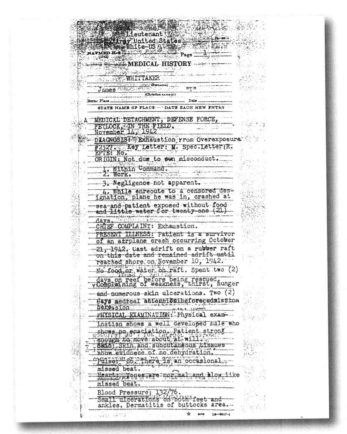

After James Whittaker was taken to the newly built Funafuti hospital, Doc Hall prepared this medical report, sent to the class by one of the medical corpsmen.

you have indicated a post office box in San Miguel de Allende, I have forwarded your letter to our Consular Agent in that city." Once again, two pathways merged.

Dr. Hall continued, "We had a great bunch of corpsmen and we all had a lot of pride in our medical unit. We were all proud to be in the Navy also, and we felt very 'gung ho' supporting the United States Marine Corps."

From three small clues in Whittaker's book we had found William J. Hall by Christmas time, playing a cello in a string quartet in Mexico.

My husband immediately made Dr. Hall photos from the Rescue Reunion. We sent these to him, along with other information. We asked if he wanted a copy of James Whittaker's book. He wrote back that he had read the book in early days of its publications, but he did not think he had ever read Rickenbacker's. Then he added, "Actually I am not sure if I ever told my daughter, born in 1949, about the Rickenbacker incident or not."

Dr. Hall reminded me of my sixth graders who really became involved and found more questions with each answer. He wanted names of hospital corpsmen from Funafuti whom we had located. Were Doctors Fuller and Garrity still living? Had we attempted to locate the New Zealand coastwatchers who had been on Nukufetau?

This last question prompted him to remark, "Jim Reynolds was in pretty bad shape (he sure does not look it now) when I saw him in Nukufetau. I wonder if he really recalls seeing me there?" Then Dr. Hall went on to describe the conditions of the three men he had treated. He had been amazed at Whittaker's seemingly good condition when he had first seen him. "You would not of thought he had been subjected to any ordeal as I recall." He remembered DeAngelis as being in good shape, but nothing like Whittaker. "Reynolds was 'poorly.'" Dr. Hall had not described Jim's condition in detail for sixth graders, but it had been an extremely close life-death situation. We knew from Whittaker's writing that the glucose Doc Hall gave Jim had saved his life.

Mostly, Dr. Hall had questions about Funafuti. He wondered if the sixth graders in their correspondence with their counterparts in Tuvalu could clear them up. We were aware that the Tuvaluan students were on Vaitupu and might have limited access to the historical changes on Funafuti and that the time element of corresponding was lengthy, so we turned instead to our former Peace Corps friends, the Ryherds.

Dan and Donna Ryherd had been on the islands only four years before, so their knowledge from Peace Corps days was quite current. They were able to answer Dr. Hall's questions.

He first wondered if the airfield the Navy built there was still functioning or had it returned to its original status of a coconut plantation? Ryherds knew the airfield in Funafuti was still very much in use, probably close to the same conditions it was in World War II. They described it as a grassy, multi-purpose field, used for playing soccer and cricket, for grazing pigs, and as a road and bike path. When a plane was ready to land or take off, a truck with a siren would speed down the field, making sure the airfield was clear. Then "the locals line the strip to see the highlight of the day."

Doc Hall also had questions about the prefabricated huts that were built on the island and the type of housing used by the Tuvaluans today. Dan and Donna were not sure if the huts were the same as those in the '40s or not, but they wrote how they were a symbol of affluence, although many islanders desired the traditional thatch huts, which allowed better air circulation. They also told how the village on Funafuti is located along the airstrip and that on all the islands the people live together in one village, though some have a second home in the bush or on an islet where they have animals or coconuts to tend.

Doc Hall was also curious about their native clothing. Do men and women still wear the very comfortable lava-lava (colorful cloth bottom wrap) or are they in jeans now? The Ryherds reported that lava-lavas are still worn by most of the men and women, with a T-shirt or dress shirt on top. Black dress lava-lavas from Fiji are formal wear. Some youth are wearing jeans and even painter's overalls for their everyday clothes. Sunday church clothes are still a white lava-lava for men and a white dress or lava-lava for women.

Dr. Hall wondered about the change of population. And, yes, he might be interested in a photo of Toma. "He or someone just like him brought me ashore from the Kingfisher in an outrigger canoe and the next day paddled me out to the *Hilo.*" Then he added, "I find I enjoy this kind of reminiscing and I hope it helps to keep [our project] alive. Whatever happened to Whittaker and the others?" These questions we could answer.

I wrote, "Yes, it was Toma who took you ashore from the Kingfisher in an outrigger canoe." I then sent Dr. Hall copies of Toma's letters and a copy of Whittaker's book with this note, "Please accept it with my sincere gratitude for responding to my students and for all you did for the men so long ago."

Doc Hall wondered what had happened to the medical corpsmen. We had a declassified military report that referred to the medical corpsmen as part of a Detachment of the First Separate Medical Company. They were thirty-five enlisted men from the Navy now assigned to the Marines. One medical corpsman later told us it was the first medical corps unit the Marines ever had. The group worked and trained under a crew of Navy doctors. Their assignment was to provide hospital support for the military on the island. Though the unit saw little action, they were often the targets for Japanese attacks. Although this occurred after the men were rescued and treated there, we recognized how important that hospital support was.

In March 1985, just before the Rescue Reunion, Captain Cherry had called me. For years, he had played golf with the brother of a man who had helped take care of him in World War II. Would I please contact this Navy medical corpsman? Super Sleuth Amy Murphy wrote to Philip J. McAuliffe in Marblehead, Massachusetts, asking him to attend the reunion. Although he was unable to come, he wrote a detailed letter of his work on Funafuti and loaned us a few photographs, including ones of him at his medical laboratory bench. One photo showed a laboratory microscope used to evaluate blood cells and bacteria. He explained, "These laboratory procedures were the greater part of my daily routine, the lesser part was the practice of pharmacy."

Mr. McAuliffe told of having a rectangular box-like fashion of mosquito netting on their cots to keep out the mosquitoes. Though usually effective, even one pesky mosquito inside the net was not tolerable. Therefore, most of the men adopted a pet lizard, about four to six inches long, and the pet took care of any mosquitoes that sneaked inside the netting. Students could relate to the pet lizard concept. For several years we had a pet chameleon in the classroom.

Then Mr. McAuliffe concluded by saying, "It was a privilege for us to have been able to accomplish the rescue and to give medical aid to the wonderful group of men who were the survivors. Please give my best wishes to Bill Cherry and to the others attending your reunion. Wish I could be with you."

Further correspondence with the medical corpsmen began the summer after the Rescue Reunion. George Spevock, from Rivesville, West Virginia, wrote to me at Meeker School after reading a magazine article about us written by Paul Harvey, the radio broadcaster. George wrote that he had been a Navy hospital corpsman on Marine duty stationed on Funafuti at the time of the men's rescue and that he had contact with all seven of them. "I can't begin to tell you how bad their bodies had withered from this experience."

Over the years, George had tried to reach John Bartek, especially, because he had two mementos. He had a Mae West-type Army Air Force life jacket and a pair of military style oxford shoes, given to him by John Bartek, although he was not sure which of the crew they had originally belonged to. He knew John had lived in the Freehold, New Jersey area. Would I please send him John's address? He wrote that he also had addresses of former medical corpsmen who now lived in North Carolina, Tennessee, and Alabama. They had cared for the survivors on Funafuti before they were sent to another base hospital in American Samoa.

I first checked with John Bartek before giving out his address. Then I wrote to George, asking for the addresses of the other people he knew had been on Funafuti. In late February, George sent information about a "Funa Futi Medical Detachment Reunion" to be held in Tuscaloosa, Alabama. James Ellis Teer from Northport, Alabama, was organizing it. I sent a packet of information and photos to Mr. Teer that he could share at the reunion.

George had decided not to attend the reunion, but he was pleased that I had sent information to (James) Ellis Teer, who had visited him the past summer. He also had thought of a couple people from Iowa—Arthur Helland from Mason City and E. C. Ernst from Humboldt, Iowa.

After receiving my correspondence, Ellis Teer wrote that my letter, the confidential report, and other items had been copied and distributed to the twelve men and their wives who attended the reunion. At the end of that school year, Mr. Teer sent us photos of the men and their addresses.

In the summer I sent out letters to the former medical corpsmen, explaining my correspondence with George Spevock and Ellis Teer. I encouraged them to write to us and share anything they would like about their experiences on Funafuti.

Two weeks after school started for the 1986-87 term, medical corpsman Thomas W. Lenderman and his wife Marie from Wilkesboro, North Carolina, came to see us. I had not yet had time to read The Book to the class, and the students were a little overwhelmed with the school visit. However, as the third group of sixth graders doing this research project, the Lenderman's visit probably added to the students' curiosity to find both Doc Hall and then the rest of the medical corpsmen.

Tom told how he had remembered the men, particularly John Bartek and Jim Reynolds. He had daily washed out their saltwater ulcers and treated them. He related how they had first made a bed for Captain Cherry in the X-ray room, which was the only solid building they had. Tom also brought clippings from the war era that had appeared about Funafuti. Included was a citation to Thomas W. Lenderman, pharmacist's mate third class, United States Naval Reserve, for his meritorious duty with a Marine defense battalion.

In addition, Tom passed on a copy of a letter that Dr. Frank D. Sticht, from Memphis, Tennessee, had sent to him. In the letter, Dr. Sticht related how much he had enjoyed their reunion. He wrote, "I have put in one copy of the Medical Histories for you and another for the lady in Iowa— or wherever it was—which you may send on to her if you wish." In the envelope was a medical report on James W. Whittaker with a diagnosis of "Exhaustion from Overexposure," and a reference "Transferred to U.S. Naval Mobile Hospital No. 3 for further treatment." It was signed by W. J. Hall, Lt. (jg.) MC-V(G) USNR, and approved by James T. Fuller, Lt. Cdr. (MC)-V(S) USNR. Other medical reports were on John Bartek and Eddie Rickenbacker. Dr. Omar LeGant, another medical corpsman now from Albuquerque, New Mexico, who had attended one of their reunions, had signed them. When I first heard The Book from Mrs. Jacobson, I never imagined that thirty years later I would know what the men's pulse rates were when they were rescued!

After the Lendermans visited our school, students wrote them individual letters. Tom responded by saying, "They will be placed in my

Tom and Marie Lenderman visited the Zobrist Farm in Dallas County, Iowa, several times after their initial contact by the sixth graders. (*Photo Edith Zobrist*)

files and kept and cherished forever." Then he added that he intended to prepare some small memento for each one as an expression of appreciation. The students wondered what it could be.

Soon after the Lendermans left, we went back to our written research. We wanted to find the two medical corpsmen George Spevock had mentioned were from Iowa. My family had friends in Mason City, so I asked Stan and Clarice Collins if they knew any address for Arthur Helland, since we had not been able to find his listing in that city's phone directory. Stan wrote back with an address in Metairie, Louisiana.

In November, Arthur Helland, HMC USN (Ret.), wrote to our class, "I received your surprise letter several days ago. It really brought back old memories of the past, names and places I hadn't thought of in years." Mr. Helland added, "It's true I was on Funafuti at the time of the rescue of Captain Eddie Rickenbacker and other members of his mission. I did meet them, being a Hospital Corpsman attached to the Medical Unit where they were first brought after being rescued." Then he related how it seemed like everyone—Marines and Natives—kept coming by to get a glimpse of Eddie Rickenbacker, "which for a short while kept their minds off their real task."

While at Iowa State University, I had student taught at the high school in Humboldt, Iowa, as part of my training for secondary education certification. Therefore, I felt comfortable contacting people in Humboldt to find E. C. Ernst, the man George Spevock had mentioned. Mrs. (Edwin) Eunice was kind enough to write back on October 10, 1986, and let us know that her husband had passed away in 1959. On October 11, 1986, we received another letter from Tom Lenderman saying that after visiting my parents and us on the farm, he and Marie had decided to drive to Humboldt to look up the widow of another Funafuti corpsman and dear friend. Tom wrote, "Eunice is a very nice lady as would be expected of the wife of Edwin Ernst...I had not had a chance before to speak to her in person. For some, it is hard to understand the strong and lasting bonds of friendship that were forged in a relatively short time during our war." Within one day's time, we had the two letters from medical corpsmen making it obvious that Mrs. Ernst had been contacted by two sources, each without knowing what the other was doing. She must have thought it quite unreal. To me it was becoming a normal pattern of our research.

Robert W. (Red) Timian from Dunedin, Florida, responded to my letter in mid-July. I had written that Jim Reynolds had been here earlier in the summer. Red started by saying, "My dear Suzanne, I shall attempt to tell you and your class what your endeavor has meant to me." He indicated he had a vivid recollection of Jim Reynolds, probably because Jim stayed with them over two weeks on Funafuti, while the others stayed less time. Mr. Timian then wrote, "[Jim] ate constantly. He was the happiest, hungriest person I have ever known. In the many years that have passed since my tour of duty in the Pacific, whenever the subject of a hearty appetite arose, I always told the story of Jim Reynolds." Mr. Timian had been a second class pharmacist mate on night duty in the ward where Eddie Rickenbacker was being treated, so he spent four hours caring for and talking with him.

Although Mr. Timian's letter also included memories of suffering from Japanese bombing, which occurred a few months after the men's rescue, it was his humorous account of a serious situation that touched our hearts. The story involved an outrigger canoe. According to Mr. Timian, he and a Sergeant Hayes had borrowed an outrigger canoe from an island chief's daughter, Mary O'Brien, for night fishing in the lagoon. Mr. Timian wrote, "That's the night I was almost killed." Using a flashlight in the boat to look for fish, the people on Funafuti thought their outrigger canoe was a Japanese submarine, and the entire island went on "condition red" with orders to shoot if they saw the light again. "As it happened, the fish were not biting so we came ashore. As a punishment, Sergeant Hayes and I each had to dig fourteen foxholes. I recall Mary, as she and some of the other native girls watched as we dug, saying, 'You smell like a goat.'" Red Timian concluded his letter by thanking me for bringing back some of these memories.

In correspondence back to Mr. Timian and his wife Betty, I told him I was glad the fish were not biting, and he had made it ashore. I also told him I had suggested to my students that if they misbehave and think staying in for recess is terrible, it couldn't be as bad as digging fourteen foxholes. I also wrote of the coincidence of the visit with Tom and Marie Lenderman to the classroom on the very day we received a package from Tuvalu with letters from our pen pals and tapes of English and Tuvaluan singing.

After our initial contacts with some of the medical corpsmen and their subsequent annual reunions, the corpsmen wanted to contact others of their group. Thus, they turned to the sixth graders and asked if they could help track down Sherman R. (Bugle) Fairbanks, originally from Ogema,

Minnesota. He was one of the seven corpsmen who had stayed on Funafuti another six months after the Fifth Defense Battalion withdrew to Hawaii, and he had been a pharmacist's mate first class when they parted in August 1944. Tom recalled that "Bugle" had worked in a bakery. He had helped Tom make fruit pies in the mess hall. "He would weigh everything and could produce good pastry made from 24" x 30" pie crusts." Could we help locate him?

The town of Ogema was so small we could not find it on our maps. We did not know a public library to contact. Since the town was not located in the telephone book we were using, we looked up the phone company to find Ogema's phone service provider. We were given two possibilities for this city in Area Code 218—Red River Regional or Otter Tail Wide Area. Students also went to our public library for names of any elementary schools in nearby towns, or the name and address of a minister or doctor who might answer a letter from us. We did find a relative of a relative and were eventually informed Sherman Fairbanks had passed away two years earlier. We were sorry to report this to the medical corpsmen but pleased they had wanted to include "Bugle" in their reunions.

Medical corpsman Leonard Rutherford was from Huntsville, Alabama. One year we received a Christmas card from Mr. Rutherford. He wrote, "I was one of the crew [stretcher bearer] that went out to the ship and brought Captain Cherry to the island." Later we reread another declassified Report of Operations of Fifth Antiaircraft Battalion. It told of Pharmacist's Mate Third Class Leonard L. Rutherford, USNR, who was one of twenty-six members of the command who had received the Purple Heart award. This was a result of being wounded in the action on Funafuti five months after the men had been rescued there.

Another medical corpsman, Elmer Sanders, was also from Huntsville, Alabama. He shared, "I remember when Captain Cherry was brought in to our unit. I served an extra watch that night and sat by his bedside for several hours. He slept if I held his hand and would become very restless if I did not. When I realized that he was able to rest only if I held his hand, I did so for the rest of my watch."

After writing to medical corpsman H. Hazen ("Buck") Wilson, Jr. in Beaver, Pennsylvania, he wrote back about seeing a display on Eddie Rickenbacker at the Wright-Patterson Air Force Museum in Dayton, Ohio. "It seems quite a coincidence that we [the medical corpsmen] would pick the year following your project to have our first reunion." In reference to the materials we had sent to be shared, he wrote, "Thank you for adding so much to our reunion."

Although Buck had started corresponding with me, I wanted him to share with this group of students who had chosen to find the medical corpsmen. The bulletin board in our class's reading corner was becoming quite covered as students plotted their correspondence from across the country. Buck wrote to the students in December that he was pleased they had located Art Helland, because all of the corpsmen had lost track of him. Buck also added that he thought Doc Hall had originally been from McKees Rocks, Pennsylvania, and that they all used to call him "Wild Bill." Then Mr. Wilson had enclosed a special surprise—photos of the men from the war area—showing sand bagged foxholes, native huts, and even a picture of George Spevock up a coconut tree.

Just before school was out in May, two boys approached my desk with a plan. They thought we should telephone Buck Wilson. Why? They explained that it would be an educational experience—a *very* educational experience to make a long distance phone call to Pennsylvania. (Before the days of cellphones, it *was* an educational experience.) I made arrangements and then took the class to the office, so the two boys could charge the call using my credit card, and the entire class could greet in unison, "Hi, Mr. Wilson!"

The sixth graders grinned. One summed it up, "We're a whole lot of Dennis the Menaces!"—a reference to a popular television character, whose neighbor was a Mr. Wilson.

Ellis Teer from Alabama, whom we had first contacted when he was organizing the medical corpsmen for a reunion, had retired from the Navy in 1962 as a dental technician. Then he had been with the post office. Now, fully retired, he and his wife Ernestine enjoyed traveling, and on May 12 they came to visit us in Ames. They shared their correspondence with the medical men and thought they should have all the men meet in Ames for a reunion. What a novel idea! Although it was ultimately decided to hold their next reunion elsewhere, we still felt privileged to meet several of these men.

Then a package arrived in Room 14 with our "special mementos" from Tom and Marie Lenderman. Tom had designed T-shirts with a logo and "Greetings to: Kelly's Investigators." The sixth graders usually wore "Kelly green" for their annual track meet where each class sported a different color, but this year the students of Room 14 persuaded another class to exchange colors, so we could all wear our yellow T-shirts from Wilkesboro, North Carolina.

In June the Lendermans visited my parents on their farm, or as Tom put it, "We do enjoy going north for that Southern hospitality." I had a chance to ask Tom more about the medial corpsmen. I had not thought about it earlier, but I knew we had history on the Fifth Defense Battalion. Now when we analyzed it, we recognized more names, dates, and events that made a connection with us.

In the summer the students were asked to make a display at the public library. In addition to paper palm trees and the model outrigger canoe, students made another display case to show their T-shirts from the Lendermans and the story of the medical corpsmen.

Almost all the medical corpsmen wanted to know what had happened to two doctors—Dr. Fuller and Dr. Garrity. We knew Lt. Cdr. James T. Fuller (MC) USNR had been the senior medical officer with the Naval hospital on Funafuti. In the Fifth Defense Historical report, it said he was awarded the Silver Star from the Army for his actions in the enemy bombing of the island on April 22, 1943. Doc Hall wrote that he thought Dr. Fuller had entered the service in 1941 or 1942 from Mayfield, Kentucky.

Lieutenant Richard W. Garrity, USN, was the medical officer of the U.S.S. *Hilo*, the tender for the PT boats. When the ship went to Nukufetau to pick up Whittaker, Reynolds, and DeAngelis from their raft adventure and early treatment by Doc Hall, Dr. Garrity was the physician who went ashore to treat these survivors. Doc Hall, particularly, was curious if we knew anything about Dr. Garrity. We did.

In March, just prior to the Rescue Reunion in 1985, the Sixth Grade Super Sleuths had requested information from the American Medical Association. The organization responded with a partial address at that time for Dr. Garrity—a street address, but no city or state. They also indicated that he had passed away about three months earlier.

Dr. Richard W. Garrity at age 63. In 1942 Dr. Garrity was the medical officer of the USS *Hilo*, the tender for the PT boats that rescued the men.

But the week of the media blitz during the Rescue Reunion had produced an outpouring of communication across the country. In May we received a letter from Karen Stone from CBS News in Chicago. She forwarded us a letter their news office had received that they thought we might appreciate having. It was a letter from Mrs. Richard (Evelyn) Garrity.

Mrs. Garrity wrote that she had been watching the CBS April 19 noon news from San Diego, California. She told of her connection with the news story and confirmed that her husband had passed away in December. She wrote, "I was deeply moved when one survivor held up for viewers an old 1942 photo of two men, one of whom was my husband. I would so appreciate it Ms. Stone if you could help me locate Mrs. Kelly."

Evelyn Garrity and I corresponded for over a decade. Then, after her passing, I exchanged family greetings with her son, Robert. I wish I could have met Dr. Garrity, but I am grateful to have shared with his family.

Although the medical corpsmen always invited my husband and me to their reunions, we were never able to attend. Some summers I taught classes for elementary education majors at Iowa State University, and Bob was doing research for his doctoral degree. In June 1990, however, Buck Wilson sent us a note saying the men had "talked about me" at their reunion. He also sent an article from *The Beaver County Times*, a

Pennsylvania newspaper, with photos of the men and interviews with them that contained many personal anecdotes.

My sixth graders in 1992 were asked by the medical corpsmen to find another colleague they had lost touch with over the years—Dr. John J. Cloonan. At one time, he had been in New Canaan, Connecticut. By now, I was gaining many insights in teaching research skills to students. Each new group needed help in understanding how their tree of information branched and how it fit into the overall forest of knowledge we had on the people somehow connected to the raft episode.

I always started students' research by reading them The Book. Although students played on the Rickenbacker Rock Bench, it had now been eight years since the Rescue Reunion. Next, I provided a starting research packet that contained four sections about the specific research they were going to do: Background Information, Research Accomplished, Suggestions to Begin, and Other Writing Suggestions.

To help locate Dr. Cloonan, I gave students a brief background on the medical corpsmen. We had a last known address in Connecticut. Students wrote to the address, explaining we would appreciate their help. The present resident received the letter and telephoned the manager of her condominium complex. He said John's daughter Marion used to live there, but had moved. Then she called a neighbor and found another address for Marion. Although Dr. Cloonan had passed away in 1988, his daughter Marion Cloonan Uebelhoer wrote back, "…how touched I was with your letter." Then she wrote, "I'd love to learn more of my father's WWII days. Please send me Mr. Lenderman's address. Thank you for your interest in my father."

Later we sent Doc Hall more information. We learned Dr. Garrity's wife had letters from Toma and miniature photos of other servicemen. His comment, " That's a great enlargement [photo]— congratulations to your husband."

I also sent Doc Hall an update from Tom Lenderman about other medical corpsmen. One had a degree in pharmacy and dentistry and was now teaching at a medical school. One was a Red Cross director. Another had owned an appliance repair shop. One had been a farmer and worked

1986 Medical Corpsmen Reunion. *Back Row, left to right:* Elmer Sanders, Leonard Rutherford, H. H. "Buck" Wilson, Robert W. "Red" Timian, John W. Cain, and Fred Vinson. *Front Row, left to right:* Clement E. Hiigel, Thomas W. Lenderman, Frank D. Sticht, (James) Ellis Teer, and Murry M. Shipman.

in a cotton mill. Another former corpsman, John Cain, had been a supervisor at a General Motors Assembly plant and had been asked by Eddie Rickenbacker personally to supervise a car he ordered. These were their careers, but the men were also sharing with us personal hobbies and updates on their families.

I had continued to correspond with George Spevock. In 2004, I received a letter from his brother Frank Spevock in Montana Mines, West Virginia. Going through George's belongings, he had found letters and other documents from me and wrote asking about our correspondence. Frank then sent us a photo of John Bartek's life vest, before he mailed the vest to John for the museum in Freehold, New Jersey, to be housed alongside the little Testament that John had used on the raft. A year later Frank's booklet, written as a tribute to his brother, told the story of the

Rickenbacker rescue and George's part in this event. So many lives were being continually connected, not just because of the rafts' rescue, but because people cared about other people.

Chapter Thirteen

FIFTH DEFENSE BATTALION

W HEN THE JAPANESE BOMBED PEARL HARBOR, Hawaii, on December 7, 1941, they also attacked the Philippines, Wake Island, and Midway. Three days later, the Japanese had invaded the Philippines and seized Guam. Two weeks later Japan had taken Wake Island. In February, Japanese bombers sank the first carrier, the USS *Langley*. By March 1942, President Roosevelt had ordered General MacArthur out of the Philippines and appointed him commander of the Southwest Pacific Theater. Admiral Chester Nimitz was appointed as commander in chief of the U.S. Pacific Theater. In April the American forces on Bataan surrendered unconditionally to the Japanese. Although a week later, the surprise B-25 U.S. air raid by Jimmy Doolittle against Tokyo boosted the morale of the Allies, the United States was still in the defensive part of the war. In early May, Japan took Tulagi in the Solomon Islands and prepared to invade Midway Island. Then Japan took Corregidor in the Philippines, with all U.S. and Filipino forces surrendering unconditionally.

A few days later, however, Japan was dealt its first defeat during the Battle of the Coral Sea off New Guinea. Superior Allied intelligence and code breaking had led to the loss of Japanese carrier support and would have a profound effect on the next large conflict of the war.

Often referred to as a turning point in the war, the Battle of Midway in June 1942 was a decisive victory for the U.S., although not without heavy loss with the sinking of the USS *Yorktown*. In August the Marines made the first United States amphibious landing of the Pacific War and invaded Tulagi and Guadalcanal in the Solomon Islands. The next day they took over an unfinished airfield and named it Henderson Field.

In the north were the Gilbert and Marshall Islands. In mid-August a few Marine raiders, transported by submarine, attacked an atoll in the Gilberts. However, this area was heavily Japanese-controlled. It would be three more years before Japan surrendered these islands.

Although this is the larger picture of the war effort in the Pacific, a particular group of military personnel would be very involved in our story, because they would be sent to Funafuti. At this time, the Allied Forces needed some "stepping stones" between Australia and Japan. Northwest of New Zealand, and between Australia and Fiji, were the New Caledonia, New Hebrides (now Vanuatu), and Santa Cruz and Solomon Islands. West of the Solomon Islands was New Guinea and east were the Ellice Islands.

During the original search for information by the Sixth Grade Super Sleuths, classmate Jennifer Jones wrote to the Director of Marine Corps History and Museums in Washington, D.C. The Head of the Reference Section, Danny J. Crawford, sent the class two useful documents—a "Chronology of the Fifth Defense Battalion" and a "Report of Operations of the Fifth Defense Battalion." These sources provided factual details about the military on Funafuti when the men were rescued.

In August 1942 the Fifth Defense Battalion arrived in New Zealand from Bora Bora in the Society Islands. After a brief stay in New Zealand, the Marines left on the U.S.S. *Heywood* and arrived at Noumea, New Caledonia, before going on to Tongatabu in the Tonga Islands to practice amphibious landings. From there, they headed to Espiritu Santo, New Hebrides, before returning to Noumea, New Caledonia.

In mid-September, orders were received from the commander of the South Pacific. One-third of the battalion's anti-aircraft units, one-half of the seacoast artillery units, and one-half of the battalion headquarters were to proceed to Funafuti Atoll, Ellice Islands, as Marine Corps Unit #290— designated "Defense Force, Funafuti." According to the Fifth Defense Battalion report, "The sudden decision to occupy Funafuti appears to have been based upon an estimation of the enemy's intentions. South Pacific Headquarters had information which led to the belief that the Japanese, after occupying Tarawa in force in September, would move into the Ellice Group." Tarawa in the Gilbert Islands was just north and slightly northwest of the Ellice Islands.

A convoy, escorted by cruisers and destroyers, left Noumea, New Caledonia, for Funafuti, Ellice Islands. On September 30, 1942, the U.S.S. *Crescent City* and one destroyer joined the task force at sea. On the *Crescent City*, which had sailed from Pago Pago in American Samoa, were four military groups to join Defense Force, Funafuti, unaware of the part they would play in the rescue of our B-17 survivors. These groups were as follows:

• Two infantry companies "X" and "Y" of the Third Marine Regiment
• 120 man Detachment of the Second Naval Construction Battalion
• Detachment of the First Separate Medical Company (the medical corpsmen), and
• Detachment of VS-65 Scouting Squadron, consisting of operating and maintenance crews for four OS2U seaplanes.

This convoy arrived as Operation FETLOCK on Funafuti, Ellice Islands, on October 2, 1942. The total group "consisted of 33 Marine officers and 820 Marines. In addition, there were 17 Navy officers and 218 enlisted men of the Naval Administrative Group, medical detachment, construction battalion, and aviation detachment."

The report identified Funafuti as "crescent-shaped…approximately seven miles from tip to tip and a mere seven hundred yards at its widest point. The greater part of the island averaged only forty to fifty yards in width."

The convoy commander had allotted thirty hours for the unloading operation. However, three hours earlier than anticipated, he gave the orders to weigh anchor. A considerable amount of supplies and equipment was piled high and unprotected on the beach. Several reports describe how the native islanders pitched in to help.

By mid-October, the first U.S. Army troops landed on Guadalcanal, and Vice Admiral William F. Halsey was named as the new commander of the South Pacific Area (Solomons and New Guinea). But the Ellice Islands were the farthest north of the South Pacific area and the edge of the Central Pacific region.

Students were interested in the chronology of the Fifth Defense Battalion Report at the time when the men were on the rafts, starting on October 21. What was happening on Funafuti? One paragraph said, "Upon receiving a warning from Headquarters, Defense Force, Samoan Area, on 21 October, a special alert status was set. Naval intelligence reported an enemy task force under-way, destination unknown. Our alert continued through 27 October with general quarters at dawn and dusk and strengthening of watches. (Later it was learned that the enemy force moved into the Guadalcanal area)." This report provided the sixth graders with more understanding of the purpose for radio silence when the men were lost.

The Report of Operations the sixth graders received then said, "On 2 November the U.S.S. *Hilo* arrived with four motor torpedo boats. These PT Boats were from Division II, Squadron III." However, the sixth graders later had ship logs from those PT boats, which all referred to Division II, but RON ONE.

The Naval Construction Battalion completed the fighter strip by November 8, and a PBY-5A landed and took off. The base at Funafuti was supposed to be a secret, so radio silence was still maintained. But from the beginning, according to many of the men who corresponded with us, the Japanese knew. Colonel Lloyd L. Leech's group on Ellice Islands was setting up a base as a staging area for raids on the Japanese-held Gilbert Islands to the north. But the stage was also being set for the rescue of three very special rafts of men.

Following the Rescue Reunion, I received a letter from a woman who wanted to know the exact title of The Book. She said her husband had a small part in the rescue. I wrote back and invited her husband to share his story. The Marine who wrote to us was Frederick V. Johnson from Framingham, Massachusetts. He told how he arrived with his platoon on the island to prevent the Japanese advancement and takeover, and to make a chain in the Allies island- hopping to Tokyo. Instead of the usual factual style of writing, Mr. Johnson told a story for the students. "When the Marines make a beach-head, what they really do is build a city." He told how they had no fresh water supply on the island, and the rainwater was insufficient for their needs, so by now they were distilling the salt water from the sea. He added, "The Navy sent in a few P.T. boats and SOS patrol planes to guard our city..." Mr. Johnson's job was to protect the island, repair the airfield after Japanese attacks by heavy Mitsubishi bombers, clean all anti-aircraft guns, and reload ammunition.

On November 10, 1942, Mr. Johnson told how he had been injured and was in sickbay for a few days with a large bump on his wrist. When Eddie Rickenbacker was brought in, the doctor appeared with two pharmacist's mates (medical corpsmen) and asked Mr. Johnson and another patient if they were well

Lieutenant Colonel Lloyd L. Leech, USMC, was Commanding Officer of Defense Force, Funafuti, before the men were rescued.

enough to help with stretchers. In addition to his recollection of rescue events, Mr. Johnson sent us a map of the islands, photo copies of pictures of the island, and a copy of their 1942 Christmas extravaganza, "Funafuti Follies 1942." As Mr. Johnson shared, "Like all good cities, we had a movie theatre and stage theatre, so we spent the next few weeks preparing for our Christmas show." He alerted us to take special note of the show's magician. There it was in the program: "The Great Kardini—Pvt. F. V. Johnson."

We also received a letter from Charles (Chuck) N. O'Brien, Jr. from Rochester, New York. He had joined the small "Rag Tags of the Fifth" just after Rickenbacker had been found. Students always wanted to know about animals, and Mr. O'Brien shared stories of rats and huge land crabs with a body structure the size of a football. In my return letter to Mr. O'Brien, I wrote, "We just obtained three hermit crabs for the classroom. Your account of the huge land crabs and their strong claws was an interesting bit of information. The students decided, 'Now those would be crabs!'"

Mr. O'Brien described the physical properties of the island, with a reef on one side and a lagoon on the other, dark coco palms in the center, and white sand beaches. What might have looked like a picturesque tropical movie setting was a location for the Japanese to "attempt to bomb us out of the ocean." He also shared that he thought the beams from the ground-mounted searchlights tended to disturb the enemy more than the anti-aircraft explosions.

Another story Mr. O'Brien recalled was of meeting a Funafuti village leader named Henry O'Brien. The first time the two men met, the native islander approached the Marine and said, "You O'Brien—Me O'Brien—must be related." We wondered if this village leader was the same O'Brien whose daughter had loaned an outrigger canoe to Red Timian to go fishing in a lagoon and then watch him dig foxholes! Then the Marine ended his letter, "I realize that this leads away from the story of Eddie Rickenbacker but it may help your students to have a better understanding of that small dot in the Pacific called Funafuti."

So many people wrote and expressed appreciation to us for being interested in what had happened to them. One example was a letter from a Marine, Brady Hutson (B. H.) Daniel, from St. Louis, Missouri. He described the little temporary hospital on Funafuti as a partly wooden structure with screen wire windows, rather than the usual tent. He and another member of his squad had looked through the window and had seen one of the rescued men, "with a face that looked much more like a deep red basketball than a face." In another letter, Mr. Daniel expressed appreciation for all the information and material we had sent him and paid us this compliment. "Shucks, you and your students would of made dandy 1940s era caliber Marines, and that is as high a compliment as I know how to give."

At this point, we were trying desperately to have contact with any of the Naval Construction Battalion (CB) who had been on Funafuti. Although Mr. Daniel had not personally known any of them, he admired them. He explained that in early 1943 after the Japanese kept them awake at night bombing the airstrip, the CBs would jump on their earth moving bulldozers and fill up the craters. The continued goal was to maintain an

Suzanne Zobrist Kelly   185

airstrip at Funafuti for the Army B-24s that would be used to bomb Tarawa in the Japanese-held Gilbert Islands farther north. However, this bombing would not occur until after another year of conflict.

Just before our Rescue Reunion in 1985, the Marine Corps gave us the name of Hiram Quillin in Guntersville, Alabama. Mr. Quillin was presently the secretary-treasurer for the 5th and 14th Defense Battalion Association of the United States Marine Corps. Although it was too late to invite these Marines to our reunion, we sent information to be disseminated at theirs.

After Hiram Quillin encouraged members of the USMC Association to write to us if they had any connection with the rescue of the men, we received a letter from W. Keith Weston of Mt. Pleasant, South Carolina. He remembered well the survivors being brought in and all the secrecy of the island's name and location. The Marines were most impressed how the plane that had first picked up Rickenbacker and Bartek had taxied all the way to the island with Colonel Adamson. Mr. Weston had served in a heavy anti-aircraft battery (90 mm) in the fire control section. He also talked about later attending their USMC reunions and seeing General George Good, Jr.

Mr. Quillin continued to provide information to us, as well as share our story in the Marine's association newsletter, called *The 5:14 Express*. The historian and editor of the publication, John M. Hennessey, began communicating with us after W. Keith Weston asked him to run a little notice to members that we were seeking information about Funafuti. Over the years, Mr. Hennessey sent us copies of their newsletter and encouraged us with our research projects. In the association's January 1989 edition, they included an "Update—Funafuti," which we had prompted. We immediately requested a copy to send to people in Tuvalu.

Mel Brauer, one of the Marines who landed on Funafuti on October 2, 1942, corresponded with us for almost twenty years. I first heard about Mel and his family without even knowing his name. In December 1986, George Spevock, the medical corpsman who had John Bartek's life vest, wrote to me about receiving a letter from an old friend from Funafuti. This friend had recently written to him after going through some old photos and finding an address on the back of a picture. This friend had been a Marine who was also stationed on the island, but they had not contacted each other for forty years. Now this man wrote to George about recalling Eddie Rickenbacker's rescue. George told me details of this man's family from their reconnecting letters and about the man's daughter who now lives in Iowa City, Iowa. During all this correspondence, George never mentioned the name of his friend.

Eight years later in 1994, Mel Brauer, USMC (Ret.), from Ft. Mitchell, Kentucky (near Cincinnati), wrote to us about his experiences on Funafuti. He was in Headquarters and Service (H & S), was Colonel Leech's orderly, and was in aerology, where his job was to release weather balloons every morning to get trajectory data for the anti-aircraft guns. Mel asked us for help in finding a copy of Whittaker's book that I read to my students. In his initial letter, he also mentioned a daughter who lived in Iowa City and a grandson who was attending Iowa State University. By this time, I realized the connection between George and his friend Mel. I assumed that George had told Mel about us, thus initiating the contact. It was not until a phone call in May, however, that I realized our connection was not George Spevock, it was Hiram Quillin, with the 5th and 14th Defense Battalion Association. By now, copies of information, photos, and letters my students and I had collected were being circulated at Marine reunions, and our interest had sparked a reconnection among the Marines themselves. This was another example of us being reached by two sources converging, as had happened so often.

One memory Mel Brauer shared was of particular interest to sixth graders, as it connected stories related by two other Marines—Frederick Johnson (the Great Kardini) and Chuck O'Brien. Mr. Johnson had told us about the theatre they had on Funafuti, and both men had talked about the large rats. Mel recalled that unless there was an air raid, they would sit under the stars to watch an evening movie. A sheet was thrown across a line tied between two palm trees. At about 1900 the men would shine flashlights into a tree and a rat would cross the wire like a performing tightrope walker. Only after the rat had crossed, would they start the movie. Mel later wrote that he would be attending an upcoming Marine reunion, where members of the Funafuti Follies would recreate some of their World War II entertainment. They Mel added, "The tightrope walking mouse will not be able to attend!"

By mid-June, another class of Meeker students and their families were invited to a picnic in a local park to welcome our Kentucky guests. In addition, we included Mel's daughter and her husband, Joan and Tom Cook, from Iowa City. Mel brought items of interest for the students—an authentic grass skirt students could try on, beads, and shells. Afterwards, his daughter Joan wrote, "Thank you for enriching our lives and validating a time in history for a faithful WWII vet."

Lieutenant General George F. Good, Jr., USMC (Ret.) sent his photo to the class in 1985. (*Photo courtesy U.S. Marine Corps, taken Nov. 18, 1953*)

Two years later, in 1996, Joan and Tom took a trip to Fiji and then flew on to Funafuti, Tuvalu. They thoughtfully wanted to know what they could photograph for us. I particularly requested pictures of things I had heard about—the radio station where broadcasts had been made about my students, the hospital and airstrip, and of course, any of Toma's family or former Tuvaluan pen pals, who would now be in their mid-twenties.

For Joan's father Mel and us, Joan and Tom wrote a narrative of their trip and made a video of what they saw on Funafuti. Students could see the Tuvaluan flag waving at the government office, a dog crossing the airstrip, and young boys playing soccer. Our souvenirs included books, crafts, coins, shells, beads, baskets, and stamps. We were so delighted to have these items from Tuvalu and indebted to the Cooks for bridging this island country's past with the present.

My sixth graders and I had always wanted to find out more about Colonel Leech, because he had directed the rescue of the men from

George Spevock (*left*) and Mel Brauer were best buddies on Funafuti, 1942. (*Photo given to author by Joan Cook*)

Funafuti and appeared in several photos with them. Mel had saved a "Battalion Memorandum to All Units" written by Colonel Leech on September 29, 1942, telling Unit #290 that he would be leaving. He wrote so eloquently, "… and now it is with the deepest regret that, circumstances over which I have no control, require that we separate into groups for duty in distant parts." He also sent this message, "By our reputation let us be envied, by our deeds remembered." Then he closed with, "May I remind you also of our battalion motto, 'Defens ores libertatis,' [Defenders of our liberties], and that of our Corps, 'Semper Fidelis' [Always Faithful], and may we never fail either."

Mel was on the U.S.S. *Heywood* before arriving at Funafuti. An official memo from the commander, U.S. Navy and executive officer of the ship wrote this "Plan of the Day," dated "At Sea, Friday, 2 October, 1942." The plan included time for Modified General Quarters (0515), All Hands (0530), Breakfast (0600), and details for the rest of the day with Supper (1630). Two notes appeared at the end of the memo. One said, "Sunset, Dim out— use only lights necessary in handling cargo." The other was a special note: "The ship's company wishes Debarking Marines Godspeed."

Mel Brauer also shared parts of his personal diary with us. His entry for October 2, 1942, read, "We landed this morning, we still don't know whether there are Japs here or not. We arrived on the beach of Ellice Is. about 2 pm. Such wonderful coconut trees I've never seen. Worked all night."

The October 3 entry read, "We have the natives helping us and if I may say so they are very good workers. With this help we finally got all the food and equipment off the ships and they shoved off today about 3 pm. The coconuts and bananas are plentiful but the water is a problem."

The next two entries told about being extremely busy and reporting the guns were now set up, two 155s [155 mm] on each side of the beach. Mel recorded trading two bars of soap for some beads, taking a dip in the sea, and a story of caring for the colonel. Due to misinformation from a Marine gunner, Mel had been making up the major's bed each morning, instead of the colonel's. He then wrote, "The Col. didn't mind so much after I apologized."

Mel Brauer, USMC, was in Headquarters and Service and was Col. Leech's orderly.

Another entry told about going down to the native village to learn a little "lingo." Mel also told of a native girl, Paulo, who read her Bible to them in Tuvaluan. Then the Marines had gone back to their shacks, where one had a console radio with record player, and they listened to modern jive records. Mel also had written of listening to a rebroadcast of the World Series, "Sure was surprising to hear the Yanks lost 4 out of 5 games."

Mel had saved a listing of their box scores from softball leagues on the Funafuti coral atoll the year after the rescued men were there. He had played on the Palm League, opposite the Coconut League, and had been recognized for his batting average of .400.

Mel also recorded a couple of diary entries which he later highlighted "Rickenbacker Rescue." For November 12 he wrote, "Last night about 30 miles from (here) we picked up Capt. W.T. Cherry of the U.S. Army. He said that Rickenbacker along with a Colonel and several others were on 2 other rafts in the vicinity of here."

On November 13, Mel wrote in his diary, "Two planes here now, are waiting to take Rickenbacker and Co. back to the States. They all will be able to leave in about 10 days."

Then, just before Lt. Col. George F. Good, Jr. arrived to take over command and write the Rescue Report, Mel Brauer recorded this about the outgoing commander: "Colonel L.L. Leech left today on the P.B.Y. for new assignments. Everyone was sorry to see him leave…he sure was the best commanding officer in the Marine Corps."

Chapter Fourteen

THE SEABEES

S TUDENTS POURED OVER INFORMATION SENT TO THEM. They learned that early in 1942 Frank J. Iafrate, a clerk at a naval station in Rhode Island and known for his cartooning, was asked to draw an insignia for the newly established Navy's Construction Battalion. These men were to build bases, so would be trained in both military and construction, and follow the Marines ashore. Mr. Iafrate thought first of using "busy as a beaver" as an appropriate symbol, but he learned that in times of trouble a beaver will "turn tail and run." Then he thought of the bee that does not bother anybody unless they bother him, and then fights with a sharp sting. Since the CBs were to be a defensive outfit, compared to the Marines, which were an offensive outfit, Mr. Iafrate decided the bee would make a perfect insignia. He added a white hat for the Navy, a hammer and wrench to show construction skills, and a sub-machine gun to represent military powers. Thus, the CBs became the Navy Seabees—construction crews working under combat conditions.

In the Pacific Theater of the war, there was so much water and so little land. What land there was, consisted of coral atolls and often swampy dense growth of jungle-infested tropics. It was an isolated, hot, humid, disease-filled environment.

Most of the early Seabees were not as young as the men in some branches of service. They came from being experienced civilian contractors and were to fill the expansion of needed fighting forces.

Led by the Navy's Civil Engineer Corps, the Seabees were base-builders. They needed heavy equipment that was large enough and powerful enough to construct those bases quickly. They used dynamite, bulldozers, dredges, and anything they could, to get any job done. Those jobs included building roads, airfields, camps, warehouses, and artillery installations. There were no service garages or maintenance shops around the corner. The construction battalions improvised, relying on ingenuity and resourcefulness. They became the "Can Do" group and were known for making the impossible possible.

Early in 1942 the War Department decided to establish defensive positions at Samoa, Fiji, and New Caledonia. Originally, these bases were "to protect air and sea communications between the United States and Australia." The over-all plan, however, was for the development of defensive island base areas from which to launch offensive strikes against Japan.

The operation within the Samoan group of islands was designated Operation STRAW, with the defense concentrated on Tutuila, American Samoa, as STRAWSTACK and the New Zealand-mandated base at Upolu in Western Samoa as STRAWHAT. For tactical purposes, a French mandate about 350 miles west, Wallis Island, was also included in the Samoan group. It was designated STRAWBOARD.

"The Second Battalion was commissioned on April 3, 1942, at the Naval Construction Training Center, Camp Allen, Norfolk, Virginia." From this battalion, the 4th Detachment departed on April 7, 1942, for destination Upolu.

On September 25, 1942, a detachment of the Fourth Detachment, comprised of two officers and 120 enlisted men, left Samoa and joined the Marine's Fifth Defense Battalion in Operation FETLOCK at Funafuti. Under the command of Lt. (jg.) L. H. Harris, CEC, USNR, this group of Navy Seabees was also known as the Naval Construction Detachment, 5th Defense Battalion, Reinforced, Fleet Marine Force. It was referred to as the Funafuti Detachment.

Whatever it was called, this detachment in Operation FETLOCK occupied Funafuti on October 2, 1942. The group immediately began the construction of an airstrip. The 5,000 by 250-foot landing strip was completed in thirty days. Although on November 8, a PBY-5A landed and took off, later the fighter strip was expanded and broadened.

The Seabees here later built seaplane base facilities, including a thirty-foot wide ramp, small boat landing, and a floating dry-dock for PT boat repairs. They also built a road system, fifty prefabricated frame buildings for housing, four Marine warehouses, and eventually a seventy-six-bed hospital. But, not all this was completed until five months after the men's rescue.

However, to the sixth graders, it was enough the Seabees were on the island and had completed the airstrip that was necessary for the men's rescue in mid-November. After Captain Cherry was spotted in Raft #1 and taken to Funafuti, the construction battalion, along with the medical corpsmen, hurriedly worked on the hospital, and Eddie Rickenbacker was one of its first patients.

During the 1992-93 school year, a student found an address for the Navy Seabee Veterans of America (NSVA) by researching a book at the Ames Public Library. This source suggested we write to Melvin D. Ramige. The students had wanted to find a chief petty officer they had been hearing about for many years. The search started with Doc Hall writing to me in 1987, "We had an energetic Chief Petty Officer named something like Wynne (Winnie) who did a lot to make the outfit work. Did any of them (medical corpsmen) mention him?" Yes, several had, which piqued the curiosity of my sixth graders.

Five years later, we were still searching for Winnie and not finding any clues. We only knew that he was respected by the medical corpsmen for his work on the little hospital and for using his ingenuity and skill to craft needed surgical instruments out of salvaged scraps of war. Mel Ramige, National Secretary of the NSVA, responded immediately by putting us in touch with Alfred G. Don, USN, (Ret.) from Pensacola, Florida, and the National Historian and Editor of their quarterly publication, *Can Do.* Mr. Don willingly agreed to place a notice in the "Seeking" column of their national newsletter for March. Although read by 5,000 members, the publication produced no direct knowledge about this unnamed chief petty officer.

In March 1993 Mr. Don sent us a framed Seabee logo and seals, which represented the 50th Birthday of the Seabees and the 125th Anniversary of the Civil Engineer Corps. We displayed the framed gift near our red, white, and blue piano in the classroom, along with the music "The Song of the Seabees," which he had sent.

In addition to items for the classroom, Mr. Don gave us several addresses of Seabees who had been stationed on Funafuti, so we could contact them for their stories. One of these people was Archie Altman, from Astor, Florida. Mr. Altman explained how the Seabees loaded their equipment, dragline, scrapers, bulldozers, and rollers onto a big barge. A tugboat then towed this. He compared it to the barges my students might have seen near Davenport, Iowa, on the Mississippi River. The barge was sent in to the coral atoll until it went aground. Then, with the dragline on top of the barge, and by reaching out on all sides, they built a ramp to unload the equipment.

Mr. Altman worked on construction of the airstrip and described how it was made out of coral, because there was not any dirt available. He told us that, actually, the coral made a very good runway. Although there had been no attack on Funafuti before the men were rescued, there were later attacks. Mr. Altman wrote, "When we would get bombed it would just blow a hole about ten feet wide and deep and all we would have to do is push the coral back into the hole and tamp it tight."

Mr. Altman further explained how Funafuti was just a few feet above sea level. They could not dig their foxholes too deep because if the Japanese came over at high tide they might have a fox hole full of water. He admitted to us, however, "but you would jump in there anyway!"

From Savannah, Georgia, another Seabee who had been on Funafuti, John Brazzeal, sent us an audiotape. In early 1942 he had been on Wallis Island and constructed a runway and refueling station there for planes being ferried from the United States to Australia. Then he went to the Ellice Islands as part of the construction battalion. He was one of the 120 men we had read were part of the Funafuti Detachment. Mr. Brazzeal described how PBY planes transferred about fifteen people at a time. Their equipment was shipped to Funafuti by small freighters.

Mr. Brazzeal's job was to run heavy equipment. He was a cat-operator, meaning he ran the bulldozer in constructing the airstrip. He also helped

In 1993 Alfred G. Don, USN (Ret.), was the National Historian and Editor of the Seabees' *Can Do* publication. He sent this Seabees plaque to the sixth graders. (*Photo Bob Kelly*)

erect the small sick bay. We had waited a long time to find someone who was involved with the Navy's Second Construction Battalion on Funafuti. Now we had found John Brazzeal, who had helped construct both the airstrip and the little hospital. He recalled a Chief Pharmacist's Mate in charge of the hospital, but he could not remember any other people.

Jack Boyd, another member of the Second Construction Battalion who had been on Funafuti, wrote to us from Bluefield, West Virginia. He had been with the Fifth Detachment of the Second Naval Construction

Jack Boyd, a former Navy Seabee, sent the class his photo.

Battalion, leaving Wallis Island for Funafuti in April 1942. As an Electrician, 2nd Class with the Seabees, Mr. Boyd went with seventy-one enlisted men to Funafuti to reinforce the Naval Construction Detachment with the Marine's Fifth Defense Battalion there. Although he had not been on Funafuti during the men's rescue, he shared with us how the increased activity had changed the base, and with that, the increased extent of the Japanese bombing raids. Mr. Boyd wrote, "It has been said that birthdays separate the men from the boys, but I am here to tell you that a bombing raid will do the same thing."

He also wanted to put us in touch with Sergeant Southern who had participated in the search for Rickenbacker and the others. We were to hear from Sergeant Southern later.

Mr. Boyd took the time to locate a map for us of nations of the world, marked locations of our research, and sent us photos and other newspaper articles. When I asked if he needed anything returned, he answered, "I do not know of anyone else I would want to have it other than your special group of students who worked so hard on your project. It makes me feel so special to be asked right out of the blue sky to participate. I have enjoyed it so very much."

Chapter Fifteen

NEW ZEALAND
COASTWATCHERS

ROM THE MOMENT WE READ WHITTAKER'S account of the rescue of the men, students had wondered about the "friendly power" and the coastwatchers who were stationed on Ellice Islands. Our first information about them came from James W. Reynolds. I called Jim in California and said, "My sixth graders want to know what you know about the coastwatchers." Jim reported there were three New Zealanders that he could recall. One was maybe a postmaster after the war. He was the one called Tiny. He had played cards one night with Jim and "was a nice fella!" Thus began our search for Tiny, a World War II coastwatcher from New Zealand, who possibly had some connection with the postal service.

Students first wrote to the U.S. Ambassador to New Zealand in Wellington and to the U.S. Consulate General in Aukland. A librarian for the Consulate General wrote back in late May 1987 that our inquiry had been sent on to the National Archives of New Zealand with a request to work quickly, knowing our summer vacation was about to begin. The librarian concluded with, "If they cannot do it quickly, it should be there by the time you come back to school in September. You will have to be patient perhaps!"

In late July, a letter was sent to my last class of sixth graders from the National Archives in Wellington, New Zealand. The War Archives records had yielded no information about New Zealand coastwatchers on the Ellice Islands. The reference archivist wrote, "I am sorry not to be able to help you."

Looking through our research files, this class discovered a letter from John Guthrie. Students had written to him in their quest to find Toma from Tuvalu. Mr. Guthrie mentioned in his 1985 letter that he had maintained a short-wave radio station there. Now a different class of students wrote to him in Tennessee, asking this time for information on the New Zealand coastwatchers. Mr. Guthrie referred us back to Alden Harrison, who lived here in Ames, Iowa, who had been stationed in the Ellice Islands at the time. Mr. Harrison suggested we contact Noel Knutson in Auckland, New Zealand. They had also served together in New Zealand, and he thought Mr. Knutson belonged to a veteran's organization, which might provide some leads. Mr. Knutson responded in September 1988 telling us that he had searched the Auckland Public Library, the Auckland University Library, and the Auckland War Memorial Museum Library. He had found nothing.

However, Mr. Knutson made inquiries from a friend of his in Sydney, Australia, who was a world-renowned expert in rescues in the Pacific area during World War II. He wrote, "It is likely that you may already have this information, but even so, it makes interesting reading." Enclosed was a copy of Lt. Col. George F. Good, Jr.'s "Report of the Rescue of Captain Rickenbacker and Party." Three years later, we had received what we called the Rescue Report—*our* declassified report!—from Sydney, Australia. It was indeed interesting, all those connections. But there was no information on Tiny.

A major breakthrough came at the end of the 1991-92 school year. My husband was involved with emerging computer technology in education at Iowa State University. Information could now be retrieved in ways unavailable to us when we started this research in 1984. Now there was public access to library catalogs around the world. Bob searched references for "coastwatchers" at New Zealand libraries. In the library at Victoria University of Wellington, there was an entry. "Title: Report on coastwatching radio stations in the Gilbert & Ellice Islands, 1941-45 by D. L. Vaughan." Information back from the Victoria University Library System on 18 May 1992 at 15:08:53 said the book was available from D. L. Vaughan and gave an address in New Zealand. This sounded promising.

Eight classes of sixth graders had researched the New Zealand coastwatchers. We were getting closer to finding Tiny. Again, it was the end of a school year, but one student wrote a letter to the author, D.L. Vaughan, asking him if the names of the men we were seeking appeared in his 1990 publication. In June, Don Vaughan sent a six-page letter of information about the coastwatchers on the Ellice Islands. This was our first documentation of World War II history recorded by someone from an ally nation.

Why were the New Zealanders on Funafuti and Nukufetau before the United States Marines? With the prospect of a second world war, as early as 1939, there was concern with the lack of communication among smaller island groups in the Pacific. There was needed contact, not only for security reasons, but also specifically for a network of coastwatching for early reporting of shipping movements. From the Japanese-held Marshall Islands in the north, the string of islands to the south ranged from Gilbert Islands, on down to Ellice Islands, to Fiji Islands, and then on southward to New Zealand.

In July 1941 young New Zealand Post Office telegraphists were selected from the Post and Telegraph Department to go to isolated islands of the Gilbert and the Ellice Islands. (That was the postal connection Jim Reynolds had remembered.) Don Vaughan, the author of this book, had been an amateur radio operator and had previous radio station experience. Since he was good at operating radio equipment and sending messages in Morse code, he was sent to Funafuti in the Ellice Islands, and his friend A. L. Taylor was sent to Beru in the Gilberts, both being appointed as Officers in Charge of the parent coastwatching stations. Other New Zealanders had been sent to outlying islands. Soldier volunteers were also chosen for their suitability for life on isolated islands and sent to assist the younger radio operators in areas where there were no other Europeans. This was the case on the island of Nukufetau.

Since the men were going to remote areas for unspecified time, many supplies were assembled, including tinned foods, utensils, lamps, kerosene, mosquito nets, basic medical items, tropical clothing, and even writing utensils. In addition, the coastwatchers were in charge of all their equipment, so they needed to take battery operated transmitting and receiving sets, battery chargers, headsets, aerials, Morse keys, spare parts, and tools.

Because the book Don Vaughan wrote was a documentation of the New Zealand coastwatchers' role in the war, we were interested in his story of the code set up between himself on Funafuti and coastwatcher Taylor on Beru. At first, they had no common codes and had not exchanged any messages during the past year. However, by mid-July, Vaughan and Taylor finally set up a "key-word" coding system, based on passages—page, line, and word number—in a technical book they both had studied in Suva, Fiji.

By late August 1942, Mr. Vaughan and a native island assistant and interpreter, Frank Pasefika, heard the roar of a low level airplane over the lagoon, observed its "friendly" markings, so took a boat out to greet it. The delivered passenger was Colonel Vivian Fox-Strangways, Resident Commissioner of the Gilbert and Ellice Islands Colony.

In his book, Mr. Vaughan wrote that in mid-September the Resident Commissioner intimated to the coastwatchers on Funafuti that "a United States landing force would be arriving shortly" but gave no other particulars. Then at the end of the month, he advised that the landing was imminent.

By now the Resident Commissioner decided to establish additional coastwatching points at Funafuti "to guard against surprise attack." At the radio station the coastwatcher kept "a large axe, matches, and several tins of petro" in preparation for destroying the station, should an attack occur. In addition, he stored emergency supplies and radio equipment at the southern end of the lagoon.

On September 26 one of the native operators who assisted Mr. Taylor on Beru in the Gilberts sent the message, "LLLL three Jap warships." Previously the Morse code symbol LLLL had been established to mean the enemy had landed on the island. The signal AAAA would have meant enemy aircraft had attacked them. Mr. Vaughan explained to us that at the time, it was assumed the message LLLL had been sent by the native operator, because as coastwatcher, he would have been destroying their documents and the main transmitter. Then Mr. Vaughan wrote, "It was

Don Vaughan was the New Zealand coastwatcher
stationed on Funafuti. He sent the class this photo taken
in 1941.

learned, very much later, that Taylor and Murray had been unable to bring
their equipment into operation and had given themselves up a week later
to avoid threatened reprisals against the natives at Beru." Eventually,
every New Zealand coastwatcher sent to the Gilberts was either killed,
or taken prisoner and then killed.

Mr. Vaughan, on Funafuti when the American task force came to
occupy the island, wrote to us, "…and this took place on 2 October 1942
when U.S. Navy cruisers *Chester* and *Minneapolis* with four destroyers
escorted the supply ships USS *Heywood*, *Libra*, and *Crescent City* into
the 65 square mile lagoon." The lagoon was about ten miles long and

eight miles wide. From Don Vaughan's book, we gained the historical perspective of the role of the New Zealand coastwatchers as Allies in World War II. From his letters, we learned the more personal details.

Don Vaughan described the early days of the American occupation of the island. He told how the convoy made its way slowly into the lagoon through the Mateika Passage guided by the islander Pasefika. Using our detailed maps, we located the passage at the extreme southern tip of the island of Funafuti. When officers of the U.S. Navy and the Fifth Marine Defense Battalion came ashore in the early morning of October 2nd to meet with the Resident Commissioner of the Gilbert and Ellice Islands Colony, some were "surprised to learn that the coastwatching service had been in operation for over a year."

Mr. Vaughan also told how the different sorts of landing crafts bustled in and out, unloading supplies and equipment. A large area of the lagoon front was used, and then items were gradually moved inland amongst the coconut trees.

When Mr. Vaughan wrote personally to us, he knew we were researching the Americans on Funafuti, so he described in more detail how he had seen the Seabees land with all their heavy equipment— bulldozers, graders, and trucks. He wrote, "Uniforms of all types were soon in evidence from the skivvies worn by many of the unloading parties to officers of various ranks in the U.S. Navy and the Marine Corps."

Various people had described the organized chaos of the frantic unloading of cargo from the three transport vessels. We had not pictured the air full of diesel smoke from the landing craft exhausts until Mr. Vaughan described it, "…a pall of fumes permeated the island and the lagoon and rose right up into the sky." He added, "A coded message was received at Funafuti from the radio operator on Nukufetau, 64 miles away, asking what were the clouds of black smoke…" No wonder they had been in a hurry to get the equipment unloaded and off the beach.

The stated mission of the Fifth Defense Battalion was: "To defend Funafuti by providing early warning of the approach of hostile forces by covering the sea approaches, the surrounding air and the beaches by fire and observation and by attacking and destroying any hostile force effecting a landing, in order to insure the use of the atoll as an air and naval base for our forces and to deny it to the enemy."

The coastwatchers were advised by their Resident Commissioner to continue their normal activities, and for the time being, handled isolated messages for the U.S. Forces. This fact coincided with my class's previous information that the forces were keeping radio silence on Funafuti, not wanting to advertise to the Japanese that they were constructing a forward base at that location.

Mr. Vaughan explained to us more about the activity of the Seabees. Working from dawn to dusk over the next few weeks, they used bulldozers to clear away hundreds of coconut trees that were pushed to the outer side of the island. Tractors, graders, and rollers were used to fill in mosquito bogs and produce a coral surface for the landing strip. Although the coastwatchers were interested in all this activity, they remained busy with their radio watches and weather reporting duties.

Then this Funafuti coastwatcher told us about hearing the news that Captain Cherry had been found and then how the other men had been rescued. We were most interested in his account of the rescue of one of the rafts, because this involved the New Zealand coastwatchers stationed at the outlying island, Nukufetau, who comprised the nearby garrison, and who were the first to reach Whittaker, DeAngelis, and Reynolds after Toma had found them with his outrigger canoe. Don Vaughan wrote, "The three coastwatchers on Nukufetau at the time [of the Rickenbacker and party's rescue] were: Colin Davis, Radio Operator; Pte Andrew Love, Soldier Companion; and Pte Alfred Hall, Soldier Companion. I am sorry to tell you that Colin Davis passed away about seven years ago." Could one of these men be Tiny?

Mr. Vaughan wrote how a note was dropped to the coastwatchers on November 12, asking them to search the atoll of Nukufetau for a yellow raft with possible plane survivors. When Toma and the other islanders brought the men in, Colin Davis, the New Zealand radio operator on Nukufetau, sent a coded message to Funafuti asking for medical attention.

In his letter to us, Don Vaughan wrote, "A U.S. doctor arrived later the same day and treated the survivors, one of whom was in a terrible condition and was covered in sores. He looked like a skeleton and would not have lasted much longer without proper attention." That doctor was Doc Hall. That survivor was James W. Reynolds. Colin Davis and his two soldier companions had stayed up all night assisting the doctor, before the men were taken by the *Hilo* the next afternoon from Nukufetau to the Funafuti field hospital.

We had found the New Zealand coastwatchers. Had we found Tiny? I immediately contacted my former sixth graders who had worked all year to find the coastwatchers. Then I wrote to Don Vaughan and mailed him a large package with information about our research project. Of course, I also included a letter with more requests and questions. Could I purchase two autographed copies of his book, one for Jim Reynolds and one for me? Would it be possible to obtain copies of the records kept by Colin Davis?

On August 24, 1992, another school year began for my husband and me with a teachers' workshop. I was very tired after an exhausting day of meetings and room preparation for a new group of sixth graders. At 2:43 a.m. our phone rang. It was Shirley Davis calling from Papakura, New Zealand. Don Vaughan had contacted Mrs. Colin (Noeline) Davis and daughter, Shirley Davis, about our interest in the coastwatchers. That day they had received the package of information I had sent to Don Vaughan, who had then passed it on to them. They were overwhelmed and excited, and as she later wrote, "For us it was a 'spur of the moment' decision to ring you."

Shirley wrote a personal letter to my husband Bob, not intending it to be part of our research, but as she called it, "a letter of apology to you (you answered the phone!)" In her letter she wrote, "I am the 'at fault' Kiwi [New Zealander] who disturbed your night's sleep last night—and for that I apologise. Even with the help of International Tolls I managed to incorrectly calculate the time difference—mathematics was never my forte...I hope Iowa/Papakura communication has not suffered due to mathematical error!"

Shirley obviously did not understand how long and hard we had searched for her father, nor how delighted we were to have reached her.

A page from New Zealand coastwatcher Colin Davis's diary, in which he described helping Jim Reynolds through the night. The diary was sent to the students by Colin's family.

She also wrote, "We felt a deep sadness that Dad is no longer with us as he could have verbalised much about the incident that is not written." She had known of the rescue incident, because he had mentioned it in passing, but commented, "We knew Dad put himself at immense risk in breaking radio silence to alert the Americans as to the survivors' whereabouts and to access urgent medical help. The islanders of course had very limited resources."

Don Vaughan's next letter soon arrived, expressing how overwhelmed he was with the scope and contents of information we had sent him, and that he had passed it on to Noeline Davis. He also enclosed a map of the Pacific area for the students and a photo of him taken at the Funafuti coastwatching station in 1941. He thoughtfully added, "...and a spare negative of the same, as I take it that your husband Bob has photographic skills!!"

Soon we received our personal copy of Don Vaughan's book, *Report on Coastwatching Radio Stations in the Gilbert & Ellice Islands 1941-1945.* He explained to us that he had written it in third person, anticipating only limited attention to the project, but now was amazed at the interest in this account of the coastwatchers' fate. Inside the cover of the book for the B-17 radio operator he had helped rescue, he wrote, "To—Jim Reynolds—Greetings from New Zealand Jim! Doesn't life play some odd tricks. Firstly, congratulations on coming through the ordeal in 1942. I little realised then, that one day I would be writing about you all and still later with the help of Suzanne Kelly would be sending you a copy of my book! I hope you find the story of the coastwatchers of some interest. My very best wishes to you all!"

In September, Shirley wrote about the rescue her father had participated in, telling how her father had been alerted that an American plane had gone down and there could be survivors in rafts. He sent the natives out to search. When Toma found the men, her father broke radio silence, "which was a dangerous thing to do, to notify the Americans." Then she added this anecdote. In Rickenbacker's book, *Seven Came Through,* he wrote that the Americans were contacted by an "English missionary who had a small radio transmitter." Shirley Davis wrote to us, "That is a family joke as Dad was not a Missionary at all!"

Shirley then told how her father had been dropped off at Nukufetau by the ship HMFS *Viti* out of Fiji. The ship the *John Williams* was a boat that infrequently dropped off supplies. (Colin Davis had been a radio operator on the boat previously, and Toma was to travel on it after the war.)

Another story Shirley shared was that her father had kept the shirt Jim Reynolds had on when he was rescued. It had been left behind on Nukufetau when Jim was taken to Funafuti. She wrote, "If you are talking to Jim Reynolds, please give him our regards and tell him we kept his shirt for years!"

Sixth graders were very interested in codes that were used during the war. One question they had for Shirley was if she knew anything about the codes coastwatchers had sent. She wrote that there were codes recorded in her father's diaries. "The code used was called the 'Playfair Code' which was based on a square grid which you could use either numbers or the alphabet." She explained that the coastwatchers had used the alphabet, with each island having its own code or call sign. Nukufetau's code had been "Byy."

Noeline Davis wrote to me in September 1992. She enclosed copies of relevant letters she thought we might be interested in. There were two undated notes from General Good to her husband. One said in part, "Here are a couple of cartons of cigarettes to hold you for the time being. In a short while we expect some candy in and when it is put on sale I'll send you some." The other note had a reference to prints of film that Colin had sent. General Good had apologized with, "Sorry the shortage of printing paper precluded our printing more than two copies of each, but that is the best we could do." Noeline had included some of those original photos for us to have. She also wrote to us, "…when you are talking to Gen. Good could you please tell him Colin really appreciated his little acts of kindness during his time on Nukufetau."

She also enclosed copies of relevant parts of her husband's diary. Coastwatcher Colin Davis had written "Friday 13th November 1942… At 6 am this morning five aeroplanes passed over here and again at 11am, another lot came over. One circled and dropped me a note asking me to have atoll searched for shipwrecked airmen in a yellow rubber raft. I immediately sent out the canoes to search the beaches and at 3 pm we observed two canoes coming in towing a yellow raft. Of course we lost no time in getting out and found three U.S. airmen who had been adrift for 19 days without food and very little water. They had 4 oranges between eight men when they were first down."

In his diary the coastwatcher reversed the last names of Reynolds and DeAngelis, but we easily understood whom he meant. He wrote that they brought them to their house to make them as comfortable as they could.

He then documented that Whittaker and [DeAngelis] Johnny were in surprisingly good condition considering what they had been through. He wrote, "Jimmy was in a terrible state and would probably not have survived another two days. He was a skeleton and covered in sores. I sent for a doctor who arrived (about) 6 pm and he gave Jimmy a fluid which he passed in through a vein in his arm. It was marvelous to see the courage he had. I never heard a moan out of any of them and if ever three men had reason to moan and groan those did."

In another entry Davis wrote, "I did not go to sleep last night but sat up and helped the doctor. Jimmy was much better this morning and after only having a 50/50 chance last night. The doctor says he will be ok now."

Coastwatcher Davis then added, "I was sorry to see them go as we had begun to look on them as life long friends even though we had only known them a few days."

And finally, he wrote in his diary, "It will be a seven days wonder in the newspapers in U.S.A. as there were two very important people on that plane." I knew what he meant. Rickenbacker and Adamson were famous and high-ranking, but to my sixth graders and myself, there had been eight very important people on that plane. We were very grateful to the New Zealand coastwatchers who took care of three of them and who also stood guard for countless others.

Shirley Davis also sent us copies of letters that had been sent to her father. One was from James Whittaker describing what he, Jim Reynolds, and John DeAngelis were doing in the past few months since their rescue. Most importantly to my sixth graders, however, was the greeting to Shirley's father, Colin Davis. The letter started, "Dear Tiny."

I immediately phoned Jim Reynolds in California. It had taken awhile, but that confirmed we had *found* Tiny. "James W.," I joked, "it would have been a lot easier if you had just remembered his full name and address!"

Chapter Sixteen
___

NAVY SCOUTING SQUADRON

HE MILITARY REPORTS WE HAD ON OPERATION FETLOCK indicated that besides the Fifth Defense Battalion of Marines, medical corpsmen, and naval construction battalion, there was a detachment of VS-65 Scouting Squadron. Actually, according to Les Boutte, it was the Navy Scouting Squadron, VS-1-D14 (which later became VS-65) that was sent to Ellice Islands. Les Boutte, the radioman who spotted Captain Cherry's raft, explained to us the V referred to "heavier-than-air" and the S for "scouting plane." The "1" was for the first squadron. "D14" referred to District No. 14, which was the Honolulu district at the time. Boutte explained, "This was a special squadron with a made-up number, because until that time, the OS2Us [seaplanes] were used as cruiser and observation aircraft; then they were land-based."

Captain Cherry also told us about the OS2U-3 Kingfisher plane, built by Vought. During World War II, the Navy used the Kingfisher primarily as a ship-based, scout and observation aircraft. It was a compact, mid-wing monoplane, with a large central float and small stabilizing floats, and was used in support of shore bombardments. As we knew, it also played a major role in air-sea rescue.

Les Boutte told us the Bureau Number (BuNo) was 5309 for both the aircraft he flew in with Fred Woodward to rescue Bill Cherry and the aircraft he flew in with Bill Eadie for the rescue of Rickenbacker, Adamson, and Bartek. He described the two-seater, single-engine float seaplane, the Kingfisher, this way. "The OS2U was a fine little seaplane, designed for a very limited mission, search, scouting and water rescue, to a limited degree. It was not a first-line combat aircraft and was under-

On July 20, 1942, the OS2U-3s were wheeled up the ramp at Tifi Tifi, Upolu Island, in the Samoan Islands, in the establishment of a main base, and for two other bases at Wallis and Funafuti. (*Courtesy National Archives*)

powered and very lightly armed." As we researched this airplane, we found that much of the recorded information about the Kingfisher was associated with Rickenbacker's rescue.

Robert J. Eadie, pilot Bill Eadie's brother, sent us a rough draft report of the rescue that his brother had written in 1942. Shortly after the Rescue Reunion we had received this report, but as we continued to learn new information, more of the report made sense to us.

At the time of the rescue, this naval squadron consisted of twenty-one planes, eighty-six enlisted men, and twenty-six officers—operating from three separate island bases. Bill Eadie had written in his 1942 report that the squadron's commanding officer was Lt. Cdr. Clayton B. Miller, who had the main base at Upolu, British Samoa. The squadron's Flight Officer, Lt. Henry T. Hazelton, commanded the second base at Wallis Island. These two bases at Upolu and Wallis Islands had conducted special searches for the lost B-17 plane, but the one at Funafuti, Ellice Islands, had been considered "too far off their track to make a search in our area worthwhile."

Les Boutte's main base was on Satapuala Bay in British Samoa. However, at the time of the rescue, he was part of a detachment of aircraft operating out of Funafuti.

Bill Eadie had been in charge of six officers, twenty men, and seven VOS (heavier-than-air, observation-scouting) aircraft on the third base on Funafuti. He wrote that the men affectionately called this base the Salt Mines.

Late in the afternoon of November 11, 1942, Les Boutte had been flying with Lt. (jg.) Fred Woodward and sighted an object on the water, which they discovered to be a life raft containing one man. Since they were still maintaining radio silence, they flew back to the base, dropping a message, giving the raft's position, and informing the base they were returning to circle the raft.

Pilot Eadie flew out to relieve Woodward who was low on gas and arrived over the raft about the time the Motor Torpedo Boat (MTB or PT) that had been dispatched, also arrived. Captain Cherry was taken aboard the PT boat. Bill Eadie stayed with the boat until dark and then flew back to base, returning several hours before the PT boat.

Then Lieutenant Eadie included this anecdote. With no idea of the raft survivor's identity, the men had started kidding Woodward and Boutte. Besides receiving awards, they would probably be returned to the States and sent on a speaking tour. Bill wrote, "This threw a real scare into them...the idea of describing their noble deeds for crowds of civilians was too much for the boys, and they were seriously considering hiding out in the bush." My sixth graders decided that even back then they had no idea the extensive publicity that would ensue because of their rescue.

Of course, the rescue of Bill Cherry initiated a hectic, but organized, search for the other two rafts. Lieutenant Eadie wrote, "When we started the search, we had five planes, six pilots, and twelve enlisted men as our entire aviation facilities on the island. We had approximately 13,000 square miles to comb in the search." He told how one plane was torn down for routine maintenance and a second plane needed repairs. The ground crew worked all night to get both planes ready to fly by dawn.

The territory was broken into three search areas:

• Area 1 — Rectangle extending 50 miles SSW and 80 miles WNW of Funafuti (Lt. Eadie had written, "Thus, Nukufetau was at the extremity of the line dividing Area 1 and 2.")
• Area 2 — Rectangle extending 50 miles N and 80 miles WNW of Funafuti
• Area 3 — Rectangle running 50 miles WNW beyond Areas 1 and 2

There were six pilots (John Boyd, Warner Clark, William Eadie, Gaylord Forrest, Edward Pearsall, and Fred Woodward) and five radiomen (Les Boutte, Bob Floch, Edward Knight, Ian McDonald, and Stanley Staub). Eadie wrote that they decided to cut cards to see which pilot would "keep the home fires burning during the first 'round.'" Lt. (jg.) Gaylord Forrest cut the deuce of clubs and spent the morning stamping up and down the beach, and getting into the ground crew's hair."

Bill Eadie wrote that the weather had been spotty all day, alternating rain and fair with bad visibility. At 300 feet, the planes flew a scouting line spaced a mile apart, starting in Area 1. At one point Pearsall and Woodward became separated, but they all met up at the base for fuel, "all fueling having to be done by hand, pumped from drums into the planes."

For the second round of searching, Clark was to remain on the beach. Pearsall and Woodward were sent to search Area 2. On the way to Area 3, the others dropped a message to the coastwatcher on the south side of Nukufetau, directing him to search the rest of the atoll in case survivors had reached it during the night. After giving instructions for arranging a signal if there was anything to report, they proceeded to Area 3. After finding nothing in Area 3, they passed back over Nukufetau and saw their prearranged signal flying. Boyd and Forrest went on to Funafuti, and

Eadie landed in the Nukufetau lagoon to see the coastwatcher. What he [Colin "Tiny" Davis] wanted to report was "a gray painted timber from a small boat which had drifted ashore." Deciding it was a false alarm, Eadie next headed toward base to hear reports of the Area 2 search.

After only a few minutes and about twenty-five miles away from Nukufetau, Eadie spotted Forrest circling a raft with three persons. Boyd and Forrest had spotted the raft about the same time. Forrest stayed to mark the location [with a smoke flare], and Boyd flew back to base to refuel. With Forrest [and radioman Ian McDonald] about out of gas, Eadie waved them on in and stayed to circle. This was November 12, about 1600 hours.

Then Eadie was almost out of fuel, so when he lost sight of the raft during a heavy rainsquall, he started back to base, passing Boyd about ten miles out, coming back refueled and ready to circle. The PT boats and the U.S.S. *Hilo* had left the harbor of Funafuti to help with the search, but due to the heavy squalls, they had gotten off course and scattered during the day. When Eadie went in to refuel, he met Pearsall and Woodward returning from their search of Area 2, finding no raft, but having spotted a Motor Torpedo Boat. Eadie sent Clark to locate an MTB and lead it to the raft, then relieve Boyd who was still circling.

At 1730, the Nukufetau coastwatcher's radio message indicated a raft with three survivors had come ashore there. Then Eadie wrote, "It seemed to be Forrest's day to carry the jinx, because he cut cards with Woodward for the Nukufetau trip and, lost as usual. However, we cheered him up by reminding him he had sighted the raft we were all most interested in." By 1830, Lieutenant Woodward and Doc Hall had loaded their plane with blankets and medical supplies and left for Nukufetau.

Next, Boyd came in to report that Clark had not seen an MTB but was now circling the other raft, so Boyd could come in to refuel. If they were going to get an MTB to the area, they would have to break radio silence to find any within cruising range.

Then Eadie wrote, "It was now obvious that, if we were to pick up the survivors that night it would have to be done by plane. I decided to take a chance and try to land alongside the raft before dark." He arranged for a searchlight to be turned on for one minute every half hour after 2200, to help guide him back to the base in the dark.

At dusk, with light failing fast, Clark spotted Eadie and, by the Aldis (a signal light) directed him to the raft. Eadie wrote,"I dropped two float lights to make my landing by, taxied up to the raft, and cut the engine. We secured the raft to the plane at about 1930." Lt. Eadie described the three men as being in "bad shape." He wrote, "Adamson was completely irrational and Bartek seemed to be in a semi-stupor from exposure and fatigue. Rickenbacker had stood the ordeal better than the others."

Les Boutte gave the men water and a little soup. Since the weather had been bad all day, the sea was choppy, and taxiing over forty miles all the way back to the base was going to be difficult. Yet, Rickenbacker felt that was more desirable than another night in the raft. Since Adamson was in need of the greatest care, he was placed in the rear seat, and Bartek and Rickenbacker were each lashed to a plane wing. They began taxiing. Eadie then wrote, "It was blacker than the inside of a miner's hip pocket, but after bouncing along in the dark for ten miles, we made contact with one of the MTBs who had picked up our radio directions."

As we knew, Rickenbacker and Bartek were then transferred to the PT boat with Bill Wepner on board. Eadie, with Colonel Adamson still in the rear of the Kingfisher too sick to move, continued taxiing back to base. They came in somewhere along the barrier reef, but it was difficult to find one of the passes. By watching the white of the breakers on his wing tip, Eadie finally saw an in-swerving of the white line of foam, indicating a current passing from the ocean to the lagoon. He wrote, "Following it, we passed over the reef at about 0230 and beached the plane at the base at 0330." This, of course, was 3:30 a.m., so his next writing was especially meaningful. "Our faithful ground crew was standing by, 'at ready,' and we had Colonel Adamson out of the plane and made as comfortable as possible in a very short time."

Lieutenant Eadie praised the enlisted men in that outfit. "For over thirty-six hours they had labored unremittingly to keep our five planes in the air. With the rescue accomplished, they kept right on plugging, and at dawn the regular patrols went out on schedule, just as though nothing had happened to break the routine."

Members of the Navy Scouting Squadron, VS-1-D14. *Left to right:* Ian McDonald, radioman; Edward Pearsall, pilot; Bill Eadie, pilot; and Lester Boutte, radioman. (*Photo courtesy Lester Boutte*)

Eadie commended the land, air, and sea units who had all worked together from the time Les Boutte sighted Captain Cherry's raft until the U.S.S. *Hilo* brought the men from Nukufetau back to Funafuti. Eadie wrote it this way, "This episode should prove conclusively to any who place undue emphasis on any particular phase of naval aviation, that a well-trained ground crew is as important to the successful completion of any operation as well-trained pilots. It also proves that the operational efficiency of any squadron will be greatly determined by the operational efficiency of the men who serve the planes. It is hardly necessary to add that for my money, on any job, I'd pick the boys who were on the beach at Funafuti to keep me flying."

I was always grateful to Lieutenant Eadie's brother who sent this rough draft of a report with hand-written notes to me in 1985. It told much about the raft rescues from 1942, but it told even more about the men who made those rescues possible.

In 1987 my sixth graders decided they wanted to find more Kingfisher pilots. Of the six pilots, we had contacted families of Lieutenants Eadie and Woodward. Les Boutte was our best source, and he wrote to the class that he thought Pearsall and Clark had been killed in action later in the war. He had no information on Boyd. Although we had followed some leads, we were never able to find anything on John G. Boyd. That left Gaylord Forrest.

A letter from Les Boutte, Captain, U.S.N. (Ret.), gave students this information, "The last time I saw Gaylord Forrest was about 1966 in Norfolk, Virginia. His rank at that time was Captain, U.S. Navy, and he was attached to a major Fleet Staff there. I believe that he was originally from Tennessee or Kentucky and married a girl from that area. He must be retired from the Navy by now."

Students knew that libraries were a great starting place. Not only did librarians have information readily available, but also they were as curious as the sixth graders. We discovered they usually had a soft spot in their educational hearts to encourage that thirst for knowledge in young people. So one student wrote to the public library in Norfolk, Virginia, explaining that we understood Gaylord T. Forrest no longer lived there but asked for help in locating any of his relatives who might still be in the area. How could any librarian resist when the student closed the letter with, "Thank you for taking time to read this and we appreciate you helping us find Lt. Gaylord T. Forrest."

Certainly, Peggy A. Haile, librarian in the Sargeant Memorial Room of the City of Norfolk, Department of Libraries, could not resist. She had enjoyed reading the *Reader's Digest* article the students had sent and wished them luck with their "school's detective work." Most importantly, she had found a listing in a 1966 city directory for Gaylord Forrest, not for Norfolk, but for Virginia Beach. No listing appeared in that city or for Norfolk in subsequent years.

How should we proceed? Students decided to send a letter to the Navy hoping that if Captain Forrest had not retired, we could still reach him through military channels. Secondly, students wanted to try a large newspaper. Their reasoning was that since Captain Forrest was active with a major fleet staff, there might have been articles written about him in area publications. Thirdly, the sixth graders wanted to do something with that

The sixth graders worked hard to find Gaylord Forrest, one of the Kingfisher pilots. (*Photo was sent to the author by Gaylord's son*)

twenty-year-old former address they had been given by the librarian.

We held a class-brainstorming meeting. I remembered how I enjoyed as a child receiving mail that came unspecified to our home. I had an idea, but I wanted the students' input. I started our discussion by stating the obvious. "We know Gaylord Forrest does not live at that address in Virginia Beach any more." The sixth graders quickly added ideas.

"Right. But somebody does."

"But we don't know who."

"Well, you can't write to somebody if you don't know their address."

"But you can write to somebody at that address."

"What do you mean?"

"Don't you ever get mail that says, 'Occupant?'"

"Oh, yeah! Sometimes it says, 'Resident.'"

"But that's junk mail."

"Not if it comes in an envelope like a regular letter."

"I get it. We could send a letter to the people who live at that address now and call them 'Occupants.'"

"That doesn't sound very nice."

"It's probably a family. Make it sound good, so a nice family will get our letter."

"How about, 'Family in Residence?'"

"That's good. If you send it to the family, they won't just toss it in the trash."

It was decided how the letter would be addressed. One student wrote the letter asking if they or anyone in their area knew anything about Gaylord Forrest. He also suggested that if that family did not know anything, maybe a neighbor who was a long-time resident might have known the previous resident at this address. Students also agreed that enclosing a stamped, self-addressed envelope for a reply was a good idea.

We had two other responses to our requests for information on Gaylord Forrest. An editor of one newspaper had checked recent city directories for us but found nothing. He also wrote that a policy did not permit him to use pages of the newspaper to locate missing persons. The second source was from the Department of the Navy, Naval Reserve Personnel Center in New Orleans, Louisiana. Two groups of sixth graders' research had crossed paths. The director at the personnel center, D.A. Guichard, informed us, "This is the second letter I have received from your school." Although they were still working on the first request (to find Dr. Fuller), they indicated that if we would write a letter to Gaylord Forrest and send it to them, they would forward it.

Soon the student who had written to "Family in Residence" had a reply. The family's ninth grade daughter had followed our suggestion and visited with her next-door neighbor. It just happened that the day before, her neighbor had sent a letter to Gaylord Forrest, and, yes, he certainly knew the address. The girl closed by saying, "Best of luck and please let me know what you find out."

In March 1988 Gaylord Forrest received the letter that had been forwarded by the military, and he wrote to us on the 47th anniversary of his joining the Navy. He had retired in 1966 as a captain. "I did indeed participate in the Rickenbacker rescue back in November of 1942 and have just checked my Navy flight log book of that era to refresh my memory."

The sixth grade boy wrote back to the ninth grade girl, "The same day I received your letter, my friend got a letter from Gaylord Forrest." He then explained about our research and how the forwarded letter had reached Captain Forrest before her letter reached us. The sixth grader then wrote, "I hope you write back soon and please send a picture. I have enclosed a picture of myself...P.S. My classmates think it's neat that I got a letter from a ninth grade girl." In a follow-up letter, the girl wrote that she had shared our class project with some friends, and they thought the Iowa students were quite "dedicated." As an experienced sixth grade teacher, I understood "dedication" and quickly decided that although the girl's enclosed basketball picture was supposed to go into the class research folders, that a copy of the photo would do just as well—especially since a particular sixth grader had a billfold ready for the same photo.

Another letter written by the same sixth grader included a home address and a personal note, "P. S. You're a great pen pal, too." I then had a private conference with the student who grinned at me when I indicated that any further correspondence he had with the girl of the "Family in Residence" would *not* need to be documented, nor a duplicate filed in the class research file.

We sent Gaylord Forrest items from the Rescue Reunion and a copy of Lt. Good's Rescue Report, which he thought was very accurate as he recalled the episode of forty-six years ago. Forrest also wrote to the class about the other men, confirming what Lieutenant Eadie had written. In addition he said, "I have always felt that the airmanship and seamanship (after all, the Kingfisher *was* a seaplane!) of Lt. Bill Eadie and Les Boutte was exceptional...Also, Fred Woodward deserves special praise, for without his initial sighting of the Cherry raft on November 12, it is very probable that the subsequent rescues would never have transpired. A life raft in the open ocean is very hard to see—even when you know that one is in the area."

Although Eadie's chronological account of the search and rescue by the Kingfisher pilots indicated that both John Boyd and Gaylord Forrest spotted the raft about the same time, Captain Forrest wrote, "Also, John

Boyd merits special mention since, while he and I, flying in a scouting line (abreast—about a mile apart) spotted the Rickenbacker raft—I am convinced that John saw it *first* and then I followed suit."

We had wanted more information on Dr. Fuller, the Funafuti island physician. Captain Forrest informed us that Dr. Fuller had returned to Mayfield, Kentucky, to practice medicine in his hometown, but was now deceased. Captain Forrest wrote, "He was at my wedding on April 6, 1949, when I married at Murray, Kentucky, some twenty miles from Mayfield."

This former Kingfisher pilot also reminisced about the great strides in Naval Aviation and how within his career he had gone from bi-planes to jets. He said, "However, the man in the cockpit is still the most important factor, I believe." He then paid tribute to the other pilots who had searched so hard to find the rafts.

Finally, Captain Forrest concluded with a salute to the seaplanes, "They did serve us well in WWII and the little Kingfisher was a tough machine. It had to be in order to take the water landings and takeoffs and to remain—many times—tied afloat to a buoy (when not flying) in remote locations when there were no ramp facilities for beaching. To carry the large main float and two wing floats was a terrific handicap to performance in the air. However, it did its job in many a locale in the Pacific and Atlantic Theaters." Gaylord Forrest and Bill Cherry never knew each other, but they shared a love of flying, and a deep loyalty to those who kept the planes in the air and the crews that flew them.

John Bartek had asked for Gaylord Forrest's address, so he could write a proper thank-you for his part in John's rescue. Forrest later wrote, "Just received a nice letter from John Bartek—which I shall answer with pleasure!"

In December 1988 I wrote to Captain Forrest, "I received a lovely letter from John Bartek this week. His grandson, Jonathan, calls him 'Pop-Pop.' I still receive a special 'warmness' when I hear from these men, and continually marvel at the job you men did so long ago. I feel truly privileged to have had some contact with all of you. How different all our lives are because you passed our way."

Although we were unable to locate any more information about the Kingfisher pilots, students were still interested in the Naval Aviation unit that had been on Ellice Islands during the time of the rescue. They wanted to know about the airplane mechanics, the radiomen, and others.

One class wrote over one hundred letters trying to find radioman Ian McDonald. We never found him, or the other two radiomen, Edward Knight and Stanley Staub.

However, in 1993 Captain Forrest did provide us with an address for Bob Floch in Roseville, California. He wrote, "Bob himself was one of these capable and wonderful workers and crewmen." We then realized that this Robert C. Floch was the same radioman "Flock" Lt. Bill Eadie had mentioned in his rough draft of the rescue, spelling the name with a "k."

We discovered Bob Floch was not only one of the Kingfisher radiomen, but he had also served as a rear-seat gunner and an unofficial radio mechanic. He repaired and installed aircraft electrical and radio equipment on the Kingfisher or Duck (J2-F) airplanes on the bases they occupied. Mr. Floch wrote, "One of my most challenging tasks then was to install IFF (Identification Friend or Foe) equipment in all our aircraft. IFF made it easier for all U.S. (and Allied) ships, aircraft, etc. to early-on determine if approaching objects were friendly or enemy."

Now, eight years after we first read about him in Lieutenant Eadie's rough draft, Robert Floch provided us with a typed copy of Eadie's report. This was the same report that we had shared with Les Boutte, and he had passed it on where it had been put together for the U.S. Navy Scouting Squadron's history in 1990. When students wrote to Mr. Floch, they asked if he remembered Les Boutte and Bill Eadie. Yes, he did. He wrote back to the students and shared a story of how he, Boutte, and Eadie, all came to be on Funafuti.

In December 1941, Bob Floch had been in Aviation Radioman School at the U.S. Naval Air Station in San Diego, California. Two weeks after the bombing of Pearl Harbor, he was in a communication class "to which a huge, stern, second class petty officer, Radioman Les Boutte, was teaching Morse Code." A Navy lieutenant (jg.) came to the class and

Robert Floch was one of the Kingfisher radiomen in the Navy
Scouting Squadron. (*Photo given to author by Robert's son*)

asked to speak to the top two "code men." Robert Floch was one of the
two men selected. And who was the man asking? Lt. Bill Eadie.

Eadie explained there was to be a newly formed Navy Air Scouting
Squadron, VS-1-D14. The U.S. Navy Aircraft Carrier, U.S.S. *Yorktown*,
would be shepherding a Task Force of many warships to the South Pacific,
and the squadron would be ferried to Samoa, "to provide surveillance around
the barrier islands to warn of any enemy action against them." Would he be

Principal members of the Naval Squadron VS1-D-14 who rescued the men. *Left to right*: Lieutenant William F. Eadie (pilot), Aviation Radioman 2nd Class Lester Boutte, and Lt. (jg.) Fred Woodward. This photo was taken Dec. 16, 1942 on Samoa. (*Courtesy National Archives*)

interested? Mr. Floch then wrote, "At 21? Yes!! Not only yes, but h_____ yes!"

When Robert Floch arrived at Pago Pago harbor in American Samoa, he found that both Bill Eadie and Les Boutte were there, also. They were stationed at the small native village of Mulifanua on the island of Upolu on the west coast of British Samoa. Navy Seabees had just completed a seaplane ramp there for their daily launch of Kingfisher seaplanes to search for the enemy.

Bob Floch described their time on Funafuti as TDY (temporary duty)—part of the "hopping" from one target island to the next—until each island was occupied by the Navy, Army, or the Marines. While on

Funafuti he had been patrolling the surrounding seas, searching for enemy ships and submarines. When word came that the B-17 was lost, they had been requested to search for the men in adjacent areas. Mr. Floch confirmed he had been part of the "searchers" but had been recalled to headquarters on British Samoa the day before Captain Cherry's first raft was found.

Then Robert Floch wrote this tribute to the rescue plane that had taxied back to base, "And, how about that little ole magnificent Kingfisher? She was none the worse for wear except the propeller was two inches shorter and each blade-end was split wide open from beating through salt water spray for 40 miles. Maybe, as we all might have to do some day…the little Kingfisher just held her head up (above the water) and did the very best she could."

We learned that Mr. Floch was the present editor of a newsletter for squadron personnel who had served in the area. They had held their first squadron reunion in 1990. Les Boutte had written to me about it, but I had not made all the connections.

As part of our correspondence with Mr. Floch, he sent a Kingfisher model kit to the class. One student and her father put it together. In the February 1994 issue, the sixth grader's photo was published with the story of our research in the squadron association's newsletter, the *Tifi Tifi Tattler*. (Tifi tifi is a species of fish on Tuvalu.) After sending the picture to Mr. Floch, he wrote back, "*Talofa lao uo* (Hello, my friend)… I think that red, white, and blue piano is great…Also, the Seabees plaque brings back old memories…the CBs built our seaplane ramps and the aircraft landing strips…they were a great bunch of guys." Yes, they were—and so were the men of the Navy Scouting Squadron.

Chapter Seventeen

PT BOATS AND
THE U.S.S. *HILO*

O NE GROUP OF SIXTH GRADERS BECAME very interested in the PT boats, also called Motor Torpedo or Patrol Torpedo Boats. These boats were torpedo-armed, fast attack naval crafts used in the war. We knew some information from Bill Wepner, who had served on one and had shared with us at the Rescue Reunion.

The U.S.S. *Hilo* and PT Boats #21, 23, 25, and 26 left Pearl Harbor for Palmyra Island in July 1942. This South Pacific District, MTB Division 2 of Squadron 1 was under the command of Lt. Jonathan Rice, USNR, with Lt. Cdr. Frank A. Munroe, Jr., USNR, the commanding officer of the USS *Hilo*. When they left Palmyra for Ellice Islands on October 25, they were asked to keep a look out for the B-17 plane that had gone down four days earlier.

We also knew from the "Report of Operation of the Fifth Defense Battalion" that "on 2 November (1942), the USS *Hilo* arrived [at Funafuti] with four motor torpedo boats. Nightly, two boats conducted grueling twelve and thirteen hour patrols outside the reef during the hours of darkness." While the men were drifting in their rafts, the *Hilo* and PT Boats #21, 23, 25, and 26 were patrolling the waters near the Ellice Islands.

The sixth graders wanted to know more and eventually sent for blueprints of the PT boats used in the rescue of the men. The PT Boat Museum and Library of Memphis, Tennessee, that had originally sent us addresses for several of the men we had already corresponded with, now provided us with information on the PT boats. Elco Naval Division of the Electric Boat Company had built them. Although a seventy-foot version was used earlier by the United States military, a new seventy-seven foot PT boat had been designed to be faster, to enable it to get closer to strike larger enemy warships. It still needed to be a smaller boat, though, to avoid being spotted as quickly and hit by gunfire.

Already in production at the time of Pearl Harbor's bombing, a government contract was issued for the company to build twenty-four of the boats, with numbers PT 20-44. Each boat had three Packard 4M-2500 engines. At top speed, it went a little over 40 knots, using 484 gallons of fuel per hour.

The primary mission of the PT boat was attack of surface ships and craft. Their orders were "in the event of a surface attack, to seek and engage the enemy." However, throughout their service in the Pacific, PT boats were used effectively to lay mines and smoke screens, carry out intelligence operations, and conduct rescue work in vicinity of islands. As far as the sixth graders were concerned, the main job of these four particular PT boats had been to search and help rescue a few downed aviators we happened to know.

In November 1987 we received a letter from Captain Gaylord B. Lyon, USN (Ret.), from Cedar Mountain, North Carolina. He had read about the class in the *Reader's Digest* and thought we might be interested in contacting his brother-in-law. He sent the address for William W. Rucker. Gaylord Lyon wrote, "I think if you contacted him he just might come to one of your reunions." When the letter arrived at Meeker School, the students were ecstatic. Were we really going to have another reunion? There were times when sixth graders wore me out.

Mr. Rucker, we learned, had been a torpedoman aboard PT #26 that picked up Rickenbacker and Bartek. In February 1988 William W. Rucker from Tampa, Florida, wrote more details about the story the sixth graders already knew. "Rickenbacker had been located by a seaplane which sent their location, by radio, to the island headquarters of our base at Funafuti." That confirmed what Bill Eadie had told us about the decision to break radio silence and contact a PT boat in the vicinity.

Then Mr. Rucker wrote, "By this time it was getting a little rough, the sea that is, and the seaplane could not take off, so it taxied back to Funafuti with our boat leading the way." Then he summarized, "The seaplane delivered its passenger [Adamson] and we delivered ours [Bartek and Rickenbacker] to the island of Funafuti and the next day or so most of them flew away."

William Rucker thought the class might like to write to another PT crewman, one who had been on the boat that had picked up Captain Cherry. He sent us the address for V. F. Scribner.

Mr. V. F. (Vivian) Scribner was from Pharr, Texas, and had, indeed, been a crewmember of PT #21. He quickly wrote back, "I am answering your letter in a hurry so that you will know I have received your letter and will be gathering some materials that I think you will be interested in." He then told us he had a Very pistol flare case that came out of the life raft. We knew the Very pistols were flare guns named after its inventor, and not guns designed as a weapon. The men in the rafts had used them to send a nightly distress signal.

In further communication, Mr. Scribner recalled knowing the crew members of other PT boats, including Tex Featherling, Bill Wepner, and "an officer named Green" from PT #26. We had located these men four years earlier and were thrilled to give him an update on them, including Father Green, and of course, Bill Wepner, who had come to the Rescue Reunion with his wife.

In 1988 the sixth grade students received information from the Military Archives Division of the National Archives about the USS *Hilo*. We were sent a copy of the logbook page listing officers and enlisted personnel when the ship was commissioned on June 11, 1942. Students quickly looked down the list of names and were elated to find "Lt. Richard W. Garrity, M.C. U.S.N." As one student said, "I just knew Dr. Garrity was on that ship!"

The archivist also sent us information about the USS *Hilo* from the *Dictionary of American Naval Fighting Ships*. Originally built in 1931 as the yacht *Caroline*, she was then purchased by the Navy in November 1941 as *Moana*. In 1942, when the USS *Hilo* (PG-58) was commissioned, Lt.

William W. Rucker was a torpedo man aboard PT#26 that picked up Rickenbacker and Bartek. He sent this photo to the class.

Cdr. Frank A. Munroe, Jr. D-V(G), USNR, assumed command. The ship was first sent to Palmyra Island to tend a torpedo boat squadron there, fueling and providing supplies to boats then under training. In mid-October, she went from Palmyra to Canton, in the Phoenix Island group, arriving on October 29. Then the USS *Hilo* proceeded to Funafuti, arriving on November 2.

Important to our research was the information from the ship's log. We also learned that each of the four PT boats had ship's logs, so we also analyzed the recorded history contained in them. For four days, the PT boats and their PT boat tender, the USS *Hilo*, patrolled the area near the Ellice Islands and were directly involved in the rescue of the men. Sometimes it was hard to visualize where each vessel was, but the logs provided missing details of the rescue accounts, and we wanted to piece the story together.

A.P. Cluster, Lt. U.S.N, wrote the log of PT #21 for November 11, 1942. We knew exactly who Lt. Alvin Cluster was. We had located him just before the Rescue Reunion and had passed on his greeting to Captain Cherry the night the men and Super Sleuths had presented a program for the community.

Now we had a factual account of the rescue from what he had written in the ship's log:

Attached to the MTB Ron One, for Nov 11, 1942. Moored low to a buoy in lagoon at Funafuti Atoll, Ellice Islands. 0630 Underway. 0645 Moored port side to PT-26 at Funafuti Atoll, Ellice Islands 0800 Mustered crew—on stations. No absentees. 1725 Underway. 1805 Sighted scout plane hovering over a life raft. 1816 Stopped and picked up W.T. Cherry, Jr., Captain, U.S Army Air Corps (#0-0380222) and the raft he was in. 1820 Underway. 2110 Moored portside to USS *Hilo* at Funafuti Atoll, Ellice Islands. 2115 Transferred Capt. Cherry to the sick bay of USS *Hilo*. 2200 Commenced fueling from USS *Hilo*. 2230 Completed fueling, having received 1087 gallons of 100 octane gasoline.

That was the Navy's record of Bill Cherry's rescue. It sounded so factual...common...ordinary. Mixed with the time of day and routine fueling of the craft, Captain Cherry's rescue was only a small line in history. "Stopped and picked up." There must have been thousands of such rescues during World War II. But each was more than facts. Each was anything but mundane to the men who survived. One moment Captain Cherry was alone in the vast Pacific Ocean with the waves, sharks, and sun his only companions. Now Captain Cherry had been rescued.

The log for the USS *Hilo* for November 11, 1942, the same day, documented the event by John S. Weiler, Lt. (jg.) USNR:

2115 PT 21 moored alongside to starboard. Captain William Cherry, Jr., U.S. Army Air Corps was brought aboard and admitted to sickbay, cause, exposure due to twenty days at sea on life raft after plane was forced down. 2130 started master gyro. 2205 PT's 23 & 26 moored alongside to starboard. 2220 commenced fueling PT 21. 2255 Finished fueling PT 21 having delivered 1087.5 gals. of aviation gas at 86° F.

The next day, November 12, 1942, the log for the USS *Hilo* indicated that Captain Cherry was taken to the little hospital on Funafuti:

0557 Captain William Cherry, Jr., U.S.A. was transferred to sick bay, Fifth Marine Defense Battalion. 0600 Made all preparations for getting underway. 0610 PT's 21, 23, 25, &

26 cast off. 0630 Got underway in accordance with decision of Commander Task Unit 4-5-5 to engage in search for remainder of plane's company. Captain conning, navigator on the bridge, steaming at various courses and speeds to conform with the channel.

We researched that "conning" meant "at the helm." Captain Cherry indicated there were two more rafts out there somewhere, and everyone was on a high level of alert to locate them. All day the *Hilo* searched. According to Good's Rescue Report, "At 1830 a message was received from Nukufetau via coastwatcher radio that a raft and three survivors had been located there…"

Log 2234 for the *Hilo read*, "Steaming at various speeds searching for plane and rafts on surface. Average R.P.M. 245." They had searched all day and were continuing to search into the night.

We knew from Good's Rescue Report that by 0640 that morning, not only the USS *Hilo*, but also all four torpedo boats had gotten underway to search for the other rafts. We read each PT boat's log for a record of their day's activity.

Lieutenant Al Cluster recorded this log for PT #21 for November 12, 1942:

Moored in company with MTB Div. Two port side to USS *Hilo* at Funafuti Atoll, Ellice Islands. 0600 Mustered crew on stations. No absentees. 0605 Underway in company with MTB Div. Two in accord with verbal orders of Com. MTB Div. Two. 0645 Took departure and set course 273° true and 263° psc. Speed 30 knots. 0830 Commenced steaming on various courses to search for life rafts believed to be in vicinity. 1910 Stopped and layed to.

That same day, the log for PT #26 for November 12, 1942 read:

Moored starboard side to P.T. 25 adjacent to USS *Hilo* at Funafuti Island, Ellice Group in company with M.T.B. Div.

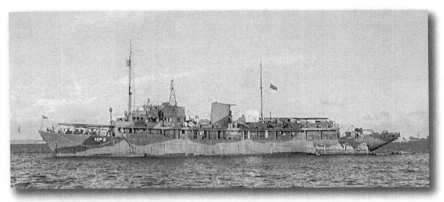

The USS *Hilo* in 1944. (*Courtesy National Archives*)

Two. 0600 Underway in company with M.T.B. Div. Two in search for life raft with missing aviators aboard. Various courses and speeds. 1855 Received Posit. of Missing aviators from USS *Hilo*. Bearing 023° T distance 45 miles from USS *Hilo*. Underway on course 023°T. 2010 Sighted seaplane with life raft secured to float. 2015 Took aboard from Seaplane two missing army aviators, Capt. E. V. Rickenbacker and Pvt. Bartek, J.B., U.S.A., suffering from exhaustion, exposure, hunger, & thirst. Administered bouillon and shock treatment. 2130 Underway on course 120° T. for Funafuti Island, Ellice Group.

Now Eddie Rickenbacker and John Bartek were aboard a PT boat and being taken care of by the crew as they headed back to base. The log for PT #23 for November 12, 1942 read:

Moored in nest alongside USS *Hilo*, Funafuti Island, in company with (MTB Ron One Div.Two). 0600 Underway with company of Div. Two, to search for lost flyers. 1835 All engines died out, due to water and dirt in fuel strainers. 1855 Underway and received location of missing men. 1925 Engine trouble, water and dirt in fuel strainers, stopped to clean

PT boat similar to the ones used at Funafuti, 1942. (*Courtesy National Archives*)

strainers. 1935 Underway for given location. 2000 sighted lights ahead. 2015 Engine trouble, stopped to repair leak in water jacket on port engine. 2030 Underway. Headed toward lights. 2040 Reached rendezvous point, contacted PT 26 and a seaplane. PT 26 had two of the missing men aboard, and seaplane had one. 2130 Guided seaplane back to Funafuti island, course 120° T.

We had always given so much attention to the men of the two PT boats who actually took the survivors aboard. But having read the log for PT #23, I realized how much effort had been expended to find the men. Engine trouble and more engine trouble! There were days like that in teaching, and I wondered how tired those men must have been after their sixteen-hour day.

Lieutenant John L. Mote, (jg.) USNR, recorded the log for PT #25 for November 12, 1942:

> Moored in company MTB DIV Two, in nest, portside to USS *Hilo* (SOPA) off Fongafale Village, Funafuti Island, Ellice Group. 0600: Pursuant to verbal order of Com MTB Div. got underway in company MTB Div. Two to carry out search for Lt. Colonel "Eddie" Rickenbacker, U.S.A. and party reported in life raft southwest of Funafuti Island. 1300: Contacted USS *Hilo* and continued search in conjunction with that ship. 1900: Upon orders of C.O. Hilo (SOPA) took course 049° T at 30 knots. 2100: Arrived at scene of rescue. PT 26 had taken survivors to port. 2130: Went ahead 30 knots course 120° T 111° psc. 2330: Moored to aircraft buoy of Fongafale Village, Funafuti Island.

By the next morning, Friday, November 13, 1942, the log for the USS *Hilo* recorded: "0639 Landfall, Funafuti Atoll." By 0723 the entry described course changes and said, "working for Te Ava I Te Lape channel entrance." Although the ship had sighted land, it took expertise to enter the narrow channel of the lagoon on the north side of the atoll between the smaller islets of Paava and Te Afualiku, then cross the lagoon and reach the base on the Central Eastern area of Funafuti. At 0847 the entry indicated, "Anchored in lagoon off Fongafale, Funafuti Atoll, Ellice Islands in 15 fathoms of water, coral bottom with 30 fathoms of chain on port anchor..."

The log for PT #26 for November 13, 1942 read:

> Underway on course 120° T. Speed 12 knots for Funafuti Island, Ellice Group. 0320 Moored to buoy in lagoon at Funafuti Island, Ellice Group in company with M.T.B. Div. Two, less PT 21. 0400 Delivered Capt. Rickenbacker and Pvt. Bartek, J.B. U.S.A. to Medical officer, Funafuti Island. 0900

Underway. 0915 Moored portside to P.T. 23 adjacent to USS *Hilo*. 1010 Underway. 1020 Moored to buoy in lagoon at Funafuti Island. Ellice Group.

That meant Eddie Rickenbacker and John Bartek had now rejoined Col. Hans Adamson at the base hospital on Funafuti, where Capt. Bill Cherry had also been taken. But the log had also recorded that when they moored to buoy in the lagoon in company of their Motor Torpedo Boat Division Two, it was "less PT 21."

We knew from the Rescue Report that PT #21 had not returned during the night of the 12-13 of November and that the aviation unit had been directed to conduct a search to locate them. Kingfisher planes piloted by Pearsall and Clark had taken off at 1045 and found the missing PT boat at 1240. A message drop informed the base, and the PT boat returned under its own power to base on the afternoon of November 13. The log of PT #21 confirmed this detail by recording, "1245—Underway on course 080° true and 075° psc at speed 20 knots. 1445 Sighted southern tip of Funafuti Atoll, bearing 070° true; distance about 11 miles…"

A log entry from USS *Hilo* for Friday, November 13, 1942, read:

0850 PT 23, 25, & 26 came alongside. PT 25 to port, others to starboard. 0900 Commenced fueling PT 25. 0939 Cable, H.H. AMM 2/c USN 372-32-81 reported aboard for transportation in accordance with the verbal orders commanding officer Fifth Marine Defense Battalion. 0950 Finished fueling PT 25 having delivered 2650 gals. of aviation gas at 86° F. 1001 Got underway."

The four PT boats had been involved in the search for rafts. Two of those boats had directly transported survivors. Now the PT tender was to play a major role in the rescue of the raft that landed on Nukufetau. The ship was headed for a specific destination, and James W. Reynolds would soon see what he always remembered about the USS *Hilo*.

The ship's log at 1305 indicated they had sighted Nukufetau. At 1453 the entry said, "Changed course...steaming at various speeds and on various courses approaching Nukufetau Island. Captain at the conn. Navigator on the bridge." The 1518 entry said, "Motor Launch [whale boat] put in water to take rescue party to the beach. Executive officer in charge of party. Cable, H. H, AMM 2/c left with rescue party. All engines stopped lying to off Nukufetau Island awaiting survivors of lost plane to be brought aboard."

Then the *Hilo's* entry for 1714 read, "Hoisted motor launch aboard with following plane survivors, put in Sick Bay, Diagnosis: EXPOSURE: 2nd Lieut. John J. De Angelis, USA 0-434651, and James C. Whittaker USA, 0-49-49-off; Staff Sgt. James W. Reynolds, USA. Lt. (jg.) W. J. Hall (M. C.), USN reported on board for transportation. 1717 Got underway..."

The Navy Scouting Squadron had taken Doc Hall to Nukufetau. Now he would be going back to Funafuti via the USS *Hilo*. It was Friday the 13, and James W. Reynolds always believed that in their family from then on "Friday the 13th" always meant "good luck." We knew from the Rescue Report that due to low visibility the ship had not attempted passage into the lagoon until the following morning.

The log for the USS *Hilo* for November 14, 1942, read, "0926 Anchored in lagoon, Funafuti, Ellice Island in 16 fathoms of water with 60 fathoms of chain out on port anchor...0945 Survivors of plane crash Second Lt. John J. De Angelis, USA, and Second Lt. James C. Whittaker, USA, were transferred to Marine Hospital Fifth Defense Battalion, Funafuti, Ellice Island. Lt .(jg.) W. J. Hall (M. C.), USN left the ship." That confirmed that James W. Reynolds was still aboard the ship, too ill to leave.

Three days later the log for the USS *Hilo* for November 17, 1942, said, "1345 Staff Sgt. James Reynolds, USA, was transferred to Marine Hospital, Fifth Defense Battalion, Funafuti, Island." And what did James W. Reynolds remember about his time aboard the former yacht? The beautiful Philippine mahogany paneling and railings!

The Ship's Log of PT #21 for Nov. 11, 1942, described picking up Capt. Cherry from his raft. (*Courtesy National Archives*)

Chapter Eighteen

FLIGHT OV-369

I N THE ARMY AIR CORPS, BILL CHERRY and his crew were members of the Air Transport Command, which had been established as an air supply system that moved military personnel and supplies where they were needed during the war. Originally, it had started in May 1941 by General Hap Arnold as the Air Corps Ferrying Command to deliver aircraft overseas from the United States. During this time four major air routes were developed. One, the South Pacific air ferrying route, connected the U.S. via Hawaii with Australia and other Western Pacific islands.

Major Sliter from Maxwell Air Force Base had sent a declassified report, "The Air Transport Command in the Pacific—1942," to Super Sleuth David Jurgens. This report indicated that Bill Cherry, John J. DeAngelis, and James Reynolds had formerly been assigned to the South Pacific Wing Headquarters at Hamilton Field, but they had been transferred to the 6th Ferrying Group, Long Beach, California, in August 1942, as part of the reorganization of the 28th Ferrying Squadron.

Thomas O. Beauchamp, from the same group, wrote to us from Clinton, Louisiana. He knew both Bartek and Reynolds, as they were in the same squadron and had flown together. Mr. Beauchamp later sent us photos of the men in a plane taken from his plane's window on a flight from Honolulu to Australia.

When pilot Bill Cherry, radio operator Jim Reynolds, and engineer John Bartek came to Meeker Elementary for the Rescue Reunion, we had four sixth grade classes gather in the school media center to hear their stories. Sixth Grade Super Sleuths and the men also spoke at a community presentation. Transcribed videotapes from these events in 1985 have recorded what they recalled about their raft adventure. Those memories, along with other military documents, helped us tell the story of their flight.

In October 1942 Bill Cherry had been to Australia with a flight of B-24s back into Hawaii and was to fly these planes on to San Francisco. He was to return to the States with what was called a "war weary" airplane—one that was obsolete. The day before this mission started, the commanding officer summoned Bill Cherry into his office and explained he needed a flight to go down over the Southern Pacific bases, flying two dignitaries for an inspection tour. As Captain Cherry told the story, "Since I was the senior pilot there and available, I was it—get my crew ready."

The Air Transport Command had assigned them an older model B-17 C. Since the C and D models did not have guns in the tails and no dorsal fin on top of their rudder, the plane was more vulnerable to fighters, so the Army Air Corps had declared them obsolete. Therefore, these C and D models of the B-17 were removed from combat in the Pacific and used primarily for transport and training.

After checking out the airplane and loading supplies, the crew had to wait until about 1:00 in the morning for their flight to take off for their Destination: HOLLY, code word for Canton Island. Although the men tried to get some rest, they were too excited to sleep. After settling the two dignitaries, Rickenbacker and Adamson, into the plane, they added a third person. Alex had been on a combat ship going through Hawaii and had been delayed in a hospital with jaundice and an appendectomy. Now he was also being transported back to his group in the Pacific.

As they taxied out ready to take off, the rubber expander tube inside the brake drum, and known for bursting, did just that. Captain Cherry had no brakes in one wheel, so he had to ground loop it at the end of the runway to stop the plane. Ground looping was a procedure of rapidly rotating the fixed-wing aircraft in circles while it was still on the ground for it to lose momentum. Instead of repairing the brake, the crew was given another plane that they had not flight checked—a B-17D—an older

B-17 D in flight (*Courtesy National Museum of the Air Force*)

plane, No. A.P. 40-3084. Captain Cherry was told by his commanding officer (Brigadier General William E. Lynd) to use the plane provided and to get going. Rickenbacker was also in a hurry to proceed. Since radios were turned off at midnight in Hawaii for security purposes, Capt. Cherry explained he did not check the radio and assumed things were okay.

Flight OV-369 started at Hickam Field, Hawaii, just outside of Honolulu, near Pearl Harbor. They were headed for Canton Island in the Phoenix group, just north of the equator, about 1,700 miles south-southwest of Hawaii with a nine hour flight plan. The flight was uneventful, except that they were on top of an overcast most of the trip, so John DeAngelis could not get many navigational shots to verify their bearings.

Captain Cherry identified two ways to navigate over water—radio and octant. An octant is similar to the navigational instrument called a sextant on a ship, except the sextant uses the horizon to read, but because there is no horizon for the plane, the octant has a "built in bubble for the horizon."

Since the navigator DeAngelis was unable to utilize the octant during the night using the stars for position, he was anxious to get a shot in the morning of the sun. Bill Cherry explained, "When you take a shot on a heavenly body, it gives you a line of position, perpendicular to the body itself. If it's off to the left of you, you get a course line. If it's ahead of you, you get a speed line. We were getting a course line, since we were going south."

As their estimated time of arrival (ETA) drew closer, they made radio contact with Canton Island. Whittaker and Rickenbacker had written about this in their books, so we could visualize what was happening. But we had other information that could tell more of the story.

Since 1991, the sixth graders had obtained documents from the National Archives in Washington, D.C. They had copies of extracted logs of radio operators on duty at the time, as well as a diary of events put together by Headquarters of the Holly Defense on Canton Island. In addition, we had some of the many documents gathered by the military in the first week after the plane and crew were missing. Commanding Lt. Gen. Delos C. Emmons, of the Headquarters Hawaiian Department of the Army Air Corps, had prepared papers for the Commanding General of the U.S. Army Air Forces in Washington, D.C.

Sixth graders wanted to interpret the radio logs, but they found deciphering them was a daunting task. In the early 1990s, we were just a few years ahead of the commercialization of the Internet, and finding sources to answer our questions was extremely difficult.

My father's cousin, Hubert Zobrist, had served in World War II, and he put us in touch with a former B-17 radio operator, John Chopelas. Students next wrote to Mr. Chopelas, who had remembered his Army buddy "Zobe," and agreed to help us if he could.

John Chopelas from Killeen, Texas, sent a "Study Sheet for Basic Code." Since the "Z" signals used in early 1942 had been replaced that December with "Q" signals, most of the war years used a different code. However, Mr. Chopelas did help us understand that DF/STN meant direction finding station, and JW3 Suva referred to a ground station on Suva in the Fiji Islands, located southwest of the Phoenix Islands and directly south of the Ellice Islands. He explained that MR/for/BG, or S for MR referred to the radio operators on duty. When one left and the other took over, the letters indicated the change. A final clue from Mr. Chopelas referred to the middle letter of the "Z" signals: ZAP was answering, ZCE for calling, ZDC was directions, and ZFJ or ZFK for frequency.

Mr. Chopelas next sent us a reference called "Elementary Telegraph Procedure." It contained enough "Z" signals to keep the students interested in their decoding. Mr. Chopelas also had contacted a fellow radio operator in his group, and they both expressed how frustrating it was to realize that at one time they had been very knowledgeable of this material but, as Chopelas put it, "now it has become barely recalled memory. To be honest, I've forgotten 99 per cent of what I used in the way of radio procedure. As I look at these signals, I do remember seeing them back then but couldn't for the life of me 'translate' a single one today."

There were many obstacles to piecing together, not only what happened, but also, when it took place. How time was recorded was one problem. We had learned that Flight OV-369 had departed at 0130 HWT, which was 1:30 in the morning Hawaiian War Time, and that Whittaker had made a first entry in his diary in the raft at 1630 HWT. But what had happened in those fifteen hours in between had changed lives and would change them more in the days to come. The radio logs we had were on Greenwich Mean Time (GCT) or Zulu (Z) Time. However, by subtracting ten-hour differences, we were able to approximate when events were happening and to visualize what was taking place in the plane and on the ground, as the B-17 soared over the Pacific Ocean for the last time.

The radio log from Operator 1 said, "1915— CTC 369 OK ZAP FJ/NM OK ASKED ETA HE SAY EST. 200 MILES OUT AT 1910 GAVE ETA AS 2025 PHONE OPER AN CONTROL ZCF 1945...MR.." That meant that at 1915 Greenwich Mean Time or Zulu Time, minus approximately ten hours, would be at 0915 or 9:15 a.m. James W. Reynolds, the radio operator on the B-17 of Flight OV-369, had contacted the Canton station. When asked for their estimated time of arrival (ETA), John DeAngelis, the flight navigator, estimated the plane was 200 miles out and gave an ETA of 2025, or 10:25 a.m.

When their ETA for Canton Island had passed, there was no island in sight. The crew was beginning to worry.

At Meeker School Bill Cherry said it this way. "The octant was bad. The octant was a cheap training octant with mirrors instead of prisms. Any sudden jar could make them off thirty, forty, or fifty miles. We didn't have time to check after the ground loop. Should have had time, but didn't." They figured the octant that had been in the first plane and then carried by DeAngelis aboard the second plane must have been bumped when Captain Cherry had done the ground looping. When the octant indicated they were on course and over the island, they were not over it, but probably east or west of it.

Captain Cherry recalled, "We were so close, we could hear the tower talking to us with the volume turned down. But do you go left, right, straight ahead, or what? We had been briefed, that if you get in trouble, don't start looking around for the island, ask for a variance. They'll have direction finding equipment. We thought we had pretty hot cargo, so we asked for a bearing."

The tower he was talking about was the Canton Island Radio Station WYVA. The volume referred to was a VHF radio, or a short distance radio. And the hot cargo was Eddie Rickenbacker.

The radio log from Operator 1 read, "2025—CTC 369 HE WANTS A ZDC TOLD HIM NO SOAP HERE ASKED HIM HOW FAR OUT HE WAS WAIT HE SAY..." Flight 369 had contacted Canton again, requesting a radio bearing, and was told they did not have a radio direction finding station there. Then the Canton radio operator asked them how far out they were, and he was told to wait.

At 2045 the plane's crew reported that they were lost. They were sending out signals to get a bearing, but because the Canton station did not have equipment set up that was needed to take a bearing, it contacted NIX, a direction finding station at Palmyra in the Line Islands, about halfway between Hawaii and Canton. The 1st Operator's log from Canton recorded, "2045—HE SAY HE LOST G GOT NIX TO TAKE A ZDC ON HIM TOLD HIM TO ZDA OK HE DOING IT MIN...MR..." Then..."NIX CANT PICK HIM UP YET"

From this point on, it was clear that a three-way communication was necessary. Palmyra could not communicate by radio with the plane, but could with the radio station at Canton. The plane's signals could be picked up by Palmyra, however. Therefore, Palmyra could get a bearing on the plane's position with their RDF (radio direction finder) and send it by radio to Canton. Canton could then relay the bearing back to the plane.

The 1st Operator's extracted log read, "2100 — GOT BEARING FROM NIX AS 126 HE FLYING NOW TRUE BEARING AS 215 TO HERE GAVE IT TO HIM HE SAY OK WILL TRY IT...ASKED HIM IF RADIO COMPASS WAS WRKIN HE SAY HE TRY ZDC NOW." Palmyra had given a bearing of 126 so asked the plane to fly a true bearing of 215 to Canton. Flight OV-369 responded they would try that. Was their radio compass working? They would check it out now.

The radio direction finder was used to help navigate before radar. This worked by taking bearings from two or more broadcasting stations. It was possible to locate the plane's relative position by finding where these bearings intersected.

The plane's antennae for receiving a message had been working for part of the flight, but now seemed jammed. To receive a message the radio operator in the plane would tune the receiver to the correct frequency and then manually turn the loop of the antenna that was mounted above the plane's fuselage and determine the direction of signal. It identified the correct degree heading marked on the radio's compass as well as its 180 degree opposite, but the navigator still needed to know if his location was east or west of the sending station, so he wouldn't go in the opposite direction.

Why did Canton not have any direction finding station? At the Meeker Elementary Media Center, the former radio operator Jim Reynolds told us, "Canton had DF equipment, but it wasn't operational. Keep in mind this was the early part of the war in 1942, and there weren't too many things that were operational." Jim also shared how the crew he flew with pioneered the route the commercial airlines later flew. On their trips across the Pacific, Jim always sent back weather reports every hour on the hour. This information built up a background of weather data at different times of the year. Then he said, "I had operated with these people at Canton Island before and at Hickam. It wasn't their fault they didn't have the equipment operational."

Military reports we obtained from the National Archives explained that the "HF/DF equipment was inoperative, but under reconstruction." The station had originally belonged to Pan American Airways, which had abandoned Canton after the outbreak of fighting with Japan. The Navy was in the process of developing an air base there and was relocating the station during the time of the men's flight.

Could two other stations take a bearing on the plane's location? The 1st Operator's extracted log read, "2156—CALLED NANDI TOLD THEM TO TAKE BEARING ON 369 FROM STN JW3 AT SUVA." Radio station, WYVB at Nandi Airport in Fiji contacted JW3, a direction finding station at Suva, also in the Fiji Islands, southwest of Canton. They both reported that the plane's signal was too faint to obtain a bearing.

But was the plane's compass working? The 1st Operator's log recorded, "2217—ASKED 369 IF HIS RADIO COMPASS WORKING/SED AS./ THE RADIO COMPASS IS NOT ACCURATE. /R ZZA/ R." The radio station at Canton asked the plane and the plane answered. It was not working. The Canton operator acknowledged R (receipt) of the message and sent ZZA (stand by).

What should they do now? Without the plane's octant and the radio compass working properly, even if given a bearing by an Army Air Corps station or a Navy station, the plane would not know where it was along that bearing. As a military report written by Henry Luna from the Air Transport Command said, "…there was no other bearing available to resolve the airplane's position from a line of Position into a fix." But as sixth graders interpreted it, "Mrs. Kelly, they *were* in a fix!"

Then Canton thought they had the plane on radar. In a document from the National Archives, the station reported that at "approximately 2226

This Western Union message relayed that James W. Reynolds was missing in the Pacific. (*Courtesy Jim Reynolds*)

Radar set 270 had picked up an echo and continued to pick it up on each of 3 complete rotations of the antennae. This was the only echo at the time and we tentatively assumed it was Flight 369."

Captain Cherry had explained it this way: "They called up radar, without telling me this. Radar was brand new then. It had just come out. They said, 'Hey! We got one of those Air Force jockeys lost. Where is he?' Well, they turned that scope round and round. They picked up a target. They did not have it identified. They only knew it was on radar. They said to fly 240 degrees." The plane had continued to get new bearings, and Captain Cherry had responded each time.

By 2247 the Canton station admitted, "We told 369 to fly a course of 240 degrees that he was 10 miles out. The Radar echo was lost as an airplane came into land, but it was a B-24 and not Flight 369 as anticipated."

Four years before we had this information, my sixth graders had received a letter from Albert Miceli from Wading River, New York. After the article about our school research project appeared in the *Reader's Digest*, Mr. Miceli had contacted the magazine and asked that we write to him.

He wrote to the editor, "After reading, 'A Gathering of Legends' in the July issue of your great *Digest*, I find myself being the 'Missing Link' in the presentation of your story about the Rickenbacker incident. It made my heart very heavy." He went on to say that when this incident occurred he was with Air Control and was stationed on Canton Island. "I was a crew chief of a radar crew, (radar was very secret then)."

He indicated to us that his superiors would not allow him to make radio contact with the plane they thought was Rickenbacker's, due to the proximity of Japanese held islands. Whether that was the case, or if the radar station was following a wrongly identified plane, is unclear. But I did sense that Mr. Miceli had intended to do his job well, had been distraught that he could not have done more, and was relieved that he could write to John Bartek to explain his view of the incident. Perhaps our research in putting him in contact with some of the crew had eased a little of the concern Mr. Miceli had felt for forty-five years.

At our Rescue Reunion, Captain Cherry explained that for an hour and a half, he had listened to their bearings and changed his course accordingly. But the radar had not picked up Flight OV-369. As our Texan pilot put it, "In the meantime I'm getting so far away I can hardly hear him any more. So I knew there was a mistake. An old country boy does wake up eventually!"

The B-17 was becoming very low on fuel as they tried to backtrack closer to Canton and asked that the island send up anti-aircraft fire. A message at 2335 from Colonel Adamson on board Flight 369 requested that AA [anti-aircraft] guns be fired on five minutes schedule and stated the plane had climbed to 5,000 feet. This was, of course, both to observe the bursts and to avoid being hit by them. The crew saw nothing.

Captain Cherry recalled, "Now then, it becomes apparent we're going to go in the water. We had Jim on the radio for an hour and a half. He had been sending MOs for a long time. Now he's sending SOS. That means it's serious. Let's do something."

Cherry further explained, "MOs—is when you want a bearing on—it's easy to pick up. It's Dah Dah—Dah Dah, Dah—over and over. That way they can pick you up easier. And SOS is Di Di Di—Dah Dah Dah—Di Di Di." The sixth graders already knew about SOS, but the MOs—Morse code for letters "M" and "O"—were new to us.

The 1st Operator's log from Canton recorded, "2354—HE SENDING MO'S NOW—SIG VERY WEAK—"

Then the log said, "0033—TOLD 369 THAT HE WAS FLYING A COURSE OF 229 DEG AT 0030Z FROM NIX / SHIP SED HE ABT 35 DEGREES AND HALF HRS GAS LEFT." This was at 1430 HWT, or about 2:30 in the afternoon. It was the last message received from the plane.

At Meeker Elementary, Captain Cherry explained to us how he had deployed the crew to the back of the plane in safety position against the bulkhead. He, along with the co-pilot Whittaker, and John Bartek were in front. Running on vapors and estimating only about ten gallons of fuel left in a tank, Captain Cherry had John Bartek as engineer pump all fuel remaining—about eight to ten minutes of fuel—from the inboard tanks to the outboard tanks. Then he had feathered the engines on number two and three, the inboard engines, turning the propellers, so there would not be any drag, and those engines stop. He explained, "The reason I put it [the fuel] in the outboard tanks was I was afraid the prop might come off and damage us in the airplane—we were closer to it." Then he added, "It was just a matter of *when* we were going to land."

John Bartek then raced to the back of the plane. The pilot and co-pilot placed a kapok cushion under their seat belts. They were all secured in place. Then Captain Cherry told us, "I started looking for the softest water we could find."

He next made a power-on, stall landing. In his own words, he described the moment. "So we go down. We had about eight to ten miles an hour wind blowing. I elected to land crosswind, in a trough. Waves were coming toward us, but between the waves was the trough. I got down just about twenty feet high...lower and lower until I found the right swell and trough. I wanted it to be in the trough and the swell smooth. I was just above stalling—about three knots...Whittaker had ahold of the master switch for the engines. I got it just where I wanted it, at about eighty miles an hour, maybe seventy-five, and hollered, 'Cut it.' He cut the engine."

The students listening in the Meeker Media Center seemed to hold their breaths as they heard Captain Cherry explain what had happened when he ditched the plane into the ocean. He continued, "We hit tail first—quite a splash. Then the wingtips came down into the swells. Then the nose came in. That is when we hit a brick wall. Went under and then popped up like a cork."

He added, "I had prepared myself, and Whittaker had too, way back in the seat reaching like this for the control wheel, with stiff arms slightly bent, so I wouldn't break my arms. We hit so hard I pushed the wheel through the instrument panel...I figured—just guessing—in just over fifty feet at eighty miles an hour, so it was quite a rapid stop." Normally sixth graders would say, "Duh! Ya think?" But they were too engrossed in his story.

Then Bill Cherry explained how they had been briefed. If a plane were ditched in the ocean, it would break up essentially in two minutes. At that time, no B-17 had ditched and floated long, because they had guns on them and had broken into pieces. He admitted that versions vary as to length of time the plane stayed afloat...but the airplane floated for a great deal longer than ever anticipated.

Captain Cherry continued, "To me the airplane didn't look too much damaged. I thought we could just jack it up on land and fly it again." Then he flashed a resigned grin. " I just couldn't find any land!"

The men quickly climbed into the rafts—Colonel Adamson, Rickenbacker, and John Bartek in the first one. That meant climbing *up* through an opening in the fuselage and going out onto the wing of the plane and then down onto a launched raft. Captain Cherry recalled he was still inside the airplane looking for food as the others evacuated. Although they had a little orange juice and water on the plane, he had made them stop drinking water an hour earlier, thinking to save the water. Now his mouth was very dry. As he said, "I was spitting cotton!"

John DeAngelis and Alex Kaczmarczyk climbed into the little doughnut raft. James Reynolds and Jim Whittaker were in the third raft, waiting for the last person. And where was Bill Cherry? He was still inside the airplane looking for food.

Captain Cherry recalled how there was debris everywhere, but he finally found three oranges floating. (John DeAngelis had picked up one, which made a total of four oranges for the rafts.) As the first raft was already about a half mile away, Whittaker and Reynolds were anxious to get the rafts joined together. They had hollered for Bill to get out of the plane.

At our school, Bill Cherry turned to his left and asked for confirmation from Jim Reynolds. "I was in there, what—about ten minutes?"

Jim just grinned, shook his head, and replied, "You were in there longer than you should have been!" After the intensity of their recollections, this was just the humorous breather we all needed. Besides, thinking Captain Cherry might have been a "little bit naughty" endeared him even more to sixth graders.

But the reality of their situation returned quickly when he summarized, "We had been sending SOS signals for two or three hours. You expect at least one ship or station on the shore to hear it. Nobody heard us at all. We started our floating career."

John Bartek was the youngest of the crewmembers. He told us how he had always admired Eddie Rickenbacker. Growing up, he had even dreamed of talking to him. He never imagined they would be floating together on a raft. But John admitted to us that when they first realized they had a problem in the plane, he thought, "I'd just love to be back in the States right now!"

As they had prepared to ditch, John had helped throw things overboard to lighten the plane. His camera, an expensive Leica, was one of those items. But he had saved his New Testament and put it in his pocket. When they landed, it was John's job to get the life rafts out. As he shared with us at school, "I was too busy to take photographs then anyway." In the plane, the ocean looked smooth, but on a raft, the ocean was deep and rough.

At the community presentation when the men shared their personal stories, we had seated each survivor and rescuer at a different table on stage with several Sixth Grade Super Sleuths. As John shared his story, he looked across an adjoining table at the pilot he had been with on rafts over forty years earlier. John then faced the audience, "You probably wonder what goes through a man's mind about that time. Cherry never once looked like he sweated." Captain Cherry just grinned and shook his head with a you-have-to-be-kidding-me look!

John continued his recollections by lightening the mood for the audience. He pointed to the man on the other side of him, "Reynolds was sending SOS—he could spell that backwards or forwards!" I noticed a couple of sixth graders' fingers moving on their tables, unobtrusively tapping out the distress call.

Then John shared his thoughts as they had assembled in the rafts. "Captain Eddie is aboard. They'll send the Navy, the whole Air Force—and everything else they got. And if they don't…the Japanese will!" But there would be three weeks of waiting…and wondering…

It was the end of Flight OV-369.

Chapter Nineteen

THE SEARCH

F ROM THE NATIONAL ARCHIVES WE HAD COPIES of almost fifty radiograms, photos, and other documents that had been preserved about the "Rickenbacker Rescue." Researchers from the National Archives had corresponded with my sixth graders each year. I particularly recall archivist Richard Peuser. Since he was in the military reference branch of the Archives, he received the majority of the students' questions. He always responded with efficient expertise that motived the young historians.

Now, students thought they had a gold mine with the radiograms. These transcribed messages were sent in code and then deciphered, or they were messages from original penciled copies sent to or received from a code station by phone. Many of these papers were not dated. Others were stamp dated when they were filed, not when they were received. We wanted to put these radiograms in chronological order, but it was impossible.

We discovered the War Department had the same problem in 1942. After the men were lost, and before they were rescued, Maj. Arthur Finch of the Army Air Corps wrote a memorandum on November 9 to the Director of Communications for the War Department. The subject was titled, "Items of particular interest in radio log covering loss of Aircraft OV-369." In the memo he mentioned the discrepancies in the radio logs. He attributed some of them to different time zones, but he also recognized there were inconsistencies in the logging procedures. He suggested this might be due to unreliable timepieces at the various radio stations and/or attention to time signals. He recommended, "that standardized radio logs be used throughout the A.A.F. [Army Air Force]."

From the numbers on the radiograms, we thought we figured out some time documentation. The six-digit number at the top of the radiogram seemed to indicate a day and time. The first two digits referred to the day and the last four digits to GCT or Zulu time.

Even so, the search crossed the International Date Line. We were never certain even which day a radiogram was sent or received.

The radiograms were easier for us to read than the "Z" codes of the radio logs. However, they contained words that the military used which were unfamiliar to us without a military background or historical knowledge.

Another problem was the names of the defense operations for the various bases. We already knew FETLOCK referred to the Ellice Islands and STRAW meant Samoa. We had determined from the operators' logs that COPPER referred to Territory of Hawaii and HOLLY signified Canton Island in the Phoenix Islands. Now we struggled with JACKKNIFE, BRUSH, BIRCH, BUTTON, CACTUS, and ROSES. We did not know these locations. Only by analyzing many documents were we able to "put two and two together." Eventually we figured out that JACKKNIFE was for Johnston Island in the Pacific, just southwest of Hawaii. BRUSH was for Palmyra, south of Hawaii. BIRCH was Christmas Island, southeast of Palmyra. ROSES referred to Efate and BUTTON was for Espiritu Santo Island—both in the New Hebrides Island chain, and much farther southwest than even the Ellice Islands. CACTUS was for Guadalcanal in the Solomon Islands, west of Funafuti.

Names of people were also confusing. In material from the National Archives was a copy of a letter from Commanding Lt. Gen. Emmons, from Headquarters Hawaiian Department at Fort Shafter, TH (Territory of Hawaii). If Emmons was in Hawaii, then Commanding Officer Ellsworth had to be at Canton. By playing sort of a "Who's on first?" analysis, we could piece together much of the search for the downed aircraft and crew.

The documentation fell into three categories—informing people and bases of the incident, organizing the search for the men, and reporting progress of searches. Flight OV-369 was an Army Air Corps flight, but

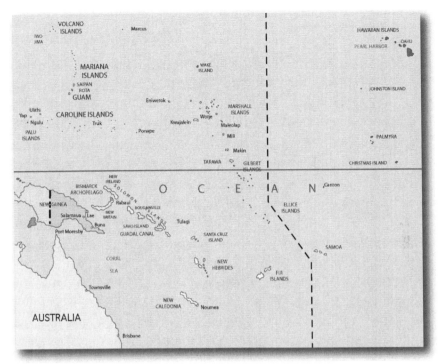

Map of South Pacific Lines of Communication to Australia, 1942. (*Courtesy U.S. Army Center of Military History*)

the rescue would involve the Army, Navy, and Marines. Help was summoned from Allied bases that dotted the vast Central Pacific Ocean—Ft. Shafter and Pearl Harbor in the Territory of Hawaii, Palmyra in the Line Islands, Christmas and Johnston Islands, Efate in the New Hebrides Islands, Upolu in the Samoa Islands, Fiji Islands, and, of course, Canton Island in the Phoenix Islands, which had been the airplane's destination. Any available plane or surface craft that could be spared from other duties was requested to help search.

Radiogram 220130 was sent from Ellsworth to Emmons, or from the Commanding Officer (CO) at Canton to the Commanding General (CG) in Hawaii. It started, "SEE HERE QQ BAKER SEVENTEEN RICKENBACKER FLIGHT DOWN AT SEA XX EMMONS FROM ELLSWORTH XX LAST BEARING FROM PALMYRA TWO TWO SEVEN DEGREES NOTIFY CINCPAC TO HAVE IMMEDIATE AIR SEARCH STARTED FROM ELLICE ISLANDS ALONG THIS LINE XX ALL AIR AND SURFACE VESSELS HERE SEARCHING" This notification was that the B-17 was down. Palmyra indicated to Canton their last bearing of 227 degrees. CINCPAC (Commander in Chief Pacific) was Admiral Chester W. Nimitz, U.S. Navy, and the southwestern most point of the search was to start from Ellice Islands.

Another message was coded KMZD V WYVA, which meant this message 220150 was sent to the Palmyra radio station (KMZD) from the Canton radio station (WYVA). "PEPSICOLA PP REQUEST YOU START IMMEDIATE AIR SEARCH PAREN CO PALMYRA FROM ELLSWORTH PAREN ON BEARINGS TWO TWO SEVEN TO TWO TWO NINE FROM YOU FOR PARTY FROM BAKER SEVENTEEN PLANE DOWN AT SEA XX PARTY INCLUDED CAPT EDDIE RICKENBACKER OO CHESTERFIELDS." Students were fascinated with the sender and receiver call names, "PepsiCola" and "Chesterfields." This message also had another name—"Rickenbacker."

The answer came back 220440, "YOUR 220150 FIVE PLANES WILL COMPLY XX TAKE OFF AT ONE SIX THIRTY ZED XX ONE PREP BAKER MIKE PLUS FOUR ROGER FOUR DOGS ALL PLANES WILL LAND CANTON ON COMPLETION SEARCH." On October 22 at 0440, Palmyra answered the radio message sent from Canton earlier. The message seemed to refer to one kind of plane, plus four other planes. But what was a "Roger Four Dog"? Sixth graders had a reference they often poured over in the reading corner. Once when Captain Cherry came back for a school visit, he had slipped me a fifty-dollar bill and asked that I buy something for the class. I had used the money to purchase an extensive book on airplanes of World War II. Now this reference indicated one of the five planes was a PBM, a seven or eight seat patrol flying boat, and four were R4Ds (referenced Roger Four Dogs), larger cargo/transport planes.

Planes from Canton and Palmyra were scrambling to search, but it was a large ocean. One early communication (220330) from Ellsworth at Canton seemed to cover the entire Pacific Ocean. "SAD NEWS. CO (Commanding Officers)—NANDI, SUVA, NEW CALEDONIA NOTIFY ALL NORTH BOUND STOP EMMONS AND CINCPAC NOTIFY ALL SOUTHBOUND STOP ALL PLANES AND SHIPS TO KEEP SHARP LOOKOUT FOR LIFE RAFTS FROM BAKER SEVENTEEN PLANE DOWN AT SEA TWO TWO ZERO ONE THREE ZERO LAST BEARING TWO TWO SEVEN FROM PALMYRA XX ELLSWORTH XX POSITION UNKNOWN X PARTY INCLUDED CAPTAIN EDDIE RICKENBACKER PERSONAL REPRESENTATIVE OF SECRETARY OF WAR EE GOOD LUCK."

Then Emmons in Hawaii sent a message (220652) to the command at Canton, "HOPE FOR BEST STOP OMIT IN FUTURE RADIOS ANY REFERENCE BY NAME TO PASSENGERS ON BAKER SEVENTEEN THAT IS DOWN AT SEA STOP SEC'Y WAR DIRECTS NO PUBLICITY BE RELEASED REGARDING THIS MISSION STOP HAVE YOU ANY FURTHER INFORMATION STOP KEEP US INFORMED STOP TEN NAVY PLANES WILL ARRIVE IN AREA TOMORROW TO ASSIST IN SEARCH."

Nobody knew exactly where Flight OV-369 went down. Radio communications continued to say, "best guess—repeat—best guess." In the diary of events put together at Canton on October 25, it was recorded that at first the location of the downed aircraft was possibly at 168° 17' W, 0°24' N, so the initial search by one Liberator-type plane and five C-47s was concentrated between Canton and Palmyra. That decision suggested that the plane went down northeast of Canton. (Ellice Islands were southwest of Canton.)

Radiogram 230335 read, "MATCHES VV SAN BERNARDINO AND PETER BURNETT DEPARTED TWO TWO TWO ONE ZERO ZERO ON SURFACE SEARCH TOWARDS PALMYRA UNTIL WEST OF XMAS THEN DIRECT TO XMAS QQ PEANUTS" Sixth graders read the call signs for the radio operators, and though we didn't know who they were, at least students appreciated the names "Matches" and "Peanuts." We knew no way to track these people down, or the sixth graders would have tried! In language arts classes, we often talked about "context clues" and the analysis that could be done based on clues given in a written passage. In this message, "west of Xmas" obviously did not refer to a December event, but to a location. Students quickly located Christmas Island in our room atlas and on our world globe. Although the message sounded like both a ship and a person left on a surface search, our class reference on U.S. ships indicated the *San Bernardino* (PG-59) was a patrol gunboat, and *Peter Burnett* (IX-104) was an unclassified miscellaneous auxiliary ship.

Not only was it imperative to send planes to the right area, it was a monumental task to get fuel where it was needed. One message said, "Gas all planes for Canton to capacity. Acute gasoline shortage here." Another message (230320) read, "Radios requesting info on date of arrival on gas unanswered…Search for lost B-17 will exhaust supply in forty-eight hours. Request immediate reply."

On October 25, 1942, the Headquarters Holly Defense Command put together a "Diary of Events Connected with the Loss of B-17 Airplane, Flight OV-369." Along with this summary, we obtained search diagrams that were compiled by the military.

By the afternoon of October 22, all available aircrafts from Canton, except fighters, were sent to search in what was documented as Search Diagram No. 1. For the last two hours or so before contact with the plane was lost, Palmyra's bearings on it had been within one or two degrees of 228. When asked how accurate those bearings were on the B-17, Palmyra answered, "Bearings considered fair with maximum error two degrees… Relative strength of signals indicated plane southwest of Canton." A decision was then made to have four other C-47s search southwest from Canton, along the same axis. These planes flew a night search, flying at twenty-five mile distances, sweeping the area lying along and north of the 228 bearing line from Canton and a distance of 600 miles to Ellice Islands, then closing to five miles apart and returning in daylight to Canton, sweeping a new strip adjacent to their night strip.

Then fourteen C-47s or D-4s, two PBY-5As, and one PBM-3 (Pan

American Airways) swept the same area. "The fourteen C-47 airplanes, en route to the south broke off at the Ellice Islands and made a dog leg to Nandi [Fiji]. The seaplanes returned on reciprocal courses to Canton completely finishing the double coverage of the area shown on Search Diagram No. 2. Results of search: negative."

On October 24 bad weather conditions limited visibility. No further searches were made. However, a radio message indicated a possibility that the airplane might have gone down within 200 miles of Wallis Island, which was about halfway between Canton and Fiji, southeast of the Ellice Islands.

A recorded Search Diagram No. 3 illustrated a plan for seven PGY-5As and three Catalinas in transit to sweep a 100-mile wide strip from Canton southwestward to Nandi and Suva on bearing 213 degrees from Canton. Then six remaining PBY-5As were to return to Canton "sweeping a section sixty miles wide adjacent to the strip searched on the southbound trip." A corner note referred to three B-24s and seven PBY-5As—"Area search: 225,000 square miles; distance flown: 15,000 miles." It was a large ocean and a small downed plane.

In May 1993 we received a letter from Ira Southern from Princeton, West Virginia. His World War II buddy, Jack Boyd, had asked that he write to us and share his part in the rescue of the men. Jack Boyd was a member of the Naval Construction Battalion and had ended up on Funafuti in April 1943, as part of a reinforcement group for the Seabees. He had written to us from Bluefield, West Virginia. Ira Southern and Jack Boyd had become friends after travelling halfway around the world and finding they both came from neighboring towns in the same state.

Mr. Southern had been stationed at Hickam Field, Territory of Hawaii, when Eddie Rickenbacker had arrived there in October 1942. Ira Southern was a member of the 19th Troop Carrier Squadron, 7th Air Force, South and Central Pacific and told us he often had the honor of flying dignitaries through the Pacific region.

As part of the search for the lost plane, he had been dispatched to Canton via Palmyra Island. He was flying co-pilot on a C-47, but he was by training a flight engineer. He explained that flight crews were in short supply in the early part of the war, so he had been assigned as co-pilot. When the C-47 arrived at Canton, they began to search. Mr. Southern described how they flew what was called the wagon-wheel search method. Starting at the hub, in this case Canton, they flew out one spoke of the wheel, then flew the gap over to the next spoke, and finally returned to base on a second spoke, and so on. The total search from hub to rim was about 250 miles, so they each covered over 500 miles with this method. We knew about his search. We had a diagram of it.

Mr. Southern also shared with the students the vastness of the Pacific Ocean, explaining that the flight from Hickam to Canton could be ten to twelve hours, depending on headwinds, tailwinds, or crosswinds. He also mentioned, "The Pacific is supposed to be the 'Quiet One'—but its storms are violent and deadly."

Then he wrote to us something that put a personal touch on all the military reports we had been reading, "We flew this method day after day until the search was called off and Rickenbacker was given up as lost. I used binoculars during the search until my eyebrows and facial surfaces became sore from the continued contact."

A couple months later Mr. Southern wrote to me again. He was worried because Ames, Iowa, had been involved in the "Floods of '93" and he was concerned about us. He added, "Nature has a way of letting us know how trivial we are to the universe. I feared the Japanese as an enemy, but I feared the weather most while flying in the Pacific."

Years earlier, in July 1987, after the *Reader's Digest* article was published, I had received a letter from Raymond M. Coveney of Marlboro, Massachusetts. He wrote that at the time Captain Cherry was still in the air, he was a navigator on a C-47 (DC3) called *Full House*, flying from Christmas Island to Canton Island. When they landed at Canton still in daylight, they were briefed, refueled, and sent up to search. All twelve planes in their 33rd Troop Carrier Squadron were involved. He wrote, "In our briefing before takeoff, we navigators were told by the Marine Captain, who was the island commander, that the B-17 radio compass was 'out' and so not usable to 'home in' on Canton's radio signal."

Then Mr. Coveney shared, "Our planes flew two separate patterns that first day, and on the second day started out at 3 a.m. local time looking for flares. After the first search on that second day, two of our planes stayed on the ground for repairs, while the others refueled and tried again, without success. On the third day at 7 a.m. we left for our next stop in the Fiji Islands and were told that other planes were taking up the search from other bases."

After an Associated Press article appeared about the Rescue Reunion, we received a letter from Capt. Elton L Knapp, USN (Ret.), from Indianapolis, Indiana. The mention of Eddie Rickenbacker in the article had caught his eye, and Capt. Knapp checked his flight logs from many years ago. In 1942 he was a Senior in Charge of patrol plane pilots for a Navy Patrol Squadron, VP-14. He was flying PBY-5As (Catalinas) out of Kaneohe Bay in Hawaii, mainly doing Hawaiian patrol. His search sector included about 700 miles out and back for twelve to fourteen hour flights.

In one letter Knapp wrote, "By the way, in those days it was easy to miss an island after flying over one thousand miles of ocean with no check points or radar or radio beams. Patrolling out of Palmyra I missed the small atoll a couple of times—hidden in a rainsquall—and had to search a little."

When the B-17 was lost, the Navy organized a search with two planes from three different squadrons, for a total of six search planes. Captain Knapp then had left Hawaii for an 8.7 hour flight to Palmyra. The next day, October 23, he flew another 6.9 hours to Canton where they started their organized search for the downed crew.

In May 1985 Captain Knapp sent us a copy of his flight log for October 1942. On the 24th and 25th of October he flew airplane PBY-5A, No. 08036 for JLXU. He explained that the last was code for the character of the flight, JLX meant patrolling, but he could not remember what the "U" stood for. As the command pilot, he had a co-pilot and a pilot navigator with him. The first day he flew 10.1 hours, and the second day he flew 11.0 hours in his "Search for Capt. Rickenbacker."

Finally, he wrote, "Apparently we had meager—wrong—info that the B-17 ditched to the northwest of Canton. We obviously were wrong and with the Japs in the Gilberts we were told to stop the search."

His diary of October 25 summarized what the command at Canton had already hinted: "If results are still negative and unless further

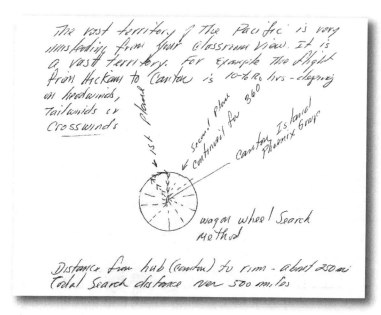

Elton Knapp drew a diagram of the wagon wheel search he conducted to find the lost men.

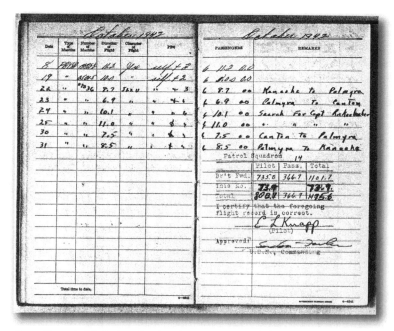

Elton Knapp's Flight Log for October 1942 recorded his search for Capt. Eddie Rickenbacker.

On October 24, 1942, the Commanding Officer at Canton sent this message. (*Courtesy National Archives*)

information is available, consideration will be given to recommending abandonment of the search." Many of the radiograms ended with "Results of Search: Negative." It was now assumed, not that the crew was just lost—but that we had lost the crew.

Chapter Twenty

THE RAFTS

FTER THE RESCUE REUNION, WE RECEIVED a letter from Katherine M. Michaelsen of Minneapolis, Minnesota. She wrote that a member of her family, the late Harold Ulrik Sverdrup, had played a role in the search for the men. Dr. Sverdrup had been a Norwegian scientist on the staff of Scripps Institute of Oceanography at La Jolla, California.

Within twelve minutes after the last radio contact with the plane, a message was sent to Wallis Island that said in part, "Request you immediately search area…inform us full radar position from Wallis of unidentified plane, direction of flight of plane until radar contact lost-also your estimate of drift of rubber life rafts that area…"

Although we tried, we were never able to obtain any specific records of ocean currents. Evidently, the military had not found anything useful, because the men had obviously drifted, what some estimated to be, over 500 miles.

The men had been adrift on three life rafts, strung together with rope Rickenbacker had brought from the plane. We knew from descriptions by the men and old newspaper photos that the rafts were not luxurious, but in our eyes, they had served their purpose well.

Whittaker described the outside dimensions of the larger raft, as four by seven feet. With the inflated gunwales, the inside measurement was about two and a half feet by five and a half feet. John Bartek had listed the inside dimensions as two feet four inches by six feet nine inches. Any way you view it, even the larger raft was very crowded to have three men in the confined space for three weeks—during rainsqualls, large wave action, and shark movement.

The raft that Captain Cherry was rescued in was much, much smaller. Whittaker had written how originally DeAngelis and Kaczmarczyk were in the little raft they called "the doughnut." Students thought of it as the size of an inner tube they would take to a swimming pool. To keep from falling out, two men had to sit facing each other, placing their legs over the other person's shoulders. At school we usually marked off this space on our tiled classroom floor and had two boys demonstrate how awkward and uncomfortable this would be. After they sat in this position as I read the description from The Book, the boys always complained how cramped their legs were. Then we discussed how the men endured the discomfort during the night as well as the day; there was no period of relief. Students always sobered at that fact.

When the men visited Meeker Elementary, they also described the rafts, emphasizing how small they were. Bill Cherry explained that the rafts that held three people were officially known as the "five-man" rafts. They were based on weight. To test them, a 1,000-pound weight had been lowered onto the raft. As Cherry clarified, "The weight could be lead, but it can't be five men. No way!"

Captain Cherry shared other limitations of the rafts besides their size. Whittaker had written about the men sitting in water in the bottom of the rafts. Cherry explained that if the raft seats were used, the center of gravity was so high that waves would overturn the raft. In addition, salt water that was always present also moistened the adhesive that fastened the first-aid kit to the floor. These materials chafed their bodies as they tried to sleep on the bottom of the raft.

Sixth graders pictured the men on the raft from their mental images created from Whittaker's writing. They could visualize how Captain Cherry's undershirt had been attached to an oar. With one man leaning against the oar in the raft, they had a makeshift mast and sail. They knew Captain Cherry had been sleeping with his head on the side of the raft when the tail of a large shark, presumably cleaning barnacles off its back,

Military personnel on Funafuti inspected two of the three rafts used by the men. Captain Cherry was rescued in the smaller one they called "the doughnut." (*Courtesy National Archives*)

hit him square in the nose. As Jim Reynolds described it, "I thought we never would get the bleeding to stop."

Students also knew of Captain Cherry's tangle with a two-foot shark. Although he did not have bait, the young shark took the barb. The men hauled it into the rafts, and Captain Cherry used his knife to capture it. In doing so, a small slit was made in the bottom of the life raft. Salt water had moistened the glue on the patching material, and the rubber cement material evaporated and would not stick to the raft. They had used a bullet from his rusted revolver to plug the hole.

But when the men came to Ames, Bill Cherry described vividly his scariest time in the rafts. He said, "We had quite a storm. Wind blowing about fifty miles per hour. Salt spray was ruining any rainwater we could catch. Waves looked like a mountain. It was very scary. It was probably a tropical disturbance—up to sixty miles per hour. We decided to get smart and sit up on the side of the boat and hold a cloth above our heads to catch more rainwater. Black night. Could not see. I had my Mae West over my left shoulder and about a third full. My life vest was not inflated. Whittaker could not swim, so his life vest was inflated. The raft turned over. I came up holding the water under the boat. Jim did, too. Whittaker came up out of the boat. I tried to turn the boat over." Then Captain Cherry expressed his frustration of working so hard to right the raft, hang on to the water, and keep Whittaker from drowning—all in the midst of a tropical disturbance. Some days are tough and some are really tough.

Goodyear Tire and Rubber Company in Akron, Ohio, had made the rafts. The two larger rafts were known as type A-2 rafts, and the smaller one was a type B-3 raft. Numbers stamped on the rafts identified assembly-line workers who had produced them. Following the rescue of the men, much publicity had been given to the raft-builders. In summer 1991, we obtained two photographs from the National Archives in Washington, D.C., identifying the four people who had helped build the rescue rafts. These factory workers were: Kay E. Thompson, Robert S. Barnhart, Elmer K. Brown, and Flossie Anson.

By the 1991-92 school year, a group of sixth graders was determined to find the raft-builders. Using phone directories from the Akron area, students wrote dozens of letters to all people with the same last name. If letters were returned stamped that no one by that name was at that address, students wrote to "People in Residence" at the address, requesting their assistance.

One of our many letters was sent to a man at the correct street address, but the wrong town. A postal worker caught the mistake and sent the letter on. The man was not related to one of the raft-builders, but he was interested and wanted to help. He suggested we contact the Goodyear Company, and he provided us with an address and phone numbers for their personnel department and corporate headquarters.

By the following school year, we still did not have contacts, but this group of sixth graders wanted to continue the search. The investigative summary I provided to the new group was five pages long. Instead of trying phone numbers and addresses, this group decided to try libraries and newspapers. Students wrote to the Hudson Library and Historical Society. The archivist wrote back that Hudson was about fourteen miles north of Akron, and although in the same county, he did not have detailed records of Akron residents. He forwarded our letter to the Akron-Summit County Public Library's local history department where that librarian had another suggestion. She provided an address for the Summit County Genealogical Society and suggested we ask a woman there to check the ancestor charts she had.

In the meantime, other sixth graders had written to the Barberton Public Library in Akron, Ohio. Mrs. Phyllis Taylor, the Barberton History Specialist at that facility, had another idea. She sent a copy of our letter to a journalist at the *Akron Beacon Journal*, telling us that a column would reach many more people than she could contact individually. In Fran Murphey's column on February 5, 1993, she ran portions of the students' letter. "We are very interested in finding the people who worked on the assembly line and made these rafts. The National Archives sent us pictures and identified the people. Is there any way you can help us find out if they or their relatives are still living in Akron?" After a list of the students' names, our school phone number was given for a place of contact.

Three days after the column ran in the newspaper, we received a call at school at 9:40 a.m. Lori Rossi from Akron had read the newspaper article and called to tell us that she had lived across the street from Elmer K. Brown, one of the raft-builders. He had passed away a year ago, but she could provide us with the address and phone number of his daughter, Doris Simmons.

We soon heard from Doris who wrote, "I was so pleased to hear from you. Thank you for your interest in my father." She told us she was four-years-old when her father had helped build the raft. They had moved to Providence, Rhode Island, when she was eight, so her father could help open a new Goodyear facility. She only knew of the incident from family stories and articles shared over the years. Her father, Elmer, had later built a replica of a plane that is now in the Smithsonian Institute. When he retired, he wrote poetry, and Doris sent us a book of his inspirational poems.

She also told us that at age eighty-seven her father had remarried a family friend whose husband had also worked at Goodyear before he passed away. She thought we might like to write to this person, Kathy Brown, and included an address for us. Students then wrote to Kathy Brown, who shared more with us, including one of Elmer's poems that had been put to music.

Working through the Goodyear Company, we did attempt to contact other factory workers and did find some relatives. The raft-builders were a special part of our research. The rafts were an essential part of the rescue. With all their limitations, the rafts had kept the men alive on the endless waves of the Pacific Ocean.

Thousands of stories exist of rescue and survival during World War II. With this particular rescue, many people who were involved told us that it was a memorable, but small event, in their total war effort. Yet, because Eddie Rickenbacker was famous and the media coverage was so extensive, this story was remembered. People wrote to us who had gathered around radio broadcasts and poured over news accounts. They recalled the moment when they heard the news that Rickenbacker had been rescued at sea.

From the 1942 "Air Transport Command in the Pacific" document the Air Force had sent us, the men's time in the rafts provided invaluable information to the military. The report summarized it this way, "The entire affair brought a great deal of publicity to the South Pacific Wing. In addition and of considerably greater importance, it taught Wing Headquarters a great many valuable lessons about the proper procedures of airplane ditching, the emergency equipment that overwater aircraft should carry, and the all-around technique of survival at sea."

According to one document sent to us, the Air Transport Command at

Hamilton Field in California had interviewed four of the survivors. Since Cherry, DeAngelis, Whittaker, and Bartek had actually "tested" the emergency provisions and life rafts, their input was important to the War Department in preparing emergency materials for future use. (One document mentioned that Jim Reynolds was not interviewed because he was too ill.)

We knew from copies of Whittaker's journal that within a few hours of being in the rafts, the men were recording suggestions, "We think all life rafts should have food and water as well as M.O. set." Food, water, emergency-signaling device — these three things were essential for survival and rescue. The men had specific suggestions.

In January 1943 a conference was held on the state of life rafts and emergency equipment. Bill Cherry provided input to members of the Engineering Division of the Materiel Center for the Army Air Forces. One of the main points he made was "that technical instructions be issued to crews operating airplanes over water, outlining procedure to follow in the event of a water landing, and that crew drills be initiated and the importance of such drills be emphasized."

A copy of the Army Air Forces Survival brochure used at the time of the men's rescue listed many tips of things to do and not to do. The section categorized "At Sea" was of particular interest to us. Even sixth graders recognized how different the men's survival was because of their lack of food, water, survival kits, and emergency equipment mentioned in the manual. The men's two goals—survival and rescue—were both hampered because the emergency rations, which were supposed to be included in all the rafts, were missing.

When the men ditched the B-17 in the Pacific, they had no idea that the plane would float as long as it did. Thinking that their rafts would be overturned by the vortex of the sinking plane, the men left in such haste that some emergency equipment and water was left behind.

Bill Cherry recommended that if time-permitted during a ditched landing, all food supplies and the radio transmitter should be taken from the cabin, and all emergency equipment, such as knives, should be retrieved from remaining parachute jungle kits. He specifically suggested taking canvas material, such as seat cushions, that could be used as protection from the sun during the day and as a cover for warmth at night.

Research tests were already being done on shoulder holsters for pilots, parachutes, rubber life suits, life vests, and rafts. Although the men survived in rectangular-shaped rafts, water ballasts (round objects) were considered promising as more stable vessels, so they would not overturn so easily in an ocean environment. Besides the rafts, other survival issues included over-all procedures and materials, techniques for obtaining food and water, and how to help facilitate a rescue.

A document sent to us from the National Archives indicated that one corrective measure was to attach emergency kits to the rafts, so they could not separate. Another document referred to investigations as to whether a darker color oar for the life rafts would less likely attract sharks. Three separate groups, including one at Wright Field, were working on a crash manual. (I personally preferred that the reference be called *survivor manual!*)

Suggestions also included other supplies, such as a hand pump with hose, forty feet of seventy-five pound test cotton cord, rings to hang equipment onto the raft, patching repair kits that would withstand salt-water and heat, flashlights, sunshades, and camouflage cloths. The men could have used a signal mirror, cans of fluorescein dye, and floating smoke candles, which might be better for day signaling. Everything needed to be waterproof—compass, flashlight, charts, and even flares. Bill Cherry suggested making the Very pistols out of brass, so they would not rust.

There was the need for more knives, possibly a solar still or other water-producing device, and extra bailing pails. The men had a pail, but they could not use it for bailing during a rainsquall and also a water storage facility at the same time. The men had devised a method of catching rainwater in their mouths and then expectorating it into their rubber life vests. Bill Cherry reported that a larger opening on the life vest would have facilitated this.

The men suggested food tablets, K-rations, and cans of water be contained in the emergency kits. Equipment also needed to be included for them to gather food and water for themselves. Fish lines and hooks should have been in the survival kits, but the lines were too lightweight and the hooks too small for ocean fishing. These had been developed for stream fishing—fine for trout, but not for fish in the Pacific. They also could have used bait, a fish spear, and net. Bill Cherry recommended a harpoon be attached to an oar as part of the survival equipment.

Of course, the men wished for an emergency radio transmitter. These suggestions led the military to test kits that would serve two purposes—give a distress signal and be a focal point used to get bearings.

All these items would help survival, but they also provided much added weight to airplanes. Both military groups and private companies went to work to test ideas and provide the best materials for future pilots and their crews. I wonder how many lives were saved because ideas were turned into products, and those items were available to other men and women who had to survive a "raft adventure."

Before the men came for the Rescue Reunion, John Bartek sent us an article from the *Freehold Transcript* from 1942, which told of a souvenir John had been given at the U.S. Naval Mobile Base Hospital No. 3, where he had been taken. Years later, John also sent us a color reproduction of the certificate entitled, "Ancient Order of the Deep" showing his membership, "having been duly initiated into the solemn mysteries in the order, having crossed the equator aboard the S.S. *Rickenbacker*." We wondered if our men were the only ones who had accomplished this in a raft!

When the survivors visited us at Meeker Elementary and highlighted their story, I asked the men, "What do you have to share with us about being on the rafts?"

To the delight of the sixth grade audience, Captain Cherry laughingly advised, "Just don't do it!"

Chapter Twenty-One

_____

THE RESCUES

E ACH OF THE THREE RAFTS HAD A SEPARATE RESCUE, and one man from
each of those rafts and two of their rescuers attended our class's
Rescue Reunion in April 1985. From transcribed tapes of that visit, we
have the men's recollections of the 1942 rescues. We also had
documentation from native islanders, coastwatchers from New Zealand,
written logs from planes and ships, and eyewitness accounts by other
rescuers. But after forty years, what did these men remember about their
ordeal?

When Captain Cherry cut loose in the small raft alone, his reasoning
was for the rafts to be in more places at one time. He also personally
stated very matter-of-factly to me, "Mrs. Kelly, I'd just as soon die by
myself as with the other guys. If I was going to die, it didn't matter
where." The men had observed the planes flying over, too high for them
to be seen, but in formation, indicating it was a regular patrol. Before
Captain Cherry untied the raft, he gave his knife to Jim Whittaker and
then began drifting away.

What little water he had, he finished by the end of the twentieth day.
There was no rain. He said, "That night I was in my quarters in my 'little
bedroom' on the raft, and found myself talking to the waves and the
waves were talking back, '*Bale the water out. Bale the water out.*'"

Then Captain Cherry told us, "On the 21st day, around noon, I was
pretty dry and my sores were hurting like mad." He had sores like boils,
called saltwater ulcers, all over his bottom, on his legs and hands. "So I
decided to take a swim. I wanted to wash them out. I stripped off nude,

was able to climb overboard, swam around with the sharks for a while, and came back."

By then he was so weak that it took him, what he guessed to be, about thirty to forty minutes to climb back into the raft. He did not think he was going to make it, so immediately he decided that was going to be the last time he left the raft. He was so weak when he climbed back in, before he put his clothes on, he lay down and dozed for a while. "I was awakened by the plane coming. He was coming straight toward me and I was a little to his right. I was naked as a bird, so I started waving my underwear, hollering, and croaking like a frog. I had an oar, and I'm waving it. Only five feet high or so, they went on by me, and I thought, *D——, criminy. Land!* They went out about half a mile or so, they started turning, and came back."

Captain Cherry continued, "They circled me for about ten minutes. I thought, *Maybe they think this is a gun.* So I threw the oar away." Then he laughed at the idea and said, "That didn't get him down."

He then admitted he thought that it was a Japanese plane and the pilot was just going to leave him out there and let him die. He did reason that from the type of airplane they were flying, he was near a land base. So, he began putting on his clothes again.

Les Boutte, the Kingfisher radioman, recalled what happened from his perspective in that patrol plane. He told how they had heard the Rickenbacker party had gone down near Canton, several hundred miles away, so they were not told to have any special lookout for this group. Boutte said, "My job as an observer, rear seat gunner, was to sit in the seat facing aft and to observe the water and horizon at all times, looking for signs of submarines, surface craft, or anything of that sort."

On that particular afternoon November 11, 1942, Boutte had launched with pilot Fred Woodward on their normal afternoon patrol. After travelling forty-five miles or so, Boutte saw a yellow object go by on the surface. Les Boutte shared, "So I called the pilot on the intercom. I told him what I had observed. He immediately made a left descending turn. We came within five feet of the water. We buzzed over Captain Cherry's head. We had radio silence, so we dropped a smoke flare near the raft, and we flew back to Funafuti." Still in condition of radio silence, because they were considered a forward area as far as the Japanese, they flew back to the island and dropped a note, giving the bearing and distance the raft was from the base. Then they went back and stuck around awhile, waiting for a PT boat to go out and pick up the pilot of the B-17.

Bill Cherry continued his recollection, telling us that not very long after that—possibly forty minutes at the most—the plane came back, this time off to one side, not over him. It had continued circling and circling over him. Then he looked up where the plane had come from and saw a ship appearing over the horizon. Bill said, "I thought it was a Japanese battleship. I thought, *I don't mind. I'll work in the mines. I'll work in the salt mines. It won't bother me at all! Just pick me up and give me water!*"

As the ship kept coming, the airplane backed off. At about ten feet from the raft, they cut the ship's engines of what he thought was an enemy battleship. Hands reached down in the water and pulled him out. Captain Cherry recalls asking who they were and then being confused when they spoke English. He told them, "I'm Captain William T. Cherry, U.S. Air Force, 03-80-222," like he had been taught to say. When they identified themselves as a PT boat with the U.S. Navy, he said he replied, "Boy, I'm sure glad to see the Navy!"

When he explained there were two more rafts out there with sick men in them, the officer of the patrol boat asked, "Would you mind if we pick up the speed, because we have an unmarked lagoon to go into, and it's going to be dark when we get back in there." Captain Cherry told them he was ready "to see some water go by me," so they kicked in all three engines.

Captain Cherry laughed, "You haven't lived until you've been in a PT boat with three full engines going!" Lying on his back on blankets, he could not breathe and had to ask them to slow a little. He drank half a cup of water, then half a cup of soup—and wanted more.

After entering the lagoon and being transferred to the sickbay of the USS *Hilo*, they fed him a couple of ounces at a time. Then Captain Cherry said, "The more they gave me, the thirstier I got, and the more delirious I got. Somewhere I got the idea that this doctor was trying to kill me, so I thought I would just play dead, not move at all, and he'd leave me alone."

But Dr. Garrity had said, "Son, I'm trying to save you. Don't worry. I'm going to take care of you."

Then Bill Cherry related how there was an electrical storm the night he was aboard the ship. He recalled the lights were off, but there was flashing light coming through the portholes. Early the next morning, they put him on some kind of small boat to go ashore and then into a brand new little hospital. He remembered how he went to bed, and the bed rocked. Bill added, "It did not stop rocking for the next two days!"

He also told about a kid waiting on him...McAuliffe...just a young kid. (This was the same medical corpsman from Massachusetts who had written to us about mosquito netting and pet lizards.) Captain Cherry recalled, "I said, 'Just give me a little more water. I need more.'"

McAuliffe said, "Captain, they're going to shoot me." Captain Cherry grinned at the sixth graders when he added, "He slipped me an extra shot of water!"

In the meantime, there were three other men on a raft, who also needed water. John Bartek recalled that after Captain Cherry left and the other raft cut loose, their raft drifted. He was worried about where the others were going. While afloat, they saw four planes, about 1,000 feet high. John told how he prayed that the planes would come back. One did. When the raft was spotted, the plane began circling, and he wondered why it did not drop food. He then admitted that they were so weak, they would have drowned going overboard to get it. But off to the side a big storm was coming through, and the plane left.

John had no way of knowing that the Kingfisher pilots were about out of fuel, could not have landed in the conditions of the sea, and certainly could not have picked up three passengers and flown them back to base.

John described how during this time Eddie Rickenbacker made him work very hard to catch more rainwater, insisting they needed the water in case they were not picked up. They caught about two quarts of fresh water. About a half hour after the storm passed, the plane came back and circled again. It started getting dark, and they dropped a few flares. The plane came down at dusk for a landing.

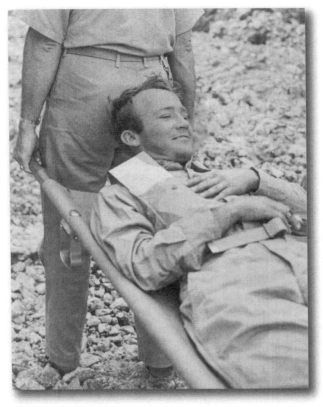

Captain Cherry was carried on a stretcher in November, 1942, after his rescue. (*Courtesy National Archives*)

Les Boutte, the Kingfisher radioman who attended our Rescue Reunion, was also involved in the rescue of this raft. He recalled that after spotting a man in the first raft, he had gone back to a native hut where he lived on the base. About 9:00 p.m. Bill Eadie, his officer in charge, came by. Lieutenant Eadie told him that the pilot of the plane Boutte spotted had been the pilot of the plane that Rickenbacker had been on, and that Captain Cherry said there were two more rafts out there. "Tomorrow morning we're going to launch all aircraft at daylight," Eadie had said, "and search as long as we have to, until we find them. You'll be flying with me."

Les Boutte then recalled that he flew three different patrols that day, including dropping a message on Nukufetau, asking they search the small islands of the atoll. Late that afternoon he had returned to base and learned that another raft had been sighted. One aircraft had stayed on the scene to cover them, while others flew back to refuel their aircraft and fly back out again. We later knew more details of this part of the story from our correspondence with other men from the Navy Scouting Squadron.

Next, Les Boutte shared, "I went to the CB kitchen and filled two canteens with water and one canteen with hot soup." They took off again, "landing in the open sea, just about dark, with pretty good ground swells and big troughs."

Describing Lieutenant Eadie as "an excellent pilot," Les Boutte told how they taxied around and lined up so they could taxi into the wind to the raft. Using the raft like they normally used a buoy to be tied up, the pilot judged his distance and speed to the raft, so when he cut his engine, the radioman could freely move on the float. Without being hit by the propeller, he reached down to tie the line that rimmed the life raft, catching it as it came by. Les Boutte secured the raft to the airplane.

He then told how Rickenbacker had stood up in the raft very feebly, put his hands on the plane, praising God. He then said, "I'd like to introduce these gentlemen. I'm Captain Eddie Rickenbacker, this is Colonel Adamson, and this is Private Bartek."

Boutte continued his story. "I had never stood in a raft before. The bottom was rubber. When you stand in it, it sinks on you." He described how he got into the raft and began hoisting the men out. Starting with Colonel Adamson, whom he described as being in "pretty bad shape," Boutte lifted him up wing height where Eadie could get his hands on his shoulder. "We put Colonel Adamson in the rear cockpit seat due to his back injury. We put Rickenbacker and Bartek on each side of the cockpit, with their legs hanging over the leading edge of the wing."

When John Bartek shared his part of the story, he recalled them putting him on the right wing and telling him to sit there. He mostly remembered wanting food. The sixth graders had a question answered. John Bartek had been strapped to the right wing of the plane and Eddie Rickenbacker had been placed on the left wing!

Les Boutte recalled, "I got a piece of anchor line from the airplane and tied them together through the cockpit. We gave each of them a little bit of water and soup—not much—and I stood on the wing in back of Bartek." With Les Boutte holding each of them by the collar, Lieutenant Eadie started the engine again, and they began taxiing back to the base. They had not taxied very long—about fifteen minutes—when they encountered a PT boat and again shut their engines down.

Bill Wepner, who had been on PT Boat #26, came to the Rescue Reunion from Wisconsin. When he shared with the students, he told how they left early in the morning to search by surface craft, at the same time Les Boutte was searching by plane. Bill Wepner said, "We had four boats in our division. Each boat had a certain area to cover. We did ground search. We couldn't see too far, because we weren't too big, and didn't stick up too far out of the water. We would cover our area, go back and forth, back and forth, and then go to another area."

Then he continued, "Late in the afternoon we got a radio message from the *Hilo*, which was our tender. We were the boat that was the closest, so we took off at full throttle. We travelled about forty-five miles to where the raft was. We learned a lot on that particular run. We found out our engines weren't as good as they were supposed to be. We had a lot of gaskets blown that afternoon." The students remembered the letter they had received from another crewmember, Ed Green, who had given so much credit to the men on the PT boat who had kept their engines going.

Bill Wepner continued, "The plane had its running lights on. That was the only way we would have found them. We didn't have any radar at that time. We had one spotlight and turned that on when we got close by. We communicated with the plane about the condition of the passengers and decided to take Bartek and Rickenbacker off."

Next, they transferred those two men back into the life raft, and Les Boutte swam with them over to the PT boat. Leaving the life raft there, he then swam back to the Kingfisher. Boutte described how sitting on the wing next to the cockpit he absorbed a great deal of salt water and spray that was constantly thrown back and up by the revolving propeller blades. They taxied forty-five miles back to base, about eight hours. He told how they stopped every half hour to give Colonel Adamson some coffee or something—not much—just encouraged him to keep going until they got back. He added, "Our engine was burned out. It was still running, but it was burned out."

Les Boutte summarized the experience. "We got back the next morning. I was so encrusted in salt water that my clothes just stood up straight. That was the last I ever saw any of these gentlemen," he said, as he gestured to John Bartek and Bill Wepner.

Bill Wepner continued with his recollections. "We got them aboard and made a place with mattresses for John up on the forward deck and covered him with blankets to keep him warm. We put Captain Rickenbacker down in the officers' quarters."

Bill added, "The plane followed in our wake. Our boat wasn't too wide—about fifteen feet wide—and flat-bottomed at the stern. By going through the water it left the water more smooth, and the plane stayed in that while they were taxiing. It wasn't that smooth, but it was a lot smoother than being away from us. That's how they taxied all the way back—for eight hours—behind us."

John Bartek grinned when Bill Wepner described how John had talked coherently all the way back to Funafuti. There the men were transferred to the little hospital.

Bill Wepner finished by saying, "That day we started out at five in the morning and didn't end up until three or four the next morning. That was one patrol I was glad I made."

The last survivors who were picked up by the military were those in the raft that landed on the island of Nukufetau. James W. Reynolds teased, "Out of all of us, I was the only one there. Maybe I should just make up something." We all laughed, but I remember thinking how the Super Sleuths would have been on the case!

Jim told how his raft with DeAngelis and Whittaker drifted a lot differently than it had been when it was tied to the other rafts. He explained that at this point they thought of things they wanted to see. So when Johnny DeAngelis happened to be facing the island and saw the palm trees, "Whittaker thought he was off his rocker."

Then Jim explained, "You don't row unless you have some place you want to go, because you'd just be wasting your strength." Although they all tried, only Whittaker, the oldest of the three, was able to row them into the lagoon and onto the windward side of the island. There was no sandy beach here, and the tide had gone out. But it had rained and left fresh water in some of the coral pockets. Jim said, "I stood up for thirty seconds, and it was the last I stood for thirty days. I had to learn to walk all over again."

They dragged the raft over to the other side of the island to a sandy beach and stayed on the leeside, or east side, of the island. They had found coconuts. And in the foliage, they found breadfruit—and lots of rats. One rat was so brave it just came right up and bit him on the finger. Then Jim announced to the audience, "I don't mean to offend anyone, but that rat tasted a lot better than any steak I've ever eaten." We understood, however, that Jim was in such a state of starvation, that his system could not have handled much.

Eventually the men were strong enough to move down the island where they found an old hut. There, they again replenished their supply of fresh water.

Then Jim described how he thought he was seeing things when Toma and the other native islanders arrived in an outrigger canoe with a banana palm sail. Jim recalled, "They could see we were dehydrated. I was lying flat on my back looking up. He had a rope made out of coconut husks, and wrapped it around his feet in a figure-eight configuration and jackknifed up the tree, knocking down three green coconuts. When he came down, he just let go and slid down."

Jim explained that in green coconuts the meat is soft, not hard like we are used to, and you can just scoop it out with your fingers. The insides

John DeAngelis (*rear*) and James Whittaker were transferred by motor launch, probably going from the USS *Hilo* that picked them up on Nukufetau and took them to the field hospital on Funafuti, Ellice Islands. (*Courtesy Auburn University Libraries Special Collections and Archives*)

had water, or coconut milk, which was the first sugar they had. He told how the natives fed it to them gradually.

Then the islanders took them over to the village on Nukufetau. This was near where the New Zealand coastwatchers were stationed. Jim told how they had a thatched hut that was open all around. The New Zealanders put them on cots there and cleaned them up. Jim said, "We had open sores that were caked with coral sand. It had dried like cement.

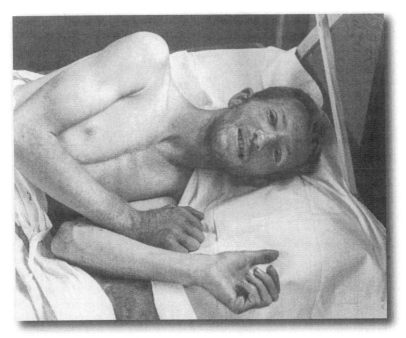

John Bartek shortly after his rescue. He suffered from sunburn, saltwater ulcers, dehydration, starvation, and exhaustion. (*Courtesy National Archives*)

The coastwatchers spent a lot of time cleaning these out." They also broke radio silence and called Funafuti.

The base flew Doc Hall in that night. Toma met the Kingfisher in his outrigger canoe and transported the doctor ashore.

When the survivors left the island, they were taken out to the USS *Hilo.* Jim remembered how Doc Hall stepped off the pontoon. "He stepped into water up to his neck—but he was holding the glucose saline solution over his head," Jim said. "Doc poured glucose into me."

Jim told us that the *Hilo* had been a yacht for Mr. Leeds, a tin millionaire, who sold it to the government for a dollar. The Navy had hung bunks off the wall, and Jim was given the "first bunk on the right."

When he was transferred to the little hospital on Funafuti, he remembered how the island natives came every day, visited, and brought him flowers. He stayed there about a month, eating soft-boiled eggs and ice cream. James W. Reynolds was the last raft survivor to leave the Ellice Islands.

Chapter Twenty-Two

GOOD-BYE, MOB-3

A S INJURIES OCCURRED DURING WARTIME, it was necessary to have a mobile hospital closer to the area where it was needed. Men could be treated there and given time to recuperate before they travelled back to the United States. MOB-3, a base Naval hospital, was at Tutuila in American Samoa. Because of various health issues, the raft survivors left the Ellice Islands at different times and were moved to MOB-3.

On November 15 John Bartek was in the field hospital at Funafuti and Jim Reynolds was in sickbay on the USS *Hilo*. However, the other five survivors had recovered sufficiently to be evacuated to Tutuila. At 0900 three PBY amphibian planes (Catalinas) left Ellice Islands for Tutuila via Wallis Island. Accompanying the survivors was Commander Durkin (MC), USNR.

A year after the *Reader's Digest* story, I received a letter at school. Charles Franklin Daniel from Kentucky, now staying in Winter Park, Florida, had picked up an old issue of the magazine and read our story. Mr. Daniel had been a U.S. Navy hospital corpsman at MOB-3 and had taken care of the men when they arrived there from the Ellice Islands. He was particularly involved with the care of Colonel Adamson, who had been seriously ill when rescued and then had developed some medical problems following his rescue.

In other phone calls and letters, Mr. Daniel helped us identify people in photographs we had collected, mainly from news clippings and archival sources. He also filled in the chronology for us.

Dr. John Durkin was chief of medicine at MOB-3 and carried most of the treatment load for the survivors. Dr. Steve Hudack was chief of surgery.

Homeward bound. *Left to right*: John Bartek, Bill Cherry, John DeAngelis, and James Whittaker. After leaving MOB-3 at Samoa, they stopped at Hickam Field in Hawaii before heading back to California. (*Courtesy Auburn University Libraries*)

According to Mr. Daniel, Pharmacist Mate 2c, Thomas J. Jones, was also heavily involved in the care of the men.

Dr. Hudack, two other corpsmen, and Charles Daniel were assigned to go to Funafuti to bring the survivors back to MOB-3. Mr. Daniel wrote of the shuffling around of personnel, and he was, what he called, a "last minute" choice. Going back to MOB-3, they took the survivors, Dr. Fuller, a war correspondent, and a photographer, making it very crowded in the PBY. The commanding officer was Capt. Robert P. Parsons.

Mr. Daniel wrote to us that after Dr. Fuller flew with the men to MOB-3 in Samoa, he stayed a few days until he could get a ride back to Funafuti. Mr. Daniel recalled that he did not see Dr. Fuller again until 1945 when they both were assigned to the USS *Rixey*, A.P.H. 3, a vessel fitted for the evacuation of the wounded, during the invasion of the Western Pacific. Mr. Daniel wrote, "He was a brave man and a brilliant surgeon and saved many lives. It was an honor to serve with him." This was Dr. Fuller, who had attended Kingfisher pilot Gaylord Forrest's wedding in Kentucky.

Colonel Adamson had to stay longer at MOB-3 than some of the others. Mr. Daniel recalled spending twelve hours a day with this very sick man, who was a mild diabetic and lacked food and water on the raft. Mr. Daniel wrote, "He [Adamson] was covered with boils when rescued and his blood chemistry was horrible. *He* was near death."

In his book, Rickenbacker wrote of his insistence to carry out the original request from the War Department. A report the Air Force sent to us said, "[Rickenbacker] was asked by Secretary of War Stimson to carry out an official survey of morale and aerial tactics in the Pacific combat theatre." Therefore, instead of coming back to the States when he had recuperated, Rickenbacker insisted on leaving Samoa and continuing on his original trip.

Sixth graders could only grasp at names in old newspaper articles and magazine pictures. In the *LIFE* magazine issue, students read Rickenbacker's account of recuperating at Tutuila and then proceeding with his mission for Secretary of War Stimson on December 1. He said, "The airplane was a Consolidated B-24 bomber, converted for transport duty. It had a crew of six, under Captain H. P. Luna…"

We had a name to start more research. We also had a report Henry Luna had written that had been sent to a sixth grader three years earlier by a researcher at he U.S. Air Force Historical Research Center. Captain Henry P. Luna, Air Corps, had prepared the report on December 29, 1942, from the Headquarters, Eleventh Ferrying Group, Army Air Forces, Air Transport Command, Hamilton Field, California.

When I talked with Jim Reynolds in January 1988, he related how Henry "Chick" Luna had taken a photo of him when he was first rescued. Jim laughed, "I had a beard a mile long!" Jim recalled that Luna had lived in San Francisco several years ago. Students were determined to track down H. P. Luna, not only to hear his story about the men, but to find the origin of that nickname "Chick."

Students used an atlas and had a list—San Francisco, Sausalito, Belvedere, San Bruno, Millbrae, Moss Beach, San Mateo, Los Altos— and they headed for the Ames Public Library after school to look at phone directories. When I returned to my classroom after a teacher's meeting on February 9, I found a note on my desk: "Mrs. Kelly, I found H P. and Virginia. No address. Phone number is…Bye!"

The next day I took two boys to the school office to make a phone call. One student asked in his follow-up letter to Colonel Luna if the class could have a photo of him to add to our research. The other sixth grader wrote, "I spoke with you on Wednesday, the 10th, about noon Pacific time. I was really excited about it and my twin brother was excited, too. I have an older sister also but she wasn't very excited about it. You're the first person that I've found since I got in sixth grade." I was more aware at this point, than ever, that students had accepted the letter writing and research as a part of their learning in my classroom and that finding someone was a special accomplishment.

It was nearly Valentine's Day, and the students decided Colonel and Mrs. Luna should receive some valentines in Atherton, California, in San Mateo County. Mrs. Virginia Luna wrote to me that her husband was busy looking through old military records to find something he thought would be of interest to the sixth graders. She also shared that Colonel Luna had a malignant brain tumor. Although his mind was clear, the tumor had slowed him down. She wanted the students to understand. Then she added that her grandmother had been born in Iowa and her great-uncle had served in the Iowa State Legislature. I felt very connected with this woman, who was linked to Iowa, cared for a family member with cancer, and liked my sixth graders.

Soon the students received letters from Mrs. Luna on behalf of her husband, Colonel Henry ("Chick") Paul Luna. He had graduated in Aeronautical Engineering from New York University, joined the Army Air Corps, and received flight training at both Randolph and Kelly Fields in Texas. In 1936 he began flying for American Airlines, before he was called to active duty.

Mrs. Luna's stories of the war added a different dimension to our understanding. She talked about rationing during the war. While being allowed four gallons of gas for the car per month, she pulled her son and daughter "a mile and a half to a store in a wagon in good weather, and on a sled in winter." She talked about saving fat for the government, raising a "Victory Garden," using coupons to purchase meat when it was available, and covering the windows at night for "blackouts." She closed her letter by letting us know she and her husband had been married for fifty-two years and, "We wish you as much happiness in your lifetime as we have had in ours."

Then in late March, Colonel Luna wrote to us himself. "After receiving twenty Valentine Day cards from your class we feel that you have made us a part of your class." He enclosed photos of himself in uniform and a picture of him and his wife, Virginia. The students were elated and immediately adopted the Lunas.

Colonel Luna shared that he was at Hamilton Field near San Francisco when the call came for him to fly a stripped-down B-24 bomber to American Samoa to fly Eddie Rickenbacker to complete the mission he was originally assigned. Colonel Luna wrote, "We landed in New Caledonia; Brisbane, Australia; Espiritu Santo [New Hebrides]; and a couple of others before heading for the States." In a personal note to me, he apologized for the typing errors. He explained that his illness affected his memory and coordination. Though the letter had been a struggle for him to write, it was a cherished item for us to receive.

Colonel Luna also sent us a "Narrative Report on Rickenbacker Trip" that contained more details about this trip with Rickenbacker from Samoa to other areas in the Pacific. On November 27, 1942, he had piloted a C-87, No. 608, which was conscripted from United Air Lines, from Hamilton Field in California to Hickam Field in Hawaii. Then his crew was instructed to leave with Captain C. Shelton, who was being sent to replace Col. Hans Adamson as Press Relations Officer for Rickenbacker, and Lt. Col. Erdman, whose "mission was to see that Captain Cherry and his crew received full consideration for their return to the mainland." With a brief stop to deliver mail at Christmas Island, they flew on to Tutuila, American Samoa, to pick up Rickenbacker.

Colonel Henry P. "Chick" Luna flew the men from Hawaii to San Francisco. (*Photo courtesy Colonel Luna*)

On December 1, Colonel Luna landed at Nandi Airfield in Fiji. The next day Rickenbacker had a conference in Suva and left in a C-53, returning to Fiji in time to leave on December 3 for Tontouta in New Caledonia and then on to Espiritu Santo, the largest island in the New Hebrides. Colonel Luna's crew stayed there, while Rickenbacker left for Guadalcanal in a B-17 combat airplane, for security purposes. When Rickenbacker returned, they left on December 11 back to Samoa. Rickenbacker had finished his mission for the War Department. It was time to head back to the States.

They arrived at Samoa, intending only to take James W. Reynolds, who was now at MOB-3, back to the States with them. However, they learned that Colonel Adamson, who had some major complications in his recovery, was also well enough to go with them. The airplane was outfitted with a regular adjustable hospital bed for Colonel Adamson, and added cots and mattresses for Rickenbacker and Reynolds. Accompanied by Lt. Cdr. Durkin (MC), USNR, they left Samoa on December 14.

After stopping at Christmas Island, and then Hickam Field in Honolulu, they were then unable to land at Hamilton Field in California due to weather conditions, so they were directed to land at San Francisco. Landing was actually made at Oakland on December 17, after a missed approach at San Francisco. Jim Reynolds recalled he spent the time "eating donuts and drinking coffee."

An hour later, they departed and landed back at Hamilton Field, where the press was waiting. Colonel Luna wrote in his report, "Colonel Adamson was placed in the station hospital. Sergeant Reynolds was met by his overjoyed parents." We had copies of government telegrams sent to Jim's parents when he was missing and then presumed lost. *Overjoyed* was probably not even close to explaining how they felt. James W. Reynolds was finally home in California.

Colonel Luna told us about flying on with Rickenbacker and Adamson, stopping at Dallas to refuel, and landing on December 19 at Bolling Field, in the Washington, D.C. area. "The flight was met by General Arnold and Rickenbacker's family and the assembled press and newsreel photographers." The next day Rickenbacker had a conference with Secretary of War Stimson and a press interview. Then Colonel Luna wrote, "We made a 1550 take-off that afternoon with Rickenbacker, his family, General Ryan, Commanding Officer of the new Pacific wing, and our party on into La Guardia Airport, where Rickenbacker was again met by the assembled press." When I read the last part of the report, I remembered the woman who wrote to us about Rickenbacker not having the proper forms for his Pacific flight. I wondered if Peg Kahn, who had been at the ticket counter at the beginning of Rickenbacker's ordeal, had read these newspaper accounts.

As interested as the students were in Colonel Luna's report, they became much more interested in Colonel Luna himself. In one letter, he answered the sixth grader's question. "Chick" Luna had been born in 1910 in New York City within three blocks of the Bronx Zoo, which at that time was a suburban area. His aunt raised a few chickens in her backyard. "As a toddler it delighted me to be allowed to feed them. I spread the corn as I called, 'Here, Chick, Chick.' From then on I have been called 'Chick' by all who knew me." Then he added, "Isn't that the corniest story you ever heard?" I remember my sixth graders laughing. Since many of them had been raised in the Iowa Corn Belt, they shook their heads and pointed to their teacher. *"Naw. We've heard cornier!"*

By April 1988, students were learning to type letters on the computer. Our school's computer lab was a great additional teaching tool. Students sent their first letters to the Lunas. An extra class picture also headed to California. In May we sent videotapes. Just before school was out, one of the boys wrote to Colonel Luna, "As you know, I am going to keep writing to you and if something happens and you can't return a letter, then that's okay cause I know it's hard. Both my grandpas have cancer."

Imagine my surprise when I received a photograph of both Jim Reynolds and Chick Luna, along with their wives, enjoying an evening at a restaurant. By mid-July Virginia wrote, "You made his life brighter."

Mrs. Luna and I continued corresponding, and each time we wrote to each other, we remembered Colonel Luna. When all the flashbulbs were going off and all the press was clamoring for an interview with the famous man he transported back to Washington and New York, Henry P. Luna was just a name beneath a photo and the signature on a military report. But to us—he was more—and he had helped bring our men home.

Although very ill, Chick Luna (*2nd from left*) was able to enjoy an evening at a restaurant in California with (*left to right*) Jim Reynolds, Margaret Reynolds, and Virginia Luna.

Chapter Twenty-Three

RIPPLES OF THE WAVES

I CHOSE TO BE A TEACHER, BUT I NEVER envisioned the many experiences I had during my professional career. Although the research for the men was a highlight, it was also a catalyst for other adventures.

Many people wrote to us originally about the World War II incident but then continued their correspondence through friendship. Quinton Stafford from Smithville, Mississippi, was one of these friends. He first wrote how he had been drafted in 1943 and enclosed a copy of a letter he had sent to his mother on December 1, when Eddie Rickenbacker had visited the drill field where he was training. Mr. Stafford wanted to know if the men at our Rescue Reunion recalled the same events he remembered Rickenbacker sharing one month after the rescue.

I answered Mr. Stafford's letter and began a correspondence that lasted with Quinton and Alice for almost twenty-five years. After purchasing a new video recorder, Quinton drove his four-wheeler "up and down the hills and hollers" to make a tape for my students. "I want them to know more about Mississippi," he explained. I particularly enjoyed the recordings of Quinton waving to his neighbors and encouraging them to "say 'hi' to Mrs. Kelly's boys and girls up there in I-oway!"

We soon learned that Quinton was a master craftsman extraordinaire. He had made bricks to build their church. He had worked in a sawmill. He had carved wood for cabinets and furniture. Sometimes he and Alice sent me things they had made, such as kitchen knives, crocheted scarves, canned fruit, and even jars of scuppernong marmalade. This muscadine grape tasted different from the concord grapes we had on the farm, but it was also delicious. Accompanying the jars of marmalade was a note, "Share these with Mr. Matson across the street." Once, a large bundle of cotton arrived. Boys and girls who knew about corn and soybeans saw their first raw cotton. For many years, students made nature designs on solar print fabric in science class. Then we sewed the fabric and stuffed it with the cotton from Mississippi to make little pillows.

Through all our correspondence, Mr. Stafford taught us more than just about the state of Mississippi. He once told me that if I didn't mind he would kind of like to continue sending us tapes and things because he believed that "you really get to know people if you take the time to share good things." We valued his friendship.

However, not all our research produced the results we wanted. As much as the sixth graders tried over the years, we never had success with two searches, one for a man and the other for a painting.

Although we tried to find Chief Petty Officer Winnie (or Wynne?), we never located him. We knew he had designed medical equipment for the doctors. If a particular instrument was needed for surgery, the medical corpsmen would show the Chief Petty Officer a picture or describe it, and soon, they had what was needed to save a life in the tiny hospital on Funafuti. One man told us that the Chief Petty Officer was interviewed for an article in a military publication about him in late 1942 or early 1943. We searched through both the Navy and the Marine Corps, but never found him to pass on the thanks from other people. However, this chief petty officer must have been a very special person for so many other men to ask if we ever found him.

Another search concerned a painting. One group of sixth graders was fascinated with a note from an unidentified source in materials John Bartek loaned us from his scrapbook. It said, "Inspired by the experience of Eddie Rickenbacker and his seven companions, Jarvis A. Stewart, art instructor at Phillips University, Enid, Oklahoma, put *Epic of Prayer* on canvas." When students asked, both Jim Reynolds and Bill Cherry recalled hearing about the painting that had been inspired by their raft ordeal.

These students desperately wanted to locate the painting for the men. Professor Paul Denny, Jr. from Phillips University wrote us that Mr.

Stewart had actually been an art student at the time he had done the painting but had since obtained a doctorate from Ohio State University. Professor Denny helped students track down Jarvis Stewart's widow, Madge Stewart, now living in Ohio.

Mrs. Stewart wrote, "It was like a voice out of the past receiving your letter concerning my husband's painting, *Epic of Prayer*." She told us that Jarvis had been commissioned by the owner of a bookstore "to make a painting of the men in the life raft at just the moment when the sea swallow perched on Rickenbacker's head." The men had shared with us that this occurred soon after they had prayed for food and read John Bartek's little Testament passage of *Matthew 6: 31-34*. Mrs. Stewart indicated the painting had been placed in the window of the bookstore, where it had drawn crowds of people. The national news wires had picked up the story, and the artist had been inundated with correspondence about the painting. Now, over forty years later, we had picked up the trail, but we never found the painting.

Paul Harvey, the famous radio broadcaster, used his signature line, "… and now, the rest of the story," to engage his audience in a meaningful follow-up to what appeared to be an interesting story. Using a line from Super Sleuth Travis Senne, I have often been asked, "And *then* what happened to the men?"

Through the years, we not only had stayed in touch, but we also had become an integral part of each other's families. Captain Les Boutte, who had made a career of the Navy, had been involved with the Mercury Space Program. Les had been the first to make contact with Col. John Glenn's Friendship Seven Space Capsule upon its re-entry from space. Then, after retirement, Les and his wife Cathy enjoyed travel to visit family and attend reunions of the many military groups to which he belonged. They sometimes sent boxes of Mardi Gras surprises to the students. Their letters were always filled with news about children and grandchildren.

After John Bartek's wife Mildred, who was ill at the time of the Rescue Reunion, passed away, John came for a visit. I had a scheduled speech in

While on the rafts, the men ate a sea swallow that landed on Rickenbacker's head. To represent this incident, the class hung a model of a sea gull in Room 14. Students often pulled the cord to make the bird "fly." (*Photo Bob Kelly*)

the community that weekend. It was fun to take John along and let him tell his own story. John later remarried, and he and Marie came to Iowa for a visit. John often sent us letters and photos of their family or the beautiful flowers Marie grew in their garden in New Jersey. Once, after John had been to the shore, a box of salt-water taffy arrived for the Meeker students. John also loved phone calls, and I cherished his excitement when he heard my voice, as he would turn to Marie and say, "It's Suzanne Kelly from Iowa," and then end with, "I love you, too."

Jim Reynolds worked in a sporting goods store after his retirement, often trying to convince me to come salmon fishing with him in Northern California. Jim, a master woodworker, made me canisters, clocks, and even a personal fishing pole. Once, when Jim, his wife Margaret, and his sister Clara had visited with us a couple of weeks, we loaded their car with scraps of walnut wood from my parents' farm, thinking Jim might enjoy working with walnut, as well as his usual myrtle wood. He immediately surprised me with a decorative walnut clock for my office.

Jim often gave my classes detailed objects he made in his shop—animal figurines, wooden toy racing cars for physics labs, and a model schoolhouse with numbered books for a calendar. Sixth graders particularly enjoyed two items we always kept in the classroom. One was a happy little caricature of a bookworm. The students promptly named it "Alameda" after Jim's California town. The second item was a large ladybug, painted red and black, with a hand-sized opening in the top. We put names in it for countless drawings. The ladybug provided a fair way of choosing names for special activities and was the best peacekeeper a sixth grade teacher could have.

Jim Reynolds usually called every other week, and to me he was a calm, kind gentleman, who provided an anchor to the busy life I led. I cherished our chats that were often filled with, "Suzanne, you had no idea what you started!"

Captain Cherry continued to play golf, travel, and enjoy his family. Occasionally, he would send us his golf scorecard, coins from his travels, or a cap from a golf course. Once, a couple of the sixth graders visited him at his home in California.

When the Super Sleuths graduated from high school, Captain Cherry came back again to see "his kids." After eating pie made from fresh rhubarb from our garden, we went to the Ames High commencement. I sat next to Bill in the audience as they played a video, filled with photos of the graduates from their earlier school careers. There were several references to the former Meeker Elementary students' sixth grade year. The music accompanying the video was one of my favorite songs, "One Moment in Time." Travis Senne, who had first asked the question about the men, gave one of the class commencement addresses, and classmate Jennifer Jones gave the "Benediction and Period of Reflection." When the Super Sleuths received their diplomas, Bill Cherry squeezed my hand as a few tears slid down my cheeks. I thought of all that had happened that had brought us together. I once wrote, "To have the privilege to educate young people is a wonderful experience. To have a fast-talking pilot from Texas care about their education, too, was a priceless gift."

Bill Cherry promised to come see "his kids" graduate from Ames High School. *Top Row:* Travis Senne. *Second Row:* Erik Smedal, David Jurgens, Ben Jackson, and David Abelson. *Third Row:* Jennifer Jones, Lisa Moore, Niki Nilsen, Christy Scott, and Amy Murphy. *Front Row:* Amy Larson, Suzanne Kelly, and Bill Cherry. (*Photo Bob Kelly*)

A few years later, Bill Wepner, the PT boat rescuer, sat at our dining table and poured over maps of the lagoon at Funafuti. However, the main reason for his visit was to take me to one of the former sixth grader's wedding. Lisa Moore and the rest of the Super Sleuths had become young adults.

One year, after our family returned from a summer vacation, we received a frantic phone call from the State Department. "Where have you been?" the man from Washington, D.C., said. I thought it quite an unusual question to be asked, until I realized he had been given an assignment to find me

Captain Cherry met the Tuvaluan Ambassador, Semu S. Taafaki, in California. The ambassador wrote a personal letter to each student in the 1989 class.

and time was running out. His Excellency, the Tuvaluan Ambassador, Semu S. Taafaki, was coming to California and had requested meeting Captain Cherry. I was the State Department's source to locate Bill, so he and Mr. Taafaki could meet. Following their visit, Captain Cherry sent us photos, and the ambassador sent a personal letter to each student in the class. I was extremely impressed. A man whose business card said "His Excellency, the Tuvaluan Ambassador" took the time to write personal, meaningful letters to sixth graders.

After I retired from teaching, the school contacted me about a phone call they had from some place called Tuvalu. The Prime Minister's office had called. They were clearing out an office and found files of correspondence from me. Would I care if they put it together for a radio broadcast to the people of their country? It has now been seventy-two years since Toma found the men. The story is still being told. People are still reaching out to one another.

In July 2008 my husband insisted I should take advantage of a restored B-17 coming to the Ames Airport. We had gone out to see it and discovered they were selling rides. When I entered the bomb bay area, I glanced at the restored radio transmitter—one just like Jim used in pounding out SOS. The crew offered me a chance to sit in the navigator's seat. As I flew over the countryside, I saw the beautiful Iowa fields. What a view! Then we landed, and instead of riding a raft on towering waves, I was back in my husband's arms. As I came off the tarmac, a former student spotted me. "Oh, Mrs. Kelly," he said, "I saw this woman coming from the plane, and I wished it was you!"

I immediately called John Bartek. With breathless excitement I announced, "John, guess what I just did! I flew in a B-17!"

There was a moment of silence on the line, and then John asked, "Why?"

I suppose from his point of view the flight had been an unnecessary adventure. To me, it was perfect.

With the passage of time, so many people in our story are now a whisper in the wind. But the Super Sleuths, now the age I was when I was their teacher, have families of their own. They have served in the Peace Corps and the military, and volunteered in Third World countries. Three have become educators—an elementary teacher, a high school teacher, and a university professor. One woman is an engineer, another a lawyer, and a third a pediatric oncology social worker. One man is a television producer and another raises beef cattle. They are business people and stay-at-home parents. I am proud of all of them.

Date	Type of Machine	Number of Machine	Duration of Flight	Character of Flight	Pilot	PASSENGERS	REMARKS
			NOVEMBER	1942			
1	OS2U-3	5309	4.3	J	LT. EADIE	SELF	
1	"	5749	2.8	J	LT.(JG) WOODWARD	"	
3	"	5309	2.5	J	LT.(JG) FREEL	"	
3	"	5309	2.5	J	LT.(JG) WOODWARD	"	
5	"	5943	2.2	J	LT.(JG) FREEL	"	
5	"	5749	2.7	J	LT.(JG) WOODWARD	"	
7	"	5749	2.5	J	LT.(JG) PEARSALL	"	
7	"	5369	2.5	J	LT.(JG) WOODWARD	"	
9	"	5943	2.0	J	LT.(JG) PEARSALL	"	
9	"	5749	2.5	J	LT.(JG) WOODWARD	"	
11	"	5943	2.8	J	LT.(JG) PEARSALL	"	
11	"	5309	3.6	J	LT.(JG) WOODWARD	"	SPOTTED 1-MAN RAFT
12	"	5309	4.0	Y	LT. EADIE	"	SEARCH FOR RICKENBACKER + PARTY
12	"	5309	5.5	Y	LT. EADIE	"	" " " " "
12	"	5309	8.0	Y	LT. EADIE	"	PICK-UP RICKENBACKER AT SEA
13	"	41356	1.2	J	LT.(JG) FORREST	"	
15	"	61356	1.0	J	LT.(JG) FORREST	"	
15	"	41351	2.1	J	LT.(JG) BOYD	"	
17	"	5749	2.1	J	LT.(JG) PEARSALL	"	
17	"	4351	2.0	J	LT.(JG) BOYD	"	
	Total time to date,						

Les Boutte sent us a copy of his flight log that recorded spotting Capt. Cherry and picking up Rickenbacker, Bartek, and Adamson. (*Courtesy Les Boutte*)

Lester Boutte's flight log for November 11, 1942, recorded that he was flying a "3.6 hr. flight" with pilot Lt.(j.g.) Woodward. Under the remarks column is listed a simple phrase—"SPOTTED 1-MAN RAFT." What an unassuming reference to an event that affected so many lives. I had once wondered which side of the plane Lester Boutte had looked out of to see Captain William T. Cherry, Jr. The former Kingfisher radioman provided the answer. "I was looking out my right-hand side, the left-hand side of the airplane, since I was facing aft, and I saw a yellow object go by on the surface."

Just what I thought—it might have been the left-hand side of the plane. But it definitely was the "*right*" side!

REFERENCES & RESOURCES

Chapter One

Whittaker, James C. *We Thought We Heard the Angels Sing*. New York: E. P. Dutton & Company, Inc., 1943: 19-21, 23, 32, 35, 40-5, 59, 60, 73-4, 78, 85-6, 94-5.

Chapter Two

Dallas/Ft. Worth Telephone Book. 1984.

Scott, Christy. "Letter to William T. Cherry, III." November 15, 1984.

Chapter Three

Abelson, David. "Letter to Dean C. Allard at Naval Historical Center." Feb. 1985.

Air Force Times. "Letter to Suzanne Kelly." Aug. 16, 1982.

—. "Locator Service." Sept. 6, 1982.

Allard, Dean C. "Letter to David Abelson." Feb. 22, 1985.

Bartek, John. "Letter to Erik Smedal." Dec. 5, 1984.

—. "Letters to Each Sixth Grader, Room 14, Meeker Elementary." Jan. 1985.

"Biographical Data on Lester Boutte." United States Navy, Sept. 29, 1969.

Boden, Derrick. "Letter to Managing Editor, *Army Historian*, U.S. Army Center of Military History." Jan 30, 1985.

Cherry, William T., Jr. "Photo of Three Generations and Notation of Broken Nose." Jan. 1985.

—. "Telephone Call to Room 14, Meeker Sixth Graders." Dec. 5, 1984.

—. "Telephone Call to Suzanne Kelly." Dec. 2, 1984.

Good, George F., Jr. "Report of Rescue of Captain Rickenbacker and Party, 11, 12 November, 1942." United States Marine Corps Headquarters, Funafuti, in the Field, 1942.

Horne, Joyce. "Letter to Suzanne Kelly." Sept. 2, 1982.

Kelly, Suzanne. "Letter to *Air Force Times*." Aug. 7, 1982.

—. "Personal Notes." Dec. 2, 1984.

Kubichek, Paul. Letter to Freehold Public Library." Nov. 7, 1984.

Novick, Karen. "Letter to Class from Freehold Public Library." Nov. 21, 1984.

Pins, Kenneth. "Sixth-graders play detective, find war fliers." *Des Moines Sunday Register*, Jan. 20, 1985.

Reynolds, James W. "Letter to Cathy Watson." Dec. 14, 1984.

—. "Letters to Each Sixth Grade Student, Room 14, Meeker Elementary." Jan. 1985.

Senne, Travis. "Letter to United States Army College Library." Jan. 30, 1985.

Slonaker, John J. "Letter to Travis Senne from U.S. Army Military History Institute." Feb. 1985.

Smedal, Erik. "Letter to John Bartek." Nov. 28, 1984.

Watson, Cathy. "Letter to James W. Reynolds." Dec. 6, 1984.

—. "Letter to Oakland Public Library." Nov. 29, 1984.

Watts, Elizabeth. "Letter to Cathy Watson." Dec. 6, 1984.

Whittaker, James C. *We Thought We Heard the Angels Sing.* New York: E. P. Dutton & Company, Inc., 1943: 21, 29, 106, 108-13, 117-29.

Chapter Four

Abelson, David. "Letter to Alvin P. Cluster." Mar. 21, 1985.
—. "Letter to PT Boats, Inc." Mar. 8, 1985.
American Airlines. "Letter to Christy Scott." Jan. 25, 1985.
—. "Telephone Call to Suzanne Kelly." Jan. 25, 1985.
Arnold, Brad. "Letter to Sam Eadie." Feb. 25, 1985.
—. "Letter to Sam Eadie." Mar. 18, 1985.
"Biographical Data on Lester Boutte." United States Navy, Sept. 29, 1969.
Boutte, Lester A. "Letter to Christy Scott." Feb. 14, 1985.
—. "Letter to Suzanne Kelly." Mar. 2, 1985.
Cluster, Alvin P. "Letter to David Abelson." Apr. 11, 1985.
Coverdale, Jeanne. "Letter to Meeker Sixth Grade and Suzanne Kelly." Jan. 21, 1985.
—. "Telephone Call to Suzanne Kelly." Jan. 21, 1985.
Eadie, Sam. "Letter to Brad Arnold." Mar. 1, 1985.
Featherling, Howard E. "Letter to Amy LeMay." Apr. 1, 1985.
Green, Edward (Father Austin). "Eddie Rickenbacker Rescue." Knights of the Sea, 1982: 117.
__. "Letter to Michele Mitchell." Apr. 3, 1985.
—. "Letter to Suzanne Kelly." May 11, 1985.
Guthrie, Alyce N. "Letter to David Abelson from PT Boats, Inc." Mar. 20, 1985.
Hefley, Mary Lu. "Letter to Christy Scott from Vermilion Parish Library." Feb. 8, 1985.
Herr, Mary R. "Letter to Amy Murphy from Davenport Public Library." Mar. 11, 1985.
—. "Telephone Call to Suzanne Kelly from Davenport Public Library." Mar. 28, 1985.
Jones, Jennifer. "Letter to William H. Wepner." Mar. 26, 1985.
Kelly, Suzanne. "Letter to Lester Boutte." Feb. 20, 1985.
—. "Letter to William T. Cherry, Jr. and others." Jan. 28, 1985.
Mitchell, Michele. "Letter to Father Edward A. Green." Mar. 25, 1985.
Murphy, Amy. "Letter to Bill Wundram, *Quad-City Times.*" Mar. 29, 1985.
—. "Letter to Davenport Public Library." Mar. 8, 1985.
—. "Letter to Mary Herr, Davenport Public Library." Mar. 27, 1985.
Nilsen, Niki. "Letter to Dale Brentnall at Fellows Elementary." Apr. 8, 1985.
Quinn, Martha. "Letter to Christy Scott from Evanston Public Library." Feb. 19, 1985.
Rickenbacker, Edward V. "Pacific Mission, Part I." *LIFE*, Jan. 25, 1943: 21-7.
—. "Pacific Mission, Part II." *LIFE*, Feb. 1, 1943: 78-92.
—. "Pacific Mission, Part III." *LIFE*, Feb. 8, 1943: 94-106.
—. *Seven Came Through.* New York: Doubleday, Doran & Company, Inc., 1943.
Scott, Christy. "Letter to Evanston Public Library." Feb. 2, 1985.
—. "Letter to Lester H. Boutte." Feb. 11, 1985.
—. "Letter to Vermilion Parish Library." Feb. 3, 1985.
Sliter, Lester A. "Letter to David Jurgens from U.S. Air Force Historical Research Center." Mar. 20, 1985.
Wepner, William H. "Photographs for Mrs. Kelly."
Wundram, Bill. "The Case of the Missing Hero." *Quad-City Times*, April 3, 1985.
—. "The Short, Tragic Life of Fred Woodward." *Quad-City Times*, Apr. 7, 1985.

Chapter Five

Arnold, Brad. "Writings from Room 14 by Mrs. Kelly's Sixth Graders." Ames, Iowa, 1985.

Beal, George. "Letter to Bikeni Paeniu, copy to Suzanne Kelly." Mar. 4, 1985.

——. "Letter to Suzanne Kelly." Mar. 5, 1985.

East-West Center Bulletin 1983-84. Honolulu: East-West Center, 1983.

Harvey, Paul. "Telephone Interview with Suzanne Kelly." Apr. 4, 1985.

Haynes, Doug. "Letter to Amasone Kilei, Sec'y. to Gov't." Feb. 20, 1985.

——. "Letter to British Embassy." Jan. 16, 1985.

——. "Letter to British High Commission." Feb. 13, 1085.

——. "Letter to British Information Service." Feb. 5, 1985.

——. "Letter to H. Panapa." Apr. 4, 1985.

——. "Letter to Prime Minister, Dr. Tomasi Puapua." Feb. 20, 1985.

——. "Letter to Tuvalu High Commissioner in Suva, Fiji." Jan. 30, 1985.

Kelly, Suzanne. "Letter to George Beal, East-West Communication Institute." Feb. 20, 1985.

——. "Letter to Gordon Tsuji." Feb. 4, 1985.

Kilei, Amasone. "Letter to Doug Haynes from Tuvalu High Commissioner." Apr. 9, 1985.

Moreland, Nicki. "Letter to Mrs. Kelly." Apr. 5, 1985.

Panapa, H. "Letter to Doug Haynes from Tuvalu Broadcasting and Information Officer." Mar. 25, 1985.

Rickenbacker, Edward V. *Seven Came Through.* New York: Doubleday, Doran & Company, Inc., 1943: 35.

Rowan, Paul. "Telephone Call to Suzanne Kelly from Reporter, *Star-Telegram.*" Ft. Worth, Texas, Mar. 13, 1985.

"Sign for Room 14 Door, Meeker Elementary." Apr. 1, 1985.

Suschnigg, Kini. "Letter to Bikeni Paeniu, copy to Suzanne Kelly." Feb. 28, 1985.

——. "Letter to Suzanne Kelly." Apr. 1, 1985.

——. "Letter to Suzanne Kelly with Telex Message from Sec'y. Ministry Commerce Natural Resources." Apr. 1985.

——. "Telephone call to Bob Kelly." Apr. 1, 1985.

Telex. "Message to Kini Suschnigg." 1985.

Tsuji, Gordon. "Letter to Suzanne Kelly." Feb. 12, 1985.

Tuvalu Fact Sheets. British Information Services, 1977.

Whittaker, James C. *We Thought We Heard the Angels Sing.* New York: E. P. Dutton & Company, Inc., 1943: 57, 61-2, 127-8.

World Almanac. 1985: 588.

Chapter Six

Blair, Richard. "Letter to Suzanne Kelly from U.S. Air Force Academy." Apr. 10, 1985.

Cherry, William T., Jr. "Television Interview." Apr. 18, 1985.

Cluster, Alvin P. "Letter to David Abelson." Apr. 11, 1985.

Good, George F., Jr. "Telephone Call to Bob Kelly." Apr. 13, 1985.

Jackson, Ben. "Letter to Iowa Air National Guard." Apr. 4, 1985.

Kelly, Suzanne. "Telephone Call to Gen. George F. Good, Jr." Apr. 13, 1985.

——. "Television Interview with *Iowa Edition*, Channel 5." Apr. 25, 1985.

Larson, Amy. "Letter to Fellows Elementary." Apr. 5, 1985.

Moreland, Jana. "Letter to Lee Himan, Meeker Elementary Principal." Feb. 13, 1985.

Smith, Diane. "Telephone Call to Suzanne Kelly." Apr. 18, 1985.
Weinberger, Caspar. "Letter to Suzanne Kelly from the Secretary of Defense." Apr. 10, 1985.

Chapter Seven

Adamson, Hans. *Rickenbacker.* New York: The Macmillan Company, 1946: 278.
Alexander, Anne. "Letter to Sixth Graders." Apr. 1985.
Associated Press. "Students Research World War II Rescue." News-Sun, Apr. 19, 1985.
Bathurst, Vera. "Letter to Suzanne Kelly." Apr. 21, 1985.
——. "Letter to Suzanne Kelly and Class." May 25, 1985.
——. "Telephone Call to Suzanne Kelly." Apr. 21, 1985.
Cherry, William T., Jr. "Telephone Call to Suzanne Kelly." June 15, 1985.
Christopher, Natalie. "Letter to Suzanne Kelly." May 14, 1985.
Crosby, Janet. "Letter to Suzanne Kelly." May 23, 1985.
Eadie, Phyllis. "Letter to Suzanne Kelly." June 14, 1985.
Eadie, Robert. "Letter to Suzanne Kelly." Apr. 22, 1985.
——. "Telephone Call to Suzanne Kelly." Apr. 19, 1985.
Eadie, William Fisher, II. "Letter to Suzanne Kelly and Class." May 1, 1985.
Eadie, William. "Rough Draft of Report of 1942 Rickenbacker, et al. Rescue." Nov. 19, 1942.
Elliott, Harry. "Letter to Suzanne Kelly from Air Force Museum, Wright-Patterson Air Base." May 1985.
——. "Telephone Call to Suzanne Kelly from Air Force Museum Wright-Patterson Air Force Base." Apr. 23, 1985.
Green, David. "Telephone Call to Suzanne Kelly from ABC Bureau Chief in Denver." Apr. 19, 1985.
Headquarters, Army Air Forces, Washington, D.C. "Orders to Captain Edward V. Rickenbacker, Special Consultant." Oct. 9, 1942.
Hughes, Marge. "Letter to Suzanne Kelly." May 11, 1985.
Hurd, Shirley. "Letter to Suzanne Kelly and Class." May 22, 1985.
Jackson, Ben. "Letter to Torrington Public Library." Jan. 30, 1985.
Jones, Jennifer. "Letter to Shirley Hurd." Apr. 26, 1985.
Kahn, Peg. "Letter to Suzanne Kelly and Class." Apr. 27, 1985.
Kelly, Suzanne. "Interview with Iowa Public Network." Apr. 1985.
——. "Letter to Diane Smith." May 9, 1985.
——. "Letter to Janet Crosby." May 1, 1985.
——. "Letter to Lillian Olmstead." May 1, 1985.
——. "Letter to Meeker Elementary Faculty and Staff." Apr. 27, 1985.
——. "Letter to Natalie Christopher." May 1, 1985.
——. "Telephone Call to Anne Alexander." Apr. 19, 1985.
——. "Telephone Call to Shirley Hurd." Apr. 21, 1985.
Mitchell, Michele. "Letter to Shirley Hurd." Apr. 22, 1985.
O'Connor, Gerald. "Letter to Suzanne Kelly." Apr. 24, 1985.
Olmstead, Lillian. "Letter to Suzanne Kelly and Class." Apr. 19, 1985.
——. "Telephone Call to Suzanne Kelly." Apr. 1985.
Reynolds, James W. "Telephone Call to Suzanne Kelly." Apr. 21, 1985.
Sixth Grade Super Sleuths, Meeker Elementary. *Souvenir Book of Rescue Reunion.* Ames, Iowa: Ames Community School District, 1985.

Smith, Diane. "Letter to Suzanne Kelly and Class." May 1985.
Smith, Linda. "Letter to Suzanne Kelly from Wright-Patterson Air Base, U.S. Air Force Museum." May 7, 1985.
Smith, Matthew. "Letter to Suzanne Kelly." May 1985.
Watson, Chad. "Letter to Burlingame Public Library." Jan. 30, 1985.
Whittaker, Irene. "Letter to Suzanne Kelly." Apr. 21, 1985.
Whittaker, James. "Diary on the Raft—Day 1." October 21, 1942.
Whittaker, Mrs. Thomas. "Letter to Suzanne Kelly." July 5, 1985.

Chapter Eight

Carter, Betty and John. "Letter to Suzanne Kelly." July 9, 1985.
—. "Letter to Teacher Suzanne Kelly and Class." Apr. 25, 1985.
Erickson, Scott. "Letter to Dan and Donna Ryherd." Aug. 15, 1985.
—. "Letter to Dan and Donna Ryherd about Interview with Toma Fakapae." Aug. 12, 1985.
Gibson, Debra. "Letter to Suzanne Kelly from ISU Alumni Association." July 1,1985.
Goodwin, George. "Telephone Call to Suzanne Kelly." July 6, 1985.
Ito, Noriko. "Letter to Suzanne Kelly." Sept. 18, 1985.
—. "Letter to Suzanne Kelly." Jan. 30, 1986.
Kelly, Suzanne. "Letter to Albert Goodwin." July 1, 1985.
—. "Letter to Donna Ryherd." July 14, 1985.
—. "Letter to Gail Linahon." July 6, 1985.
—. "Letter to Gail Linahon." July 14, 1985.
—. "Letter to Matt Smith." July 8, 1985.
Linahon, Gail. "Letter to Michele Mitchell." May 22, 1985.
—. "Letter to Suzanne Kelly." May 28, 1985.
—. "Letter to Suzanne Kelly." July 16, 1985.
"Map of Nukufetau."
McMullen, Robert. "Letter to Michele Mitchell." Apr. 19, 1985.
—. "To Funafuti and Back—Introduction."
—. "To Funafuti and Back." 8.
Mitchell, Michele. "Letter to Garner Public Library." May 16, 1985.
—. "Letter to Robert McMullen." Feb. 20, 1985.
"Note to Suzanne Kelly at Ames Noon Kiwanis Speech." Aug. 9, 1985.
Panapa, H. "Letter to Doug Haynes." May 1, 1985.
Ryherd, Dan and Donna. "Presentation on Tuvalu at Meeker Elementary School." Sept. 26, 1985.
Ryherd, Donna. "Letter to Suzanne Kelly." June 19, 1985.
—. "Letter to Suzanne Kelly." Aug. 12, 1985.
Sommerhauser, Betty and Jim. "Letter to Suzanne Kelly." Aug. 31, 1985.
—. "Letter to Suzanne Kelly." Feb. 4, 1986.
Tuvalu Echoes. Apr. 11, 1985.
Tuvalu Fact Sheet. May 1977.
Zobrist, Herman and Edith. "Telephone Call to Suzanne Kelly." May 14, 1985.

Chapter Nine

Besnier, Niko. *Ttou Tauloto Te Ggana Tuuvalu* (*A Course in the Tuvaluan Language*). United States Peace Corps, 1981.

——. *Tuvaluan Lexicon.* United States Peace Corps, 1981.

Change in Tuvalu. Directed by Stanley Dalby. Produced by Dan Murray. 1983.

Fowler, Elizabeth and Dennis. "Letter to Suzanne Kelly." Mar. 12, 1986.

Fowler, Elizabeth. "Letter to Suzanne Kelly." Sept. 1, 1986.

——. "Letter to Suzanne Kelly." June 24, 1986.

Guthrie, John. "Letter to Amy LeMay." Feb. 12, 1985.

——. "Letter to Suzanne Kelly." Aug. 11, 1985.

Harrison, Alden. "Telephone Call to Suzanne Kelly." Jan. 24, 1985.

Humberstone, Betty Jane (Woodward). "Telegram to Bill Wundram, *Quad-City Times.*" Apr. 18, 1985.

Humberstone Family. "Letter to the Kellys." Jan. 5, 1987.

Jackson, Ben. "Letter to Nelu Solomena, Headmaster Primary School, Tuvalu." Mar. 7, 1985.

Kahn, Orie. "Letter to Suzanne Kelly and Room 14." Jan. 5, 1987.

——. "Telephone Call to Bob Kelly." Jan. 1986.

Kelly, Suzanne. "Letter to Alden Harrison." July 14, 1985.

——. "Letter to Australian Consulate General." Nov. 26, 1985.

——. "Letter to Australian Consulate General." Feb. 5, 1986.

——. "Letter to Elizabeth and Dennis Fowler." Apr. 29, 1986.

——. "Letter to Elizabeth Fowler." Oct. 14, 1986.

——. "Letter to Joann Munson." July 30, 1985.

——. "Letter to Joann Munson." Feb. 5, 1987.

——. "Letter to John Guthrie." July 30, 1985.

——. "Letter to Orie Kahn." July 14, 1985.

——. "Letter to Pafini Nouata." Oct. 9, 1985.

——. "Letter to Principal, Motufoua School, Tuvalu." May 27, 1985.

——. "Letters to Motufoua Students." Mar. 2, 1987.

——. "Notes to Meeker Students." Jan. 24, 1985.

——. "Personal Notes." June 1988.

——. "Personal Notes." Nov. 11, 1985.

——. "Telephone Call to Orie Kahn." Jan. 1986.

Lausaveve, S. "Letter to Dan Ryherd." Nov. 6, 1985.

LeMay, Amy. "Letter to John Guthrie." Jan. 29, 1985.

Mercado, Victoria (Vikki) Kahn. "Letter to Suzanne Kelly." June 15, 1995.

——. "Letter to Suzanne Kelly." Apr. 26, 1995.

Munson, Joann. "Letter to Suzanne Kelly." Feb. 12, 1987.

"Note on Film," *Change in Tuvalu.* Jan. 15, 1986.

Nouata, Pafini. "Letter to Suzanne Kelly from Principal at Motufoua." June 27, 1985.

Pate, Dorothy. "Painting from Photo of Fred Woodward."

Tuvalu Bulletin South Pacific Forum. 1984.

Tuvaluan Pen Pals. "Letters to Meeker from Motufoua School, Vaitupu Island, Tuvalu." June 25, 1985.

——. "Letters to Meeker, Room 14 Sixth Graders, from Motufoua School." Mar. 12, 1986.

Wundram, Bill. "Letter to Suzanne Kelly." June 17, 1985.

Chapter Ten

Arnold, Brad. "Letter to Public Library of Columbus and Franklin County." Jan. 30, 1985.

Babcock, Eugene. "Note to Suzanne Kelly." May 1986.

Darby, Marian (Mrs. Ralph L.). "Letter to Brad Arnold." Feb. 7, 1985.

Jons, Carolyn. "Letter to Class and Suzanne Kelly." May 19, 1986.

Kelly Enterprises. "Letter to Room 14, Meeker Elementary Stockholders." Feb. 3, 1986.

Kelly, Suzanne and Former Sixth Graders. "Presentation to Ames School Board." Apr. 20, 1992.

Kelly, Suzanne. "Letter to Albert Rickenbacker." Feb. 27, 1985.

—. "Letter to Albert Rickenbacker." Aug. 24, 1985.

—. "Letter to Former Sixth Graders." Feb. 6, 1992.

—. "Letter to Room 14, Meeker Elementary Parents." Dec. 3, 1985.

—. "Letter to William C. Rickenbacker." Oct. 7, 1985.

—. "Notes on Investment Reception." May 1986.

Miller, Fred and Barb. "Letter to Suzanne Kelly." Apr. 19, 1986.

Mitchell, Michele. "Letter to William Frost Rickenbacker." Feb. 11, 1985.

Moore, Lisa. "Letter to Albert Rickenbacker." Feb. 11, 1985.

Pins, Kenneth. "6th graders forgo pizza, make investment in future." *Des Moines Register*, Apr. 17, 1986.

Potter, H. James. "These students gather no moss." *Tribune Weekender*, May 17, 1986.

Rickenbacker, Albert. "Letter to Lisa Moore." Feb. 14, 1985.

—. "Letter to Suzanne Kelly." Oct. 14, 1985.

—. "Letter to Suzanne Kelly." Sept. 13, 1985.

—. "Letter to Suzanne Kelly." Aug. 19, 1985.

—. "Letter to Suzanne Kelly." Sept. 1, 1986.

Rickenbacker, William C. "Letter to Suzanne Kelly." Sept. 16, 1985.

Rickenbacker, William Frost. "Letter to Michele Mitchell." Feb. 17, 1985.

Room 14, Meeker Elementary. "Class Meeting to Form Kelly Enterprises." 1985.

—. "Class Notes from Visit by Corbett Griffin." Jan. 24, 1986.

Room 14, Meeker Elementary Students, 1985-6 School Year. "Individual Investment Project Reports." 1986.

Roshon, Sam. "Letter to Brad Arnold from Public Library of Columbus and Franklin County." Feb. 5, 1985.

Chapter Eleven

"100 New American Heroes—The Day Mrs. Kelly's Sixth Graders Heard the Angels Sing." *Collector's Edition Newsweek*, Summer 1986: 82.

Fakapae, Toma. "Letter to Suzanne Kelly." July 13, 1985.

—. "Translation of Letter to Suzanne Kelly." July 13, 1985.

—. "Translation of Toma's Audio Tape." July 1985.

Fincher, Jack. "Letter to Suzanne Kelly." Apr. 10, 1987.

Kelly, Bob. "Samples of Latitude/Longitude Activity."

Kelly, Suzanne. "Letter to 1986-7 Room 14, Meeker Elementary Sixth Graders." July 27, 1987.

—. "Letter to Coreen Schwenk." July 30, 1985.

—. "Letter to Coreen Schwenk." Aug. 14, 1986.

—. "Letter to Coreen Schwenk." Dec. 17, 1986.

—. "Letter to Coreen Schwenk." Aug. 6, 1987.

—. "Letter to H. Panapa." May 27, 1985.

—. "Letter to H. Panapa." Oct. 9, 1985.
—. "Letter to Olinda Woods." Sept. 14, 1987.
—. "Letter to Olinda Woods." Dec. 17, 1987.
Meeker Elementary, Ames, Iowa. "Warren H. Meeker Elementary School History." 24.
Panapa, H. "Letter to Suzanne Kelly." July 11, 1985.
—. "Letter to Suzanne Kelly." Aug. 23, 1985.
—. "Letter to Suzanne Kelly." Nov. 15, 1985.
Schwenk, Coreen and Elmer. "Letter to Sixth Graders, Room 14, Meeker Elementary." Sept.
    28, 1986.
Schwenk, Coreen. "Letter to Suzanne Kelly." Aug. 8, 1985.
—. "Letter to Suzanne Kelly." Aug. 3, 1986.
—. "Letter to Suzanne Kelly." Aug. 20, 1986.
—. "Letter to Suzanne Kelly." Dec. 20, 1986.
—. "Letter to Suzanne Kelly." Dec. 4, 1986.
Woods, Olinda. "Telephone Call to Suzanne Kelly." Apr. 3, 1987.

Chapter Twelve

Cherry, William T., Jr. "Telephone Call to Suzanne Kelly." Mar. 11, 1987.
"Citation to Thomas W. Lenderman from the U.S. Navy." Apr. 22, 1943.
Collins, Stan. "Note to Suzanne Kelly." Oct. 31, 1986.
Ernst, Eunice (Mrs. Edwin C.). "Letter to Suzanne Kelly." Oct. 10, 1986.
Garrity, Evelyn. "Letter to Karen Stone at CBS News in Chicago." Apr. 22, 1985.
—. "Letter to Suzanne Kelly." Apr. 28, 1987.
Garrity, Robert. "Letter to Suzanne Kelly." Dec. 29, 1994.
Hall, William J. "Medical History—Report on James Whittaker." Medical Detachment,
    Defense Force, FETLOCK, in the Field, Nov. 11, 1942.
—. "Letter to Class." Dec. 12, 1986.
—. "Letter to Suzanne Kelly." June 1, 1987.
—. "Letter to Suzanne Kelly and Room 14 Students." Mar. 4, 1987.
Harrod, Frederick S. "Letter to Christy Scott from Chm. Hist. Dept., U.S. Naval Academy."
    Feb. 8, 1985.
Helland, Arthur. "Letter to Sixth Grade Class, Meeker Elementary." Nov. 24,   1986.
Kelly, Suzanne. "Letter to (James) Ellis Teer." Apr. 29, 1986.
—. "Letter to George Spevock." June 17, 1985.
—. "Letter to Mrs. E. C. Ernst." Oct. 4, 1986.
—. "Letter to Robert (Red) Timian." Oct. 4, 1986.
—. "Letter to Robert W. (Red) Timian." July 11, 1986.
—. "Letter to Stan Collins." Oct. 4, 1986.
—. "Letter to Tom Lenderman." July 11, 1986.
—. "Letter to William J. Hall." Jan. 10, 1987.
—. "Letter to William J. Hall." Apr. 4, 1987.
—. "Letter to William J. Hall." Sept. 20, 1987.
—. "Sample of Medical Corps Investigative Research." Sept. 1992.
Legant, Omar. "Medical History—Report on Edward Vernon Rickenbacker." Medical
    Detachment, Defense Force, FETLOCK, in the Field, Nov. 13, 1942.
—. "Medical History—Report on John Bartek." Medical Detachment, Defense Force,
    FETLOCK, in the Field, Nov. 13, 1942.

Lenderman, Tom. "Letter to Suzanne Kelly." Oct. 11, 1986.

—. "Letter to Suzanne Kelly." July 2, 1987.

—. "Letter to Suzanne Kelly." Dec. 12, 1988.

—. "Notes by Suzanne Kelly taken at Zobrist Farm." June 26, 1987.

—. "Telephone Call to Suzanne Kelly." Dec. 21, 1988.

Love, Robert William, Jr. "Letter to Christy Scott and Suzanne Kelly." Feb. 13, 1985.

McAuliffe, Philip J. "Letter to Amy Murphy and Suzanne Kelly." Mar. 10, 1985.

Mead, Diane. "Letter to Christy Scott from Dept. of Data Release Services, American Medical Association." Mar. 22, 1985.

Murphy, Amy. "Letter to Philip J. McAuliffe." Mar. 21, 1985.

"Report of Operations, Fifth Antiaircraft Battalion (Formerly Fifth Defense Battalion)." United States Marine Corps, May 16, 1944.

Rutherford, Leonard. "Letter to Suzanne Kelly." Dec. 15, 1987.

Ryherd, Donna. "Letter to Dr. William J. Hall, copy to Suzanne Kelly." Apr. 15, 1987.

Sanders, Elmer. "Letter to Suzanne Kelly." Oct. 27, 1986.

Scott, Christy. "Letter to American Medical Association in Chicago." Mar. 17, 1985.

—. "Letter to Supt. U.S. Naval Academy." Feb. 1, 1985.

—. "Letter to William J. Hall." Mar. 27, 1985.

Sixth Grader, Meeker Elementary. "Letter to David Stone at the American Embassy in Mexico." Nov. 1986.

Sixth Graders, Meeker Elementary. "Letter to Ambassador to Mexico, John Gavin." Nov. 17, 1986.

—. "Letter to Marion Cloonan Uebelhoer." Apr. 2, 1992.

—. "Letter to William J. Hall." Nov. 17, 1986.

—. "Telephone Call to H. Hazen (Buck) Wilson." May 15, 1987.

Spevock, Frank (compiled). *The Rickenbacker Story* 2004. 2004.

Spevock, Frank. "Letter to Suzanne Kelly." 2003.

Spevock, George. "Letter to Suzanne Kelly." May 4, 1986.

—. "Letter to Suzanne Kelly and Class." June 5, 1985.

Sticht, Frank D. "Letter to Tom Lenderman, copy to Suzanne Kelly." June 20, 1986.

Stone, David. "Letter to Sixth Graders from Vice Consul to Mexico." Dec. 23, 1986.

—. "Letter to Suzanne Kelly from Vice Consul to Mexico." Dec. 5, 1986.

Stone, Karen. "Letter to Suzanne Kelly and Students from CBS News in Chicago." May 13, 1985.

Sullivan, Micaela. "Telephone Call to Meeker School from American Medical Association." Mar. 26, 1985.

Swauger, Bill. "They sail through the memories of Funafuti Island." *The Beaver County Times*, June 10, 1990.

Teer, (James) Ellis. "Copy of Medical Detachment Reunion Plans from George Spevock." Feb. 27, 1985.

—. "Letter to Members of Funa Futi Medical Co. and Suzanne Kelly." Feb. 12, 1988.

—. "Letter to Suzanne Kelly." May 5, 1986.

Timian, Robert (Red). "Letter to Suzanne Kelly." July 21, 1986.

Uebelhoer, Marion Cloonan. "Letter to Sixth Graders." Feb. 6, 1993.

Whittaker, James C. *We Thought We Heard the Angels Sing.* New York: E. P. Dutton & Company, Inc., 1943: 125.

Williams, Janice. "Letter to Sixth Graders, Meeker Elementary." Feb. 22, 1992.

Wilson, H. Hazen (Buck). "Letter to Sixth Graders, Meeker Elementary." Dec. 22, 1986.

—. "Letter to Suzanne Kelly." July 16, 1986.

Chapter Thirteen

Brauer, Mel. "Letter to Suzanne Kelly." Jan. 19, 1994.

—. "Letter to Suzanne Kelly." Aug. 2, 1994.

—. "Personal Diary." Oct. 2-5, 1942.

—. "Personal Diary." Nov. 12-14, 1942.

—. "Telephone Call to Suzanne Kelly." May 1, 1994.

Cook, Joan. "Letter to Suzanne Kelly." 1994.

Cook, Tom and Joan. "Narrative of Trip to Funafuti." Mar. 7, 1996.

Crawford, Danny J. "Letter to Jennifer Jones from History and Museums Division, U.S. Marine Corps." Apr. 3, 1985.

Daniel, Brady Hutson ("B. H."). "Letter to Suzanne Kelly." June 16, 1987.

—. "Letter to Suzanne Kelly." July 11, 1987.

Executive Officer of the USS *Heywood.* "Plan of the Day." Oct. 2, 1942.

Fifth Defense Battalion on Funafuti. "Program Funafuti Follies—1942." 1942.

Good, George F., Jr. "Letter to Suzanne Kelly and Class." May 20, 1985.

Johnson, Frederick V. "Letter to Suzanne Kelly." 1985.

Johnson, Irene. "Letter to Suzanne Kelly." May 1, 1985.

Jones, Jennifer. "Letter to Director of Marine Corps History and Museums." Jan. 30, 1985.

Kelly, Suzanne. "Letter to Hiram Quillin, 5th and 14th Defense Battalion Assoc. of the USMC." Apr. 8, 1985.

—. "Letter to Irene Johnson." May 11, 1985.

—. "Letter to Joan Cook." Feb. 8, 1996.

Leech, Lloyd L. "Battalion Memorandum to All Units." Headquarters, U.S. Marine Corps Unit #290. Sept. 29, 1942.

News Sheet from Funafuti. "Box Scores of Softball League." 1942.

O'Brien, Charles (Chuck) N., Jr. "Letter to Suzanne Kelly." Nov. 5, 1985.

Quillin, Hiram. "Letter to Suzanne Kelly." Apr. 13, 1985.

—. "Letter to Suzanne Kelly." June 4, 1985.

"Report of Operations, Fifth Antiaircraft Battalion (Formerly Fifth Defense Battalion)." United States Marine Corps, May 16, 1944.

Spevock, George. "Letter to Suzanne Kelly." Dec. 19, 1986.

The History Place. "World War II in the Pacific." *Timeline of Events 1941-1945.* http://www.historyplace.com/unitedstates/pcificwar/tline-bw.htm (accessed May 31, 2013).

U.S. Marine Corps. "Chronology of Fifth Defense Battalion." Historical Section, Division of Public Information. 7.

USMC Assoc. Newsletter. "Update—Funafuti." 5:14 Express, Jan. 1989.

Wecker, David. "Helping Children Remember WWII." *The Cincinnati Post,* Aug. 2, 1994.

—. "Marine recalls days in Funafuti in World War II." *The Cincinnati Post,* Feb. 4, 1992.

Weston, W. Keith. "Letter to Suzanne Kelly." Oct. 28, 1985.

—. "Letter to Suzanne Kelly." Jan. 18, 1988

Chapter Fourteen

Altman, Archie. "Letter to Sixth Graders, Room 14, Meeker Elementary." May 12, 1993.

Boyd, Jack. "Letter to Sixth Graders." May 17, 1993.

——. "Letter to Suzanne Kelly." Sept. 6, 1993.

Brazzeal, John. "Audio Tape to Sixth Graders." Apr. 30, 1993.

Don, Alfred. "Challenge." *Can Do—Newsletter for Navy Seabee Veterans of America*, Mar. 1, 1993: 7.

——. "Letter to Sixth Graders." Mar. 11, 1993.

——. "Letter to Suzanne Kelly." Jan. 26, 1993.

——. "Letter to Suzanne Kelly and Students." Apr. 12, 1993.

Iafrate, Frank J. "The Origin of the Seabees Insignia and Name." 1942.

Matthews, C. W. (Prepared by). "United States Naval Construction Battalion 2." Aug. 26, 1969.

Ramige, Mel. "Letter to Sixth Graders from NSVA." Jan. 16, 1993.

Sixth Graders, Meeker Elementary, Room 14. "Letter to Archie Altman." Apr. 23, 1993.

——. "Letter to Jack Boyd." Apr. 23, 1993.

——. "Letter to John Brazzeal." Apr. 23, 1993.

——. "Letter to Navy Seabee Veterans of America." Jan. 4, 1993.

U.S. Government Printing Office. *History of the Bureau of Yards and Docks and the Civil Engineer Corps 1940-1946.* Vol. II, in *Building the Navy's Bases in World War II.* Washington, D.C., 1947.

Chapter Fifteen

Davis, Colin. "Personal Diaries from Nukufetau." Nov. 13-14, 1942.

Davis, Noeline. "Letter to Suzanne Kelly." Sept. 3, 1992.

——. "Letter to Suzanne Kelly." Dec. 4, 1992.

Davis, Shirley. "Letter to Bob Kelly." Aug. 26, 1992.

——. "Letter to Sixth Graders." Sept. 1, 1992.

——. "Letter to Sixth Graders." May 19, 1993.

——. "Telephone Call to Bob and Suzanne Kelly." Aug. 24, 1992.

Francis, Sherrah. "Letter to Sixth Graders from National Archives of New Zealand." July 31, 1987.

Good, George F, Jr. "Note to Colin Davis." 1942 or 1943.

Guthrie, John. "Letter to Suzanne Kelly." Jan. 15, 1988.

Harrison, Alden. "Letter to Sixth Graders, Meeker Elementary, Room 14." Feb. 14, 1988.

Kelly, Suzanne. "Letter to Don Vaughan." Aug. 4, 1992.

——. "Letter to John Guthrie." Jan. 11, 1988.

——. "Telephone Call to James W. Reynolds." 1987.

Knutson, Noel. "Letter to Suzanne Kelly." Sept. 13, 1988.

Sixth Grade, Meeker Elementary, Room 14. "Letter to Alden Harrison." 1988.

——. "Letter to Ambassador to New Zealand in Wellington." Apr. 8, 1987.

——. "Letter to D. L. Vaughan." May 21, 1992.

——. "Letter to Noel Knutson." Mar. 29, 1988.

——. "Letter to Peter Higgins, U.S. Consulate General in Aukland." Apr. 10, 1987.

U.S. Consulate General in Aukland, New Zealand. "Letter to Sixth Graders." May 27, 1987.

Vaughan, Don. "Inscription in book to James W. Reynolds." 1992.

——. "Letter to Sixth Graders." June 8, 1992.

—. "Letter to Suzanne Kelly." Aug. 31, 1992.

—. *Report on Coastwatching Radio Stations in the Gilbert and Ellice Islands* 1941-1945. 1990: Introduction, 3; Part 9, 2; Part 10, 1; Part 16, 1-2; Part 17, 1-3; Part 18, 1,3; Part 19, 1.

Victoria University Library System Search. May 18, 1992.

Whittaker, James C. *We Thought We Heard the Angels Sing.* New York: E. P. Dutton & Company, Inc., 1943: 123.

Whittaker, James. "Letter to Colin Davis." (1943).

Chapter Sixteen

Boutte, Les. "Letter to Sixth Graders." Feb. 1, 1987.

—. "Letter to Suzanne Kelly." May 27, 1987.

—. "Telephone Call to Suzanne Kelly." Apr. 19, 1988.

Eadie, William, "Rough Draft of Report of 1942 Rickenbacker, et al. Rescue." Nov. 19, 1942.

Editor. "Letter to Sixth Graders." *Virginia Pilot.* Feb. 23, 1988.

Floch, Robert. "Letter to Sixth Grader." Mar. 9, 1993.

—. "Letter to Suzanne Kelly and Class." Apr. 16, 1993.

—. "Article on Class Project with Model of Kingfisher Plane." *The Tifi Tifi Tattler*, Feb. 28, 1994: 4.

Forrest, Gaylord. "Letter to Sixth Graders." Mar. 17, 1988.

—. "Letter to Sixth Graders." Apr. 28, 1988.

—. "Letter to Suzanne Kelly." Jan. 18, 1993.

Guichard, D. A., Dept. of the Navy, Naval Reserve Personnel Center. "Letter to Sixth Graders." Feb. 22, 1988.

Haile, Peggy A. "Letter to Sixth Graders from Norfolk Public Library." Jan. 28, 1988.

Kelly, Suzanne. "Letter to Gaylord Forrest." Dec. 17, 1988.

Residence, Family in. "Letter to Sixth Grader." Apr. 28, 1988.

—. "Letter to Sixth Graders from Family in Residence." Mar. 13, 1988.

Sixth Grader, Meeker Elementary, Room 14. "Letter to Family in Residence." Apr. 15, 1988.

—. "Letter to Family in Residence." May 24, 1988.

—. "Letter to Robert Floch." Mar. 3, 1993.

—. "Letter to Robert Floch." Mar. 29, 1993.

Sixth Graders, Meeker Elementary, Room 14. "Letter to Family in Residence." Feb. 12, 1988.

—. "Letter to Department of the Navy." Mar. 3, 1988.

—. "Letter to Editor," *Virginia Pilot.* Feb. 8, 1988.

—. "Letter to Norfolk Public Library, Norfolk, Virginia." Jan. 9, 1987..

Chapter Seventeen

Ferrell, Bob and Al Ross. *Early Elco PT Boats.* PT Boats Museum and Library, 1980.

Good, George F., Jr. "Report of Rescue of Captain Rickenbacker and Party, 11, 12 November, 1942." United States Marine Corps Headquarters, Funafuti, in the Field, 1942.

Lyon, Gaylord. "Letter to Suzanne Kelly." Nov. 19, 1987.

PT #21. "Logbook." Nov. 12-14, 1942.

PT #23. "Logbook." Nov. 12-14, 1942.

PT #25. "Logbook." Nov. 12-14, 1942.

PT #26. "Logbook." Nov. 12-14, 1942.

Rucker, William. "Letter to Sixth Graders." Feb. 1, 1988.

Scribner, V. F. "Letter to Sixth Graders." Feb. 15, 1988.

Sixth Graders, Meeker Elementary, Room 14. "Letter to William Rucker." Jan. 12, 1988.
St. Louis Post-Dispatch. [Article on William Rucker], 1942-3.
"U.S. Marine Corps Chronology of Fifth Defense Battalion." Historical Section, Division of
    Public Information. 7.
U.S. Navy. *Dictionary of American Naval Fighting Ships.* Vol. III.
USS *Hilo.* "Logbook." June 11, 1942.
——. "Logbook." Nov. 6-25, 1942

Chapter Eighteen

The Air Transport Command in the Pacific, 1942. West Coast Wing, PACD, ATC, Air
    Transport Command, Hamilton Field: USAF, 1942.
Beauchamp, Thomas. "Letter to Suzanne Kelly and Sixth Graders." Apr. 22, 1985.
Budd, Bernadette. "World War II Mystery Answered in Wading River—article on Miceli."
    The Community Journal, Apr. 25, 1990: 6-7.
Canton Radio Station. "First Operator's Radio Log Extracts." Oct. 21, 1942.
——. "Second Operator's Radio Log Extracts." Oct. 21, 1942.
Chopelas, John. "Letter to Students, Meeker Elementary." Apr. 5, 1996.
——. "Letter to Suzanne Kelly." Jan. 23, 1996.
——. "Letter to Suzanne Kelly and Class." June 10, 1996.
Emmons, Delos. Command at HOLLY. "Diary of Events Connected with the Loss of B-17
    Airplane, Flight OV-369," U.S. Army Air Force, Oct. 25, 1942.
Emmons, Delos. "Ref. AG-3B to Com. Gen. Army Air Force, Washington, D.C." Oct. 29, 1942.
Finch, Arthur. "Army Air Corps Memo to Direction of Communications." Feb. 8, 1943.
Kelly, Suzanne. "Letter to Albert Miceli." Nov. 21, 1987.
——. "Letter to Hubert Zobrist." Dec. 27, 1995.
Luna, Henry. "Air Transport Command's Narrative Report on Rickenbacker Trip." Extract
    2, paragraph 3. Dec. 29, 1942.
Miceli, Albert. "Letter to Editor, *Reader's Digest.*" Oct. 27, 1987.
——. "Letter to Suzanne Kelly." Dec. 10, 1987.
Sixth Graders, Meeker Elementary. "Letter to John Chopelas." Mar. 25, 1996.
Transcribed Video Tape, "An Evening with Our Friends, Rescue Reunion," Ames, Iowa,
    Apr. 19, 1985.
Transcribed Video Tape, [A Tape the Men Made for Suzanne Kelly]. Apr. 20, 1985.
Transcribed Video Tape, "Meeker Media Center, Rescue Reunion," Ames, Iowa, Apr. 19, 1985.
Zobrist, Hubert. "Letter to Suzanne Kelly." Dec. 1995.

Chapter Nineteen

Coveney, Raymond M. "Letter to Suzanne Kelly." July 7, 1987.
Emmons, Delos. Command at HOLLY. "Diary of Events Connected with the Loss of B-17
    Airplane, Flight OV-369," U.S. Army Air Force,   Oct. 25, 1942.
Finch, Arthur. "Army Air Corps Memo to Direction of Communications." Feb. 8, 1943.
Knapp, Elton. "Flight Log of PBY-5A, No. 08036." Oct. 24-25, 1942.
——. "Letter to Suzanne Kelly." May 10, 1985.
——. "Letter to Suzanne Kelly and Sixth Graders." Apr. 27, 1985.
Nat'l. Archives and Records Services, Gen. Serv. Adm. *List of Logbooks of U. S. Navy Ships,
    Stations, and Miscellaneous Units 1801-1947.* Washington, D.C., 1978.

Office of Naval History, Navy Dept., Washington, DC. "Glossary of U.S. Naval Code Words." Mar. 1948.

Radiogram about Flight OV-369. "220130." Oct. 1942.

—. "220330." Oct. 1942.

—. "220440." Oct. 1942.

—. "220652." Oct. 1942.

—. "230320." Oct. 1942.

—. "230335." Oct. 1942.

—. "Unknown." Oct. 1942.

Southern, Ira. "Letter to Sixth Graders." May 12, 1993.

—. "Letter to Suzanne Kelly." June 29, 1993.

Chapter Twenty

The Air Transport Command in the Pacific, 1942. West Coast Wing, PACD, ATC, Air Transport Command, Hamilton Field: USAF, 1942.

Brown, Kathy. "Letter to Suzanne Kelly." June 4, 1993.

Caccamo, James F. "Letter to Students from Hudson Library and Historical Society." Jan. 26, 1993.

Davies, Marian. "Letter to Sixth Graders from Akron-Summit County Public Library." Feb. 8, 1993.

Ellsworth at Canton. "Radiogram about Flight OV-369 and Ocean Currents." Oct. 24, 1942.

Goodyear Tire and Rubber Company. "Letter to Suzanne Kelly." May 28, 1992.

"Homage Is Paid Johnny Bartek, 23, Home from Pacific." *Freehold Transcript,* Dec. 18, 1942.

Michaelsen, Katherine M. "Letter to Sixth Graders and Suzanne Kelly." Apr. 20, 1985.

Murphy, Fran. "Century of School Days." *Akron Beacon Journal,* Feb. 5, 1993.

National Archives Photos of Raft Builders. "#208 PU-162V-9 and #208 PU-162V-10."

Rossi, Lori. "Telephone call to Sixth Graders with Info on Raft Builders." Feb. 8, 1993.

Simmons, Doris. "Letter to Sixth Graders from Raft Builder's Daughter." Apr.1993.

Sixth Graders, Meeker Elementary, Room 14. "Letter to Barberton Public Library." Jan. 26, 1993.

—. "Letter to Doris Simmons." Mar. 3, 1993.

—. "Letter to Hudson Library and Historical Society." Jan. 26, 1993.

—. "Letter to Kathy Brown." May 28, 1993.

Taylor, Phyllis. "Letter to Sixth Graders from Barberton Public Library." Feb. 1, 1993.

Transcribed Video Tape, "An Evening with Our Friends, Rescue Reunion," Ames, Iowa, Apr. 19, 1985.

Transcribed Video Tape, [A Tape the Men Made for Suzanne Kelly]. Apr. 20, 1985.

Transcribed Video Tape, "Meeker Media Center, Rescue Reunion," Ames, Iowa, Apr. 19, 1985.

U.S. Naval Mobile Base Hospital No. 3. "Certificate Ancient Order of the Deep to John F. Bartek." Dec. 1942.

Whittaker, James C. *We Thought We Heard the Angels Sing.* New York: E. P. Dutton & Company, Inc., 1943: 44.

Whittaker, James. "Diary on the Raft—Day 1." Oct. 21, 1942.

Chapter Twenty-One

Transcribed Video Tape, "An Evening with Our Friends, Rescue Reunion," Ames, Iowa, Apr. 19, 1985.

Transcribed Video Tape, [A Tape the Men Made for Suzanne Kelly]. Apr. 20, 1985.

Transcribed Video Tape, "Meeker Media Center, Rescue Reunion," Ames, Iowa, Apr. 19, 1985.

Chapter Twenty-Two
Daniel, Charles F. "Letter to Suzanne Kelly." Sept. 27, 1988.
—. "Letter to Suzanne Kelly." Sept. 29, 1988.
Kelly, Suzanne. "Letter to Henry and Virginia Luna." Apr. 11, 1988.
—. "Phone Call to Charles Daniel." Sept. 28, 1988.
Luna, Henry. "Air Transport Command's Narrative Report on Rickenbacker Trip." Extract 2, paragraph 3. Dec. 29, 1942.
Luna, Henry. "Letter to Sixth Graders." Mar. 1988.
Luna, Virginia. "Letter to Suzanne Kelly." Aug. 6, 1988.
—. "Letter to Suzanne Kelly." Feb. 22, 1988.
—. "Letter(s) to Sixth Graders." Mar. 3, 1988.
Reynolds, James W. "Phone Call to Suzanne Kelly." June 3, 1988.
—. "Phone Call to Suzanne Kelly." Jan. 8, 1988.
Sixth Graders, Meeker Elementary, Room 14. "Letter to Henry and Virginia Luna." May 12, 1988.
—. "Letter to Henry Luna." Feb. 11, 1988.
—. "Note to Mrs. Kelly about Lunas." Feb. 9, 1988.
—. "Phone Call to Henry and Virginia Luna." Feb. 10, 1988.

Chapter Twenty-Three
Bartek, John. "Quote from Scrapbook about *Epic of Prayer* Painting."
Boutte, Les. "Flight Log of Kingfisher." Nov. 11, 1942.
—. "Letter to Suzanne Kelly." Oct. 19, 1987.
Denny, Paul, Jr. "Letter to Sixth Graders." Feb. 18, 1988.
Kelly, Suzanne. "Letter to the Family of Capt. Cherry." Sept. 2000.
"Program for Ames High School Commencement Exercises." May 29, 1991.
Sentimental Journey (B-17) Certificate. July 19, 2008.
Sixth Graders, Meeker Elementary, Room 14. "Letter to Art Department, Phillips University." Feb. 8, 1988.
—. "Letter to Jarvis Stewart." Mar. 4, 1988.
Stafford, Alice and Quinton. "Letter to Suzanne Kelly." Dec. 1987.
Stafford, Alice. "Note to Suzanne Kelly." Dec. 1988.
Stafford, Quinton. "Copy of Letter from Quinton Stafford to his Mother." Dec. 1, 1943.
—. "Letter to Sixth Graders, Meeker Elementary." Apr. 25, 1985.
—. "Telephone Call to Suzanne Kelly." Aug. 2, 1987.
Stewart, Madge. "Letter to Sixth Graders." Mar. 31, 1988.
Taafaki, Semu S. "Letters to Sixth Graders from the Tuvalu Ambassador to Fiji." Mar. 8, 1989.

About the Author

SUZANNE ZOBRIST KELLY RECEIVED A B.S. DEGREE from Iowa State University, with teaching licenses in both secondary and elementary education. As part of her graduate work at Purdue University, where she earned an M.S. degree in Early Childhood Education, she wrote and hosted a public television series, "Pathways of Childhood," produced by the university's telecommunications department. Suzanne went on to teach fifth and sixth grade for forty-two years, receiving several state and national awards, including the Catalyst Award and The Presidential Award for Excellence in Science Teaching. *Reaching Beyond the Waves* is her first adult, non-fiction book. Suzanne's hobby is designing and sewing fashion doll apparel, which she donates to groups and organizations. She also enjoys rambling with her husband, who photographs the Iowa landscape, and making up treasure hunts with her grandchildren.

INDEX

coordinates for locations, 27, 29, 122, 255
coral, 203, 281, 283. *See also* atoll
Coveney, Raymond M., 258-59
Coverdale, Jeanne, 39
crabs, 183-84
Crawford, Danny J., 180
Crescent City, 181, 201
Crosby, Janet, 92

Dale, Al, 93-94
Dallas County News, 49
Daniel, Brady Hutson (B. H.), 184-85
Daniel, Charles F., 285-87
Darby, Marian (Mrs. Ralph), 131-35
Davenport Public Library, 44
Davenport, Iowa, 35, 44, 194
Davis, Colin, 203-08, 213
Davis, Noeline, 204, 206-07
Davis, Shirley, 204-08
DeAngelis, John: flight, 16, 237, 239-40, 242; locating by sixth graders, 21; photo, 11, 282, 286; rafts, 9, 249, 264; recovery, 164; rescue, 23-24, 29, 31, 112, 146-47, 207-08, 235
declassified report, 27, 61, 198. See also Rescue Report
Defense Force, Funafuti, 180-81, 183
Denny, Paul, Jr., 294
Department of the Air Force, 39
Des Moines Airport, 62, 64, 66-67, 71
Des Moines Register, 34, 39, 107, 113, 132, 142
Detachment of First Separate Medical Company, 166
Dexter, Iowa, 74, 101-02
diary, 1, 95, 188-90, 205, 207-08, 241
diary of events, 240, 255-56
direction finding station, 241-44
ditched landing, 247-48, 269
Don, Alfred G., 193-95
doughnut raft, 249, 264. See also rafts, Cherry
Drew's Chocolates, 74, 101
Durkin, John K., 285, 290

Eadie, Phyllis, 89
Eadie, Robert J., 89, 210, 216
Eadie, Samuel L., 46
Eadie, William F. (Bill), 89, 211-13, 215-16, 219; history, 46, 85, 90, 221; locating by sixth graders, 43, 46, 64; photo, 90, 215, 223; rescues, 24, 28-30, 41-42, 64, 209, 213-14, 278
Eadie, William Fisher, II, 90
East-West Center, 50, 52
East-West Communication Institute, 50

Made in the USA
San Bernardino, CA
07 April 2015